D1073601

Melissa Public Library
Melissa, Texas

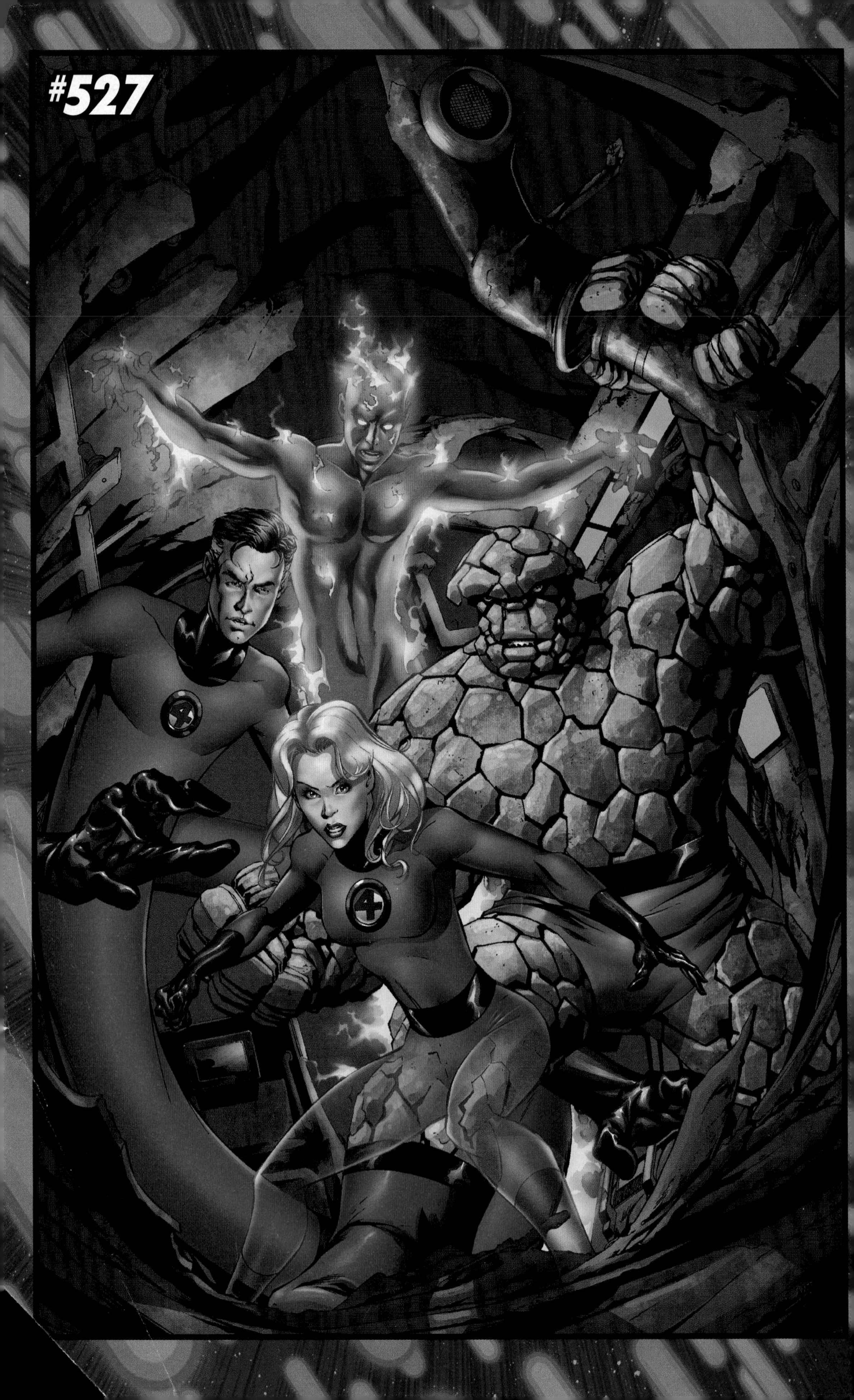
#527

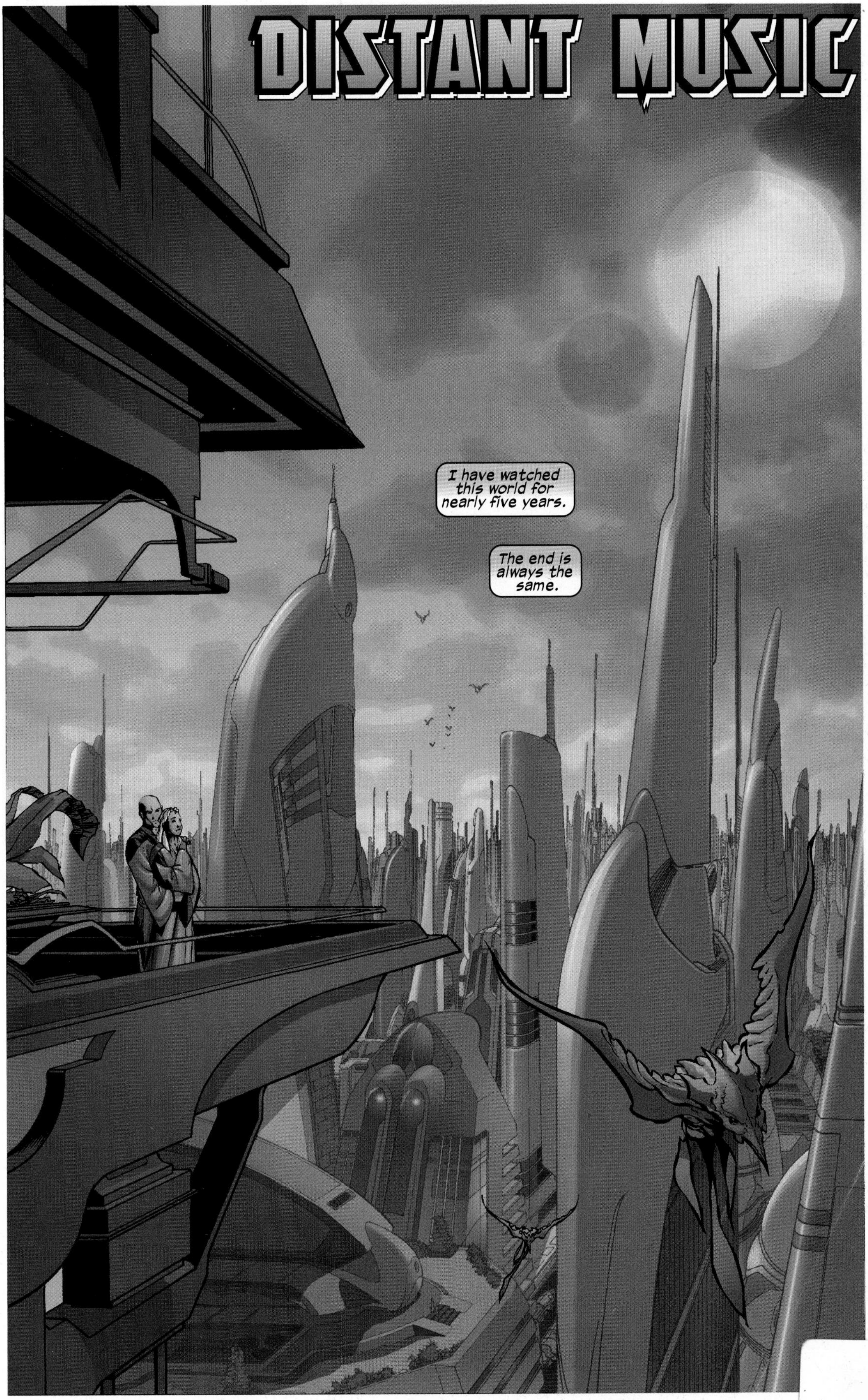
DISTANT MUSIC
I have watched this world for nearly five years.
The end is always the same.

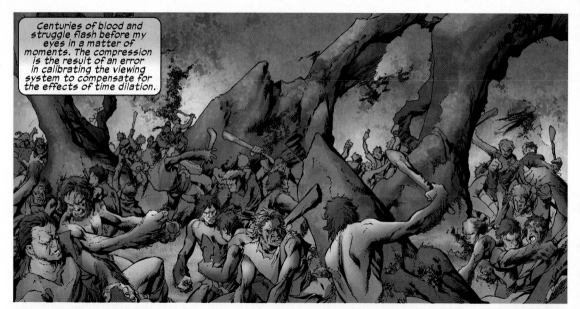

Centuries of blood and struggle flash before my eyes in a matter of moments. The compression is the result of an error in calibrating the viewing system to compensate for the effects of time dilation.

It would be a simple matter to correct the error.

I choose not to.

It takes six months here for several million years to pass there.

Then the sudden, dizzying upward climb.

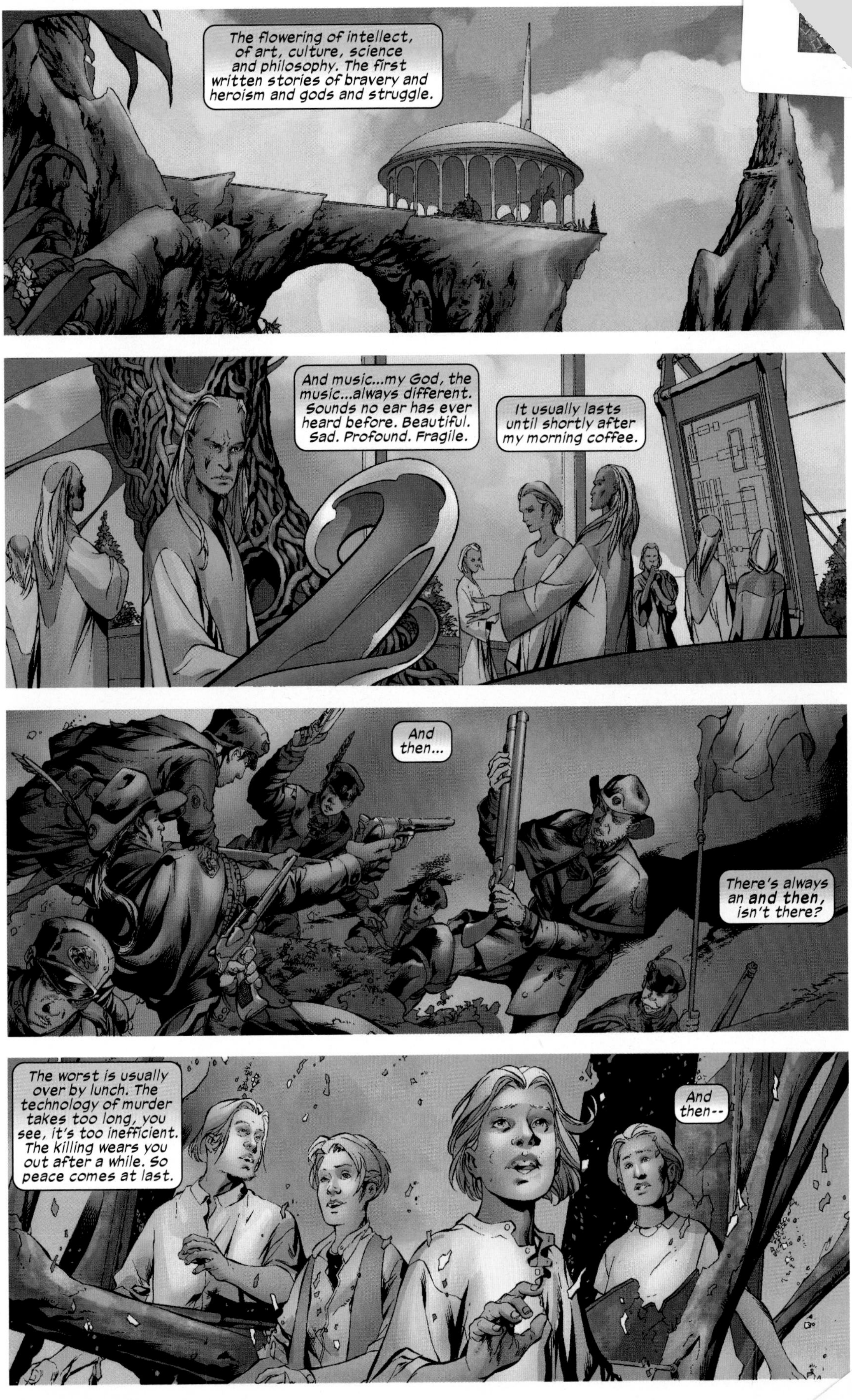
The flowering of intellect, of art, culture, science and philosophy. The first written stories of bravery and heroism and gods and struggle.
And music...my God, the music...always different. Sounds no ear has ever heard before. Beautiful. Sad. Profound. Fragile.
It usually lasts until shortly after my morning coffee.
And then...
There's always an **and then**, isn't there?
The worst is usually over by lunch. The technology of murder takes too long, you see, it's too inefficient. The killing wears you out after a while. So peace comes at last.
And then--

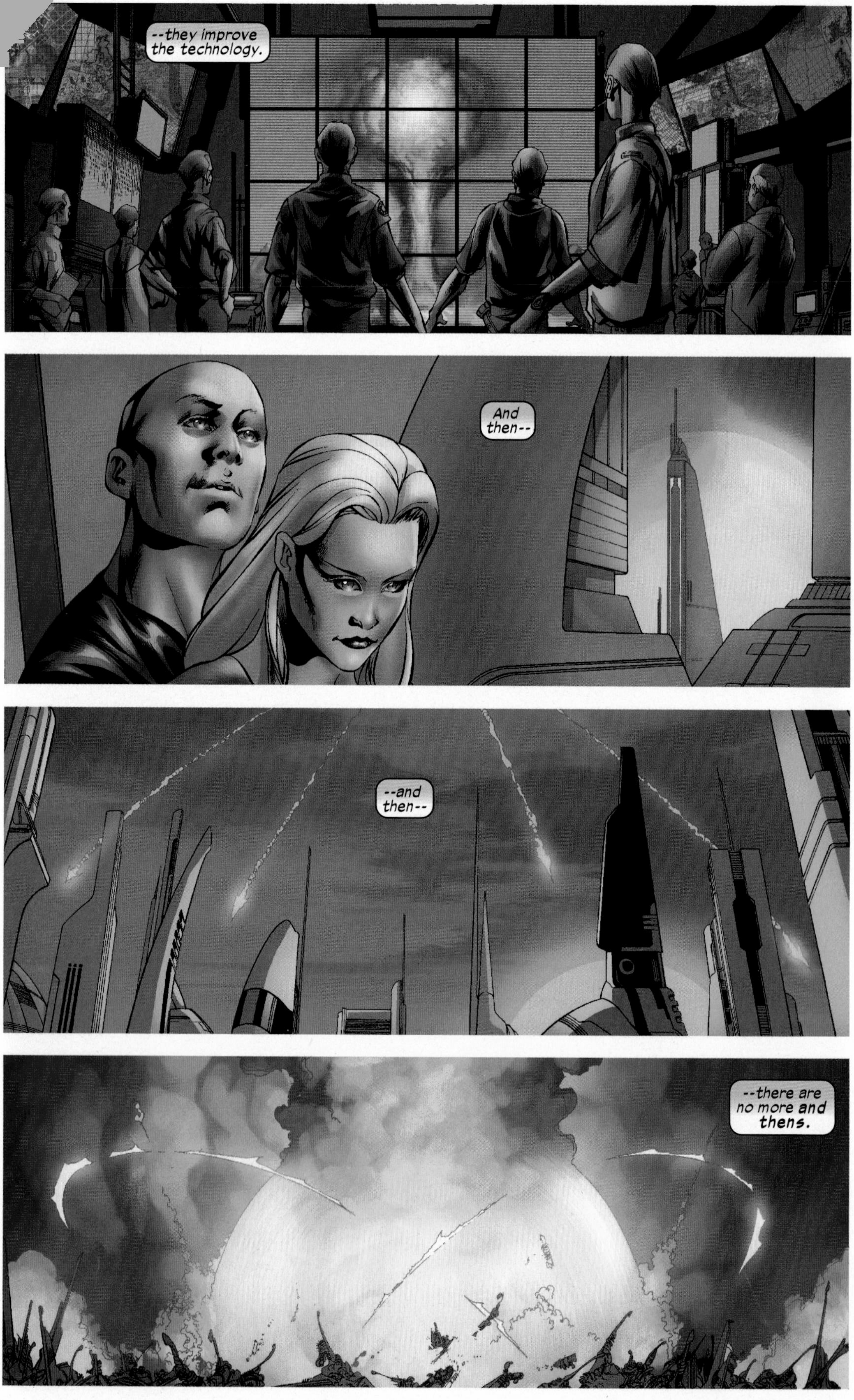
--they improve the technology.
And then--
--and then--
--there are no more and thens.

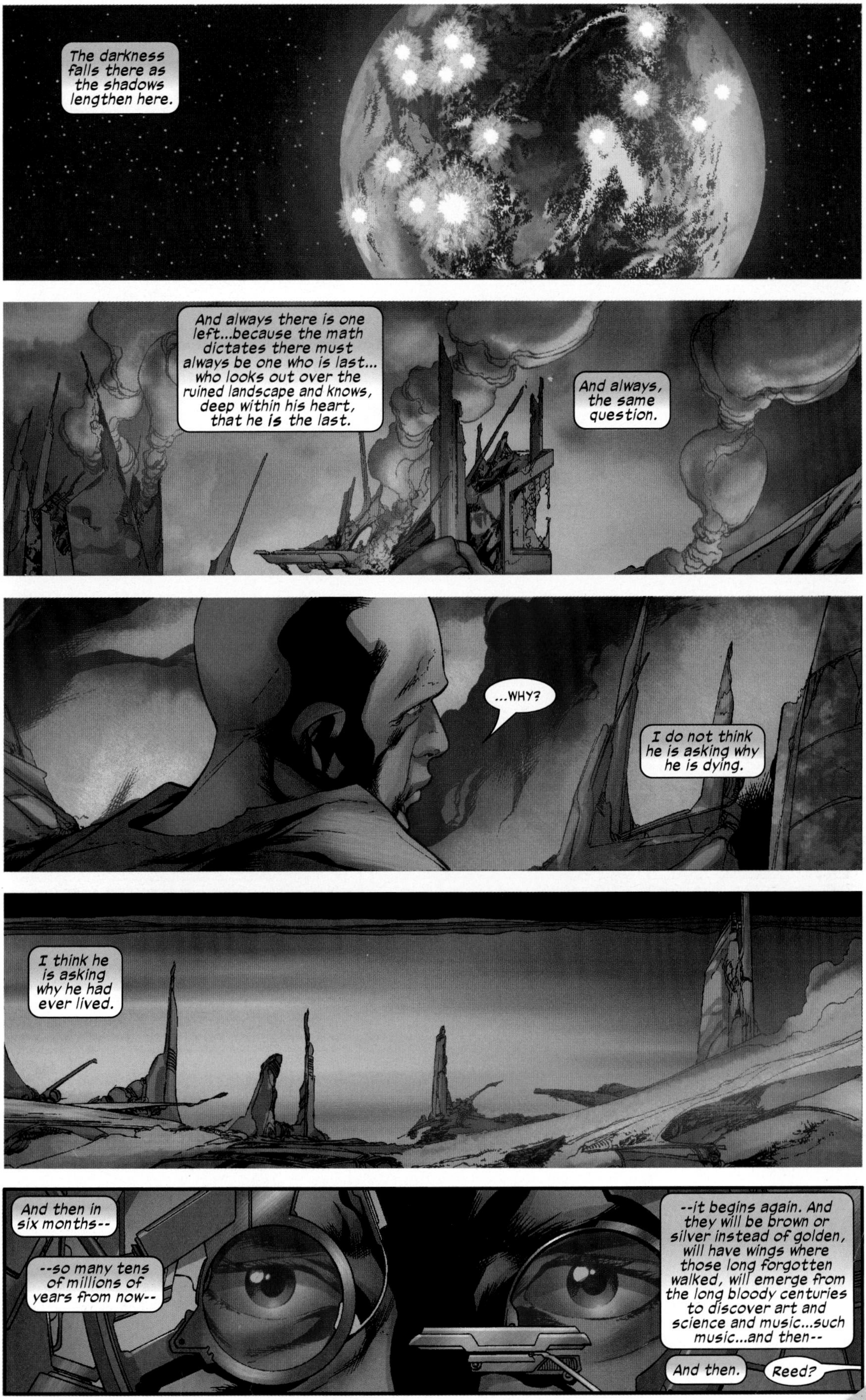
The darkness falls there as the shadows lengthen here.
And always there is one left...because the math dictates there must always be one who is last... who looks out over the ruined landscape and knows, deep within his heart, that he is the last.
And always, the same question.
...WHY?
I do not think he is asking why he is dying.
I think he is asking why he had ever lived.
And then in six months--
--so many tens of millions of years from now--
--it begins again. And they will be brown or silver instead of golden, will have wings where those long forgotten walked, will emerge from the long bloody centuries to discover art and science and music...such music...and then--
And then.
Reed?

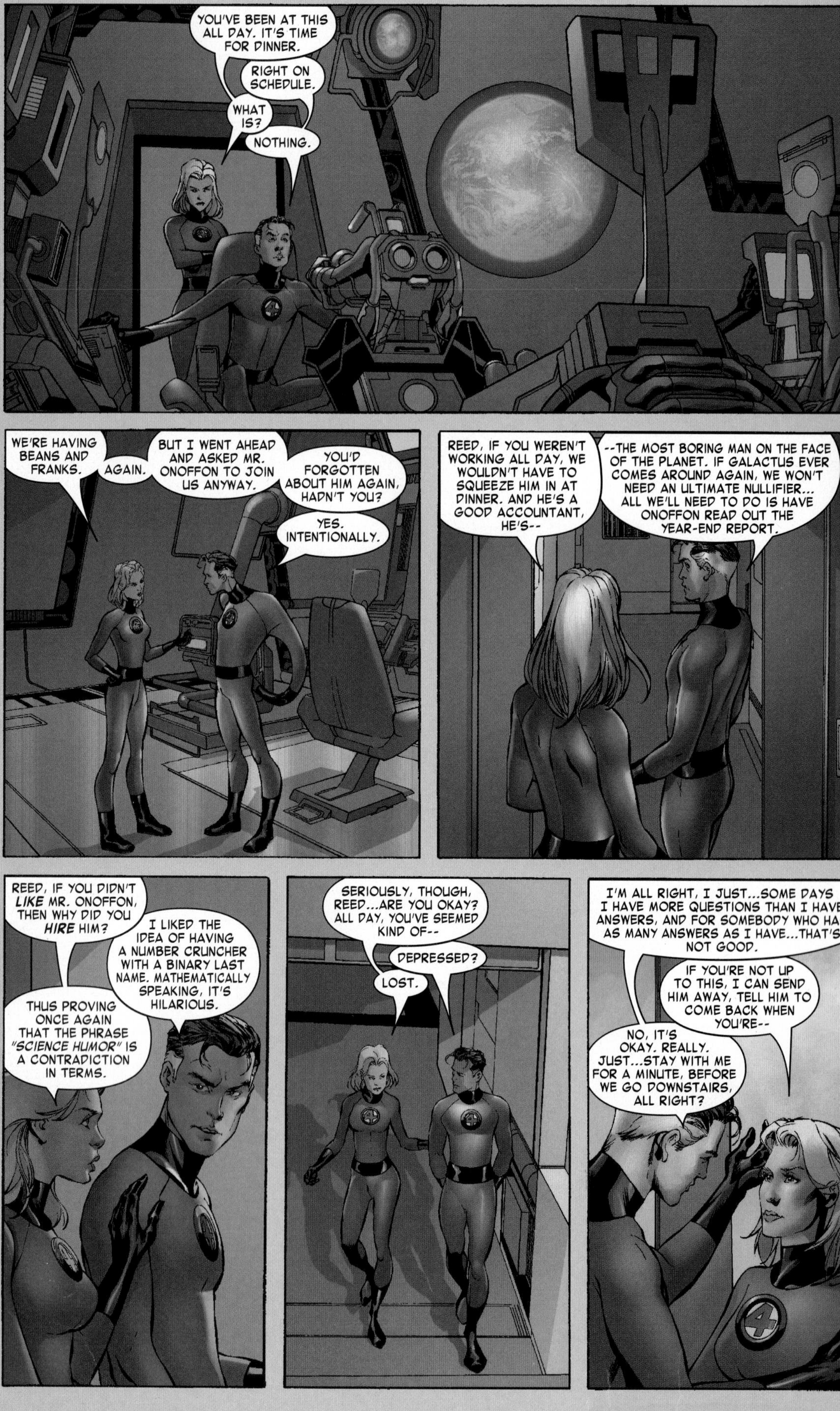
YOU'VE BEEN AT THIS ALL DAY. IT'S TIME FOR DINNER.
RIGHT ON SCHEDULE.
WHAT IS?
NOTHING.
WE'RE HAVING BEANS AND FRANKS.
AGAIN.
BUT I WENT AHEAD AND ASKED MR. ONOFFON TO JOIN US ANYWAY.
YOU'D FORGOTTEN ABOUT HIM AGAIN, HADN'T YOU?
YES. INTENTIONALLY.
REED, IF YOU WEREN'T WORKING ALL DAY, WE WOULDN'T HAVE TO SQUEEZE HIM IN AT DINNER. AND HE'S A GOOD ACCOUNTANT, HE'S--
--THE MOST BORING MAN ON THE FACE OF THE PLANET. IF GALACTUS EVER COMES AROUND AGAIN, WE WON'T NEED AN ULTIMATE NULLIFIER... ALL WE'LL NEED TO DO IS HAVE ONOFFON READ OUT THE YEAR-END REPORT.
REED, IF YOU DIDN'T *LIKE* MR. ONOFFON, THEN WHY DID YOU *HIRE* HIM?
I LIKED THE IDEA OF HAVING A NUMBER CRUNCHER WITH A BINARY LAST NAME. MATHEMATICALLY SPEAKING, IT'S HILARIOUS.
THUS PROVING ONCE AGAIN THAT THE PHRASE *"SCIENCE HUMOR"* IS A CONTRADICTION IN TERMS.
SERIOUSLY, THOUGH, REED...ARE YOU OKAY? ALL DAY, YOU'VE SEEMED KIND OF--
DEPRESSED?
LOST.
I'M ALL RIGHT, I JUST...SOME DAYS I HAVE MORE QUESTIONS THAN I HAVE ANSWERS, AND FOR SOMEBODY WHO HAS AS MANY ANSWERS AS I HAVE...THAT'S NOT GOOD.
IF YOU'RE NOT UP TO THIS, I CAN SEND HIM AWAY, TELL HIM TO COME BACK WHEN YOU'RE--
NO, IT'S OKAY. REALLY. JUST...STAY WITH ME FOR A MINUTE, BEFORE WE GO DOWNSTAIRS, ALL RIGHT?

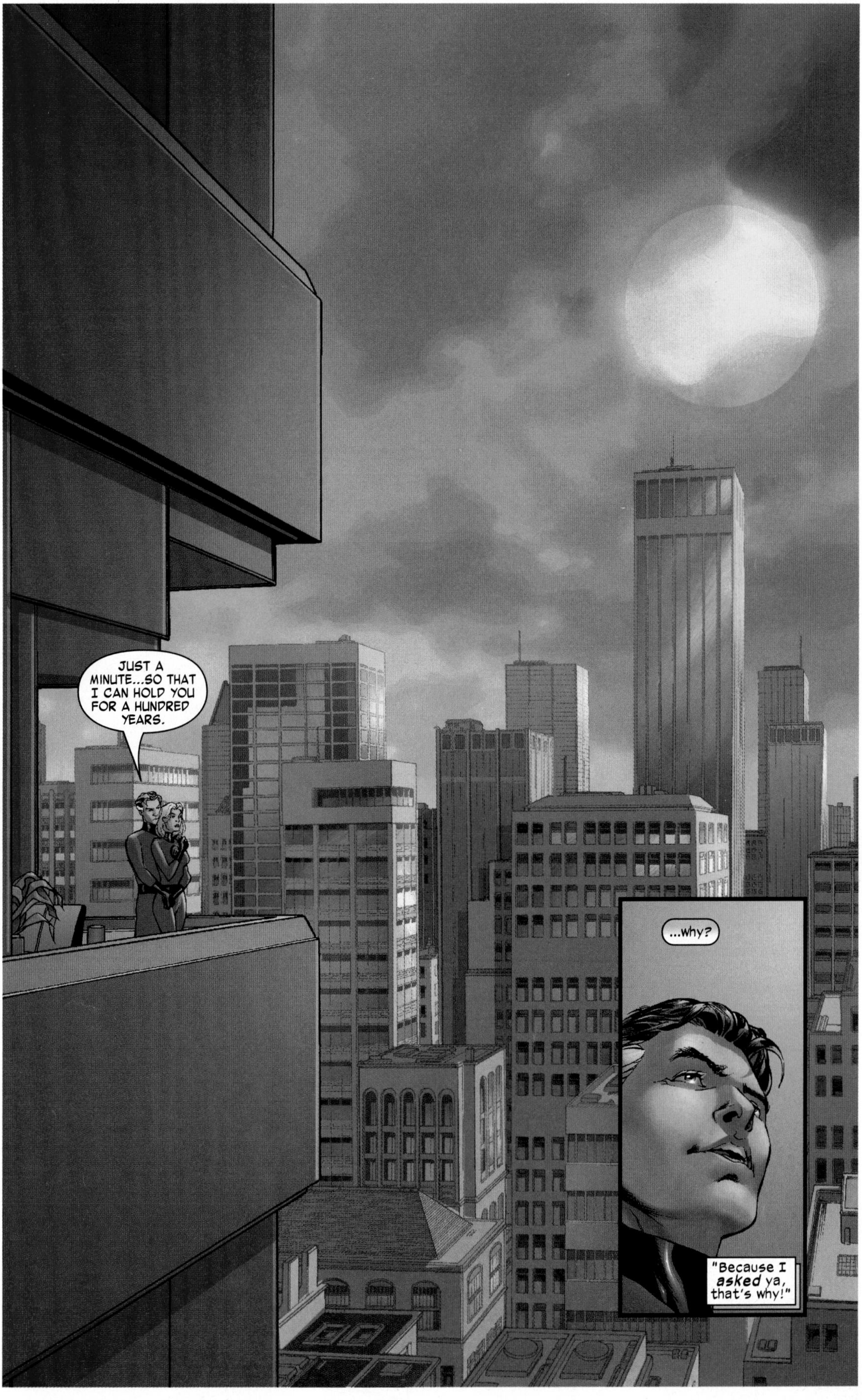
JUST A MINUTE...SO THAT I CAN HOLD YOU FOR A HUNDRED YEARS.
...why?
"Because I *asked* ya, that's why!"

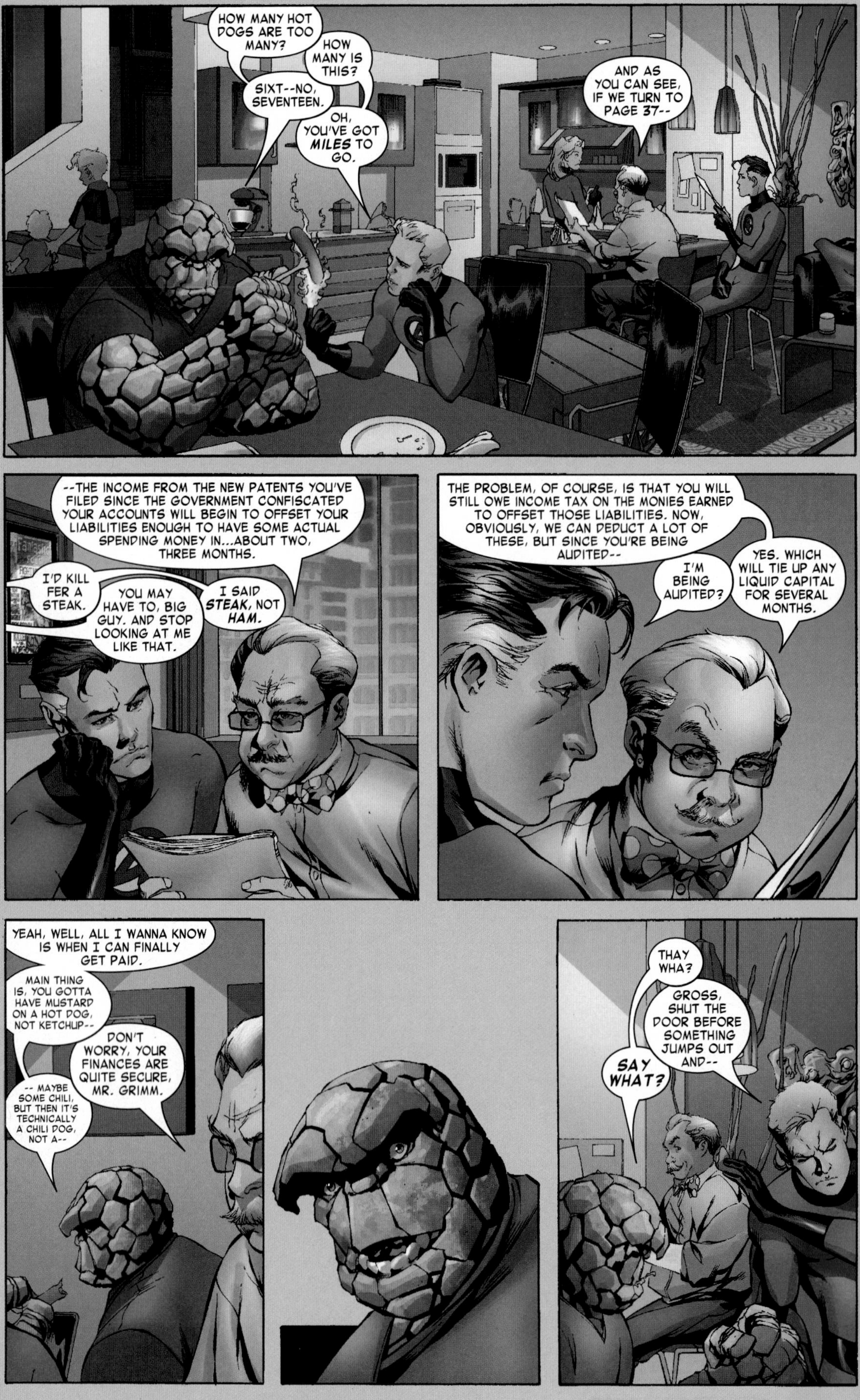
HOW MANY HOT DOGS ARE TOO MANY?
HOW MANY IS THIS?
SIXT--NO, SEVENTEEN.
OH, YOU'VE GOT MILES TO GO.
AND AS YOU CAN SEE, IF WE TURN TO PAGE 37--
--THE INCOME FROM THE NEW PATENTS YOU'VE FILED SINCE THE GOVERNMENT CONFISCATED YOUR ACCOUNTS WILL BEGIN TO OFFSET YOUR LIABILITIES ENOUGH TO HAVE SOME ACTUAL SPENDING MONEY IN...ABOUT TWO, THREE MONTHS.
I'D KILL FER A STEAK.
YOU MAY HAVE TO, BIG GUY. AND STOP LOOKING AT ME LIKE THAT.
I SAID STEAK, NOT HAM.
THE PROBLEM, OF COURSE, IS THAT YOU WILL STILL OWE INCOME TAX ON THE MONIES EARNED TO OFFSET THOSE LIABILITIES. NOW, OBVIOUSLY, WE CAN DEDUCT A LOT OF THESE, BUT SINCE YOU'RE BEING AUDITED--
I'M BEING AUDITED?
YES. WHICH WILL TIE UP ANY LIQUID CAPITAL FOR SEVERAL MONTHS.
YEAH, WELL, ALL I WANNA KNOW IS WHEN I CAN FINALLY GET PAID.
MAIN THING IS, YOU GOTTA HAVE MUSTARD ON A HOT DOG, NOT KETCHUP--
DON'T WORRY, YOUR FINANCES ARE QUITE SECURE, MR. GRIMM.
-- MAYBE SOME CHILI, BUT THEN IT'S TECHNICALLY A CHILI DOG, NOT A--
THAY WHA?
GROSS, SHUT THE DOOR BEFORE SOMETHING JUMPS OUT AND--
SAY WHAT?

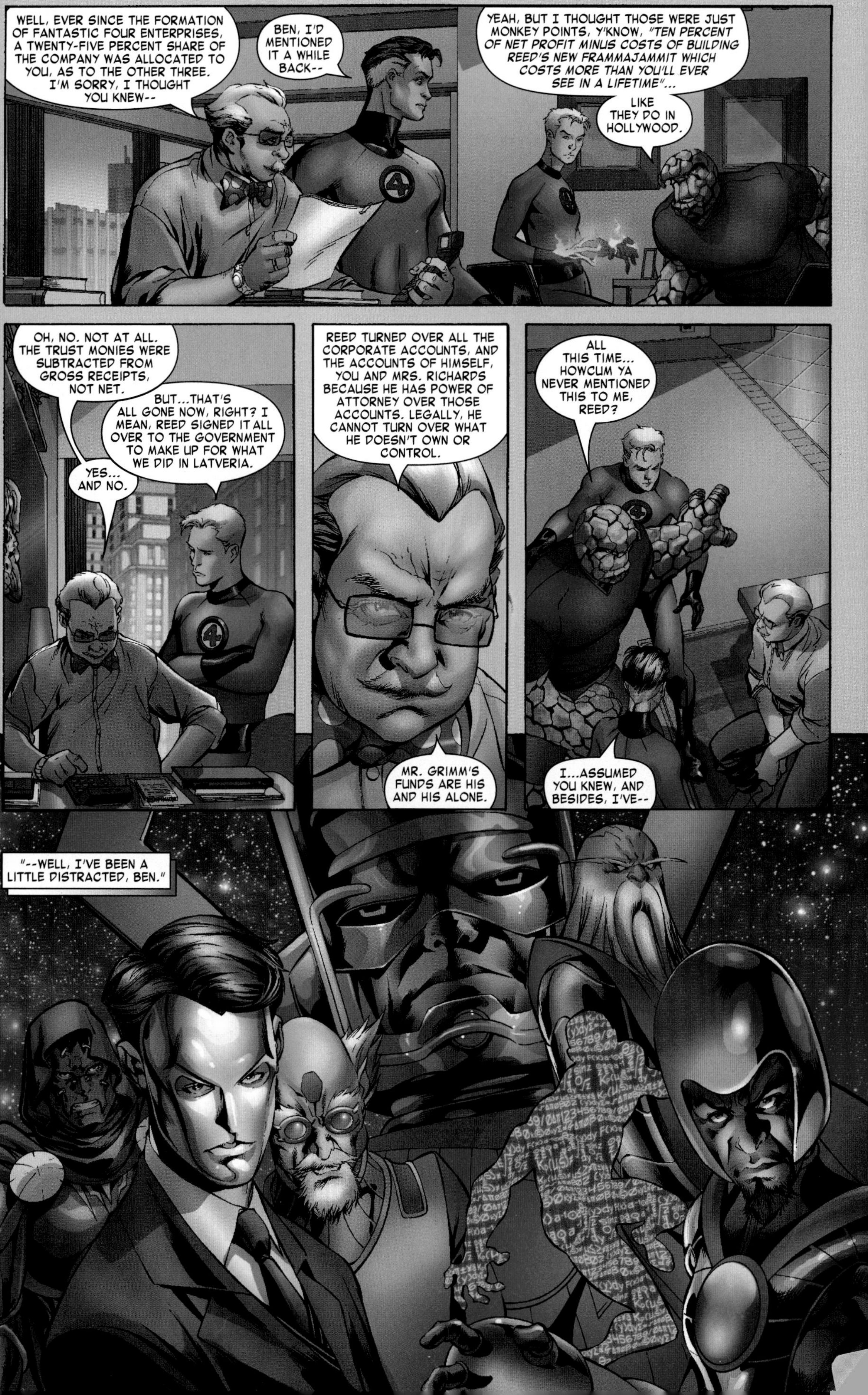
WELL, EVER SINCE THE FORMATION OF FANTASTIC FOUR ENTERPRISES, A TWENTY-FIVE PERCENT SHARE OF THE COMPANY WAS ALLOCATED TO YOU, AS TO THE OTHER THREE. I'M SORRY, I THOUGHT YOU KNEW--
BEN, I'D MENTIONED IT A WHILE BACK--
YEAH, BUT I THOUGHT THOSE WERE JUST MONKEY POINTS, Y'KNOW, "TEN PERCENT OF NET PROFIT MINUS COSTS OF BUILDING REED'S NEW FRAMMAJAMMIT WHICH COSTS MORE THAN YOU'LL EVER SEE IN A LIFETIME"...
LIKE THEY DO IN HOLLYWOOD.
OH, NO. NOT AT ALL. THE TRUST MONIES WERE SUBTRACTED FROM GROSS RECEIPTS, NOT NET.
BUT...THAT'S ALL GONE NOW, RIGHT? I MEAN, REED SIGNED IT ALL OVER TO THE GOVERNMENT TO MAKE UP FOR WHAT WE DID IN LATVERIA.
YES... AND NO.
REED TURNED OVER ALL THE CORPORATE ACCOUNTS, AND THE ACCOUNTS OF HIMSELF, YOU AND MRS. RICHARDS BECAUSE HE HAS POWER OF ATTORNEY OVER THOSE ACCOUNTS. LEGALLY, HE CANNOT TURN OVER WHAT HE DOESN'T OWN OR CONTROL.
MR. GRIMM'S FUNDS ARE HIS AND HIS ALONE.
ALL THIS TIME... HOWCUM YA NEVER MENTIONED THIS TO ME, REED?
I...ASSUMED YOU KNEW, AND BESIDES, I'VE--
"--WELL, I'VE BEEN A LITTLE DISTRACTED, BEN."

OKAY, WHATEVER, QUESTION IS, HOW *MUCH* MONEY DO I HAVE?

I'M GETTING THAT FOR YOU NOW--

BECAUSE I DON'T WANT TO GET MY HOPES UP, BUT EVEN A COUPLE GRAND WOULD BE TERRIFIC--

BOODLE-BOODLE-BREEP!

THERE YOU GO. THAT'S THE SUM TOTAL IN YOUR ACCOUNTS AS OF THIS PAST FRIDAY.

UH-HUH...

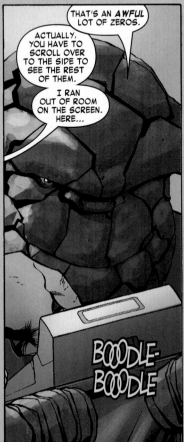

THAT'S AN *AWFUL* LOT OF ZEROS.

ACTUALLY, YOU HAVE TO SCROLL OVER TO THE SIDE TO SEE THE REST OF THEM.

I RAN OUT OF ROOM ON THE SCREEN. HERE...

BOODLE-BOODLE

BREEP!

I'VE GOT MONEY....

OH, THIS IS *SO* GOING TO BE BAD.

I'VE GOT MONEY!

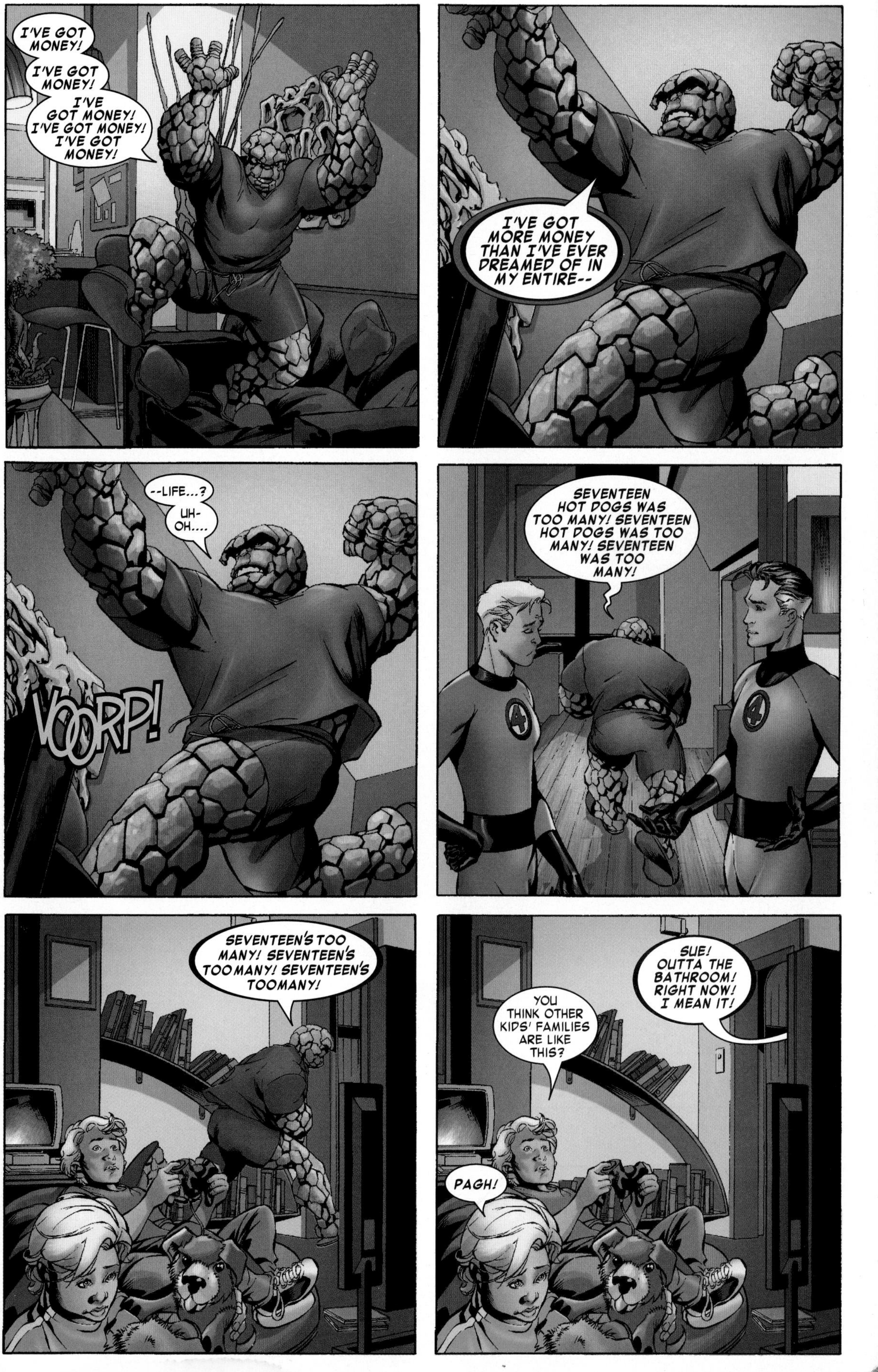
I'VE GOT MONEY!
I'VE GOT MONEY!
I'VE GOT MONEY! I'VE GOT MONEY! I'VE GOT MONEY!
I'VE GOT MORE MONEY THAN I'VE EVER DREAMED OF IN MY ENTIRE--
--LIFE...?
UH-OH....
VOORP!
SEVENTEEN HOT DOGS WAS TOO MANY! SEVENTEEN HOT DOGS WAS TOO MANY! SEVENTEEN WAS TOO MANY!
SEVENTEEN'S TOO MANY! SEVENTEEN'S TOOMANY! SEVENTEEN'S TOOMANY!
SUE! OUTTA THE BATHROOM! RIGHT NOW! I MEAN IT!
YOU THINK OTHER KIDS' FAMILIES ARE LIKE THIS?
PAGH!

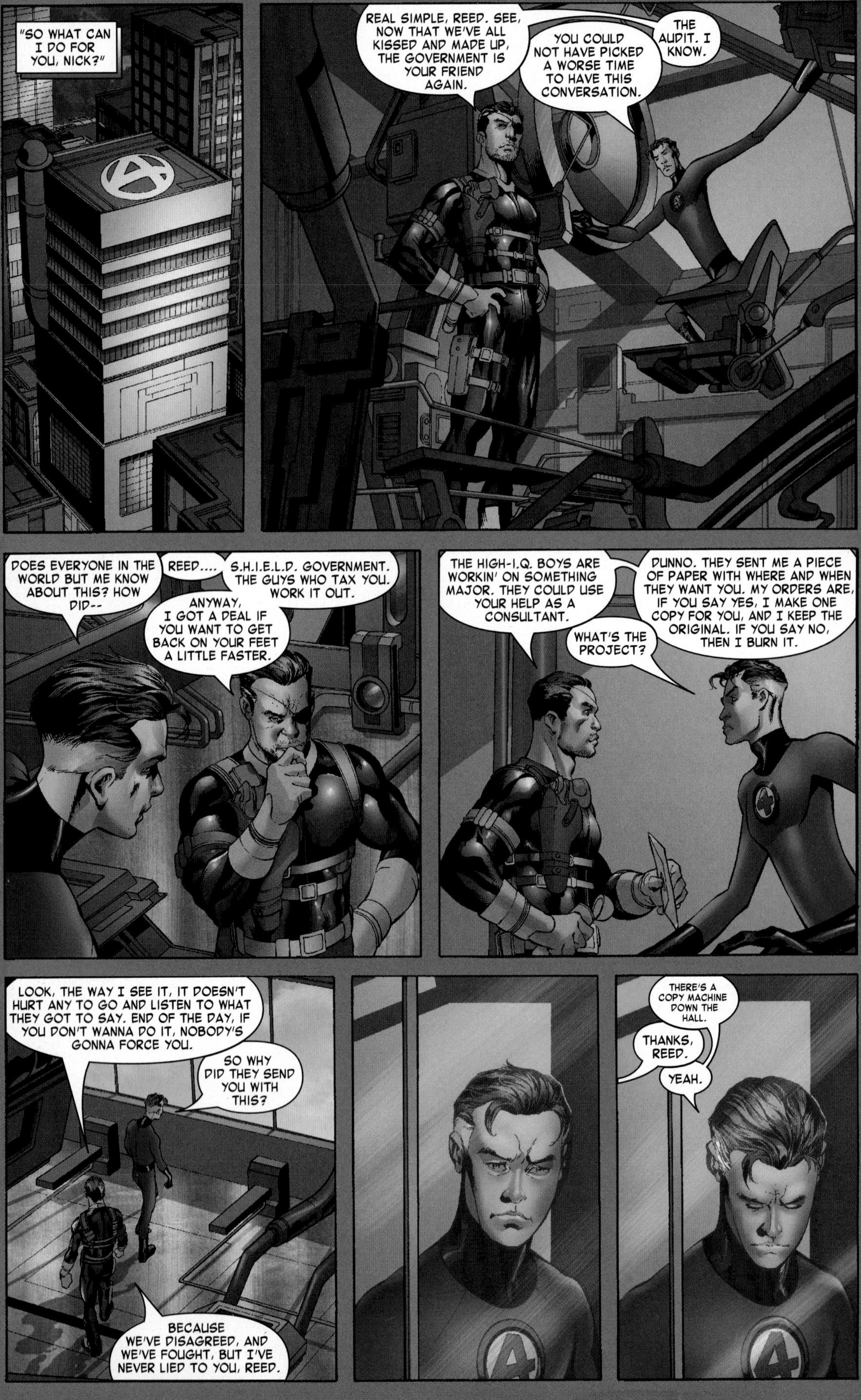
"SO WHAT CAN I DO FOR YOU, NICK?"
REAL SIMPLE, REED. SEE, NOW THAT WE'VE ALL KISSED AND MADE UP, THE GOVERNMENT IS YOUR FRIEND AGAIN.
YOU COULD NOT HAVE PICKED A WORSE TIME TO HAVE THIS CONVERSATION.
THE AUDIT. I KNOW.
DOES EVERYONE IN THE WORLD BUT ME KNOW ABOUT THIS? HOW DID--
REED....
S.H.I.E.L.D. GOVERNMENT. THE GUYS WHO TAX YOU. WORK IT OUT.
ANYWAY, I GOT A DEAL IF YOU WANT TO GET BACK ON YOUR FEET A LITTLE FASTER.
THE HIGH-I.Q. BOYS ARE WORKIN' ON SOMETHING MAJOR. THEY COULD USE YOUR HELP AS A CONSULTANT.
WHAT'S THE PROJECT?
DUNNO. THEY SENT ME A PIECE OF PAPER WITH WHERE AND WHEN THEY WANT YOU. MY ORDERS ARE, IF YOU SAY YES, I MAKE ONE COPY FOR YOU, AND I KEEP THE ORIGINAL. IF YOU SAY NO, THEN I BURN IT.
LOOK, THE WAY I SEE IT, IT DOESN'T HURT ANY TO GO AND LISTEN TO WHAT THEY GOT TO SAY. END OF THE DAY, IF YOU DON'T WANNA DO IT, NOBODY'S GONNA FORCE YOU.
SO WHY DID THEY SEND YOU WITH THIS?
BECAUSE WE'VE DISAGREED, AND WE'VE FOUGHT, BUT I'VE NEVER LIED TO YOU, REED.
THERE'S A COPY MACHINE DOWN THE HALL.
THANKS, REED.
YEAH.

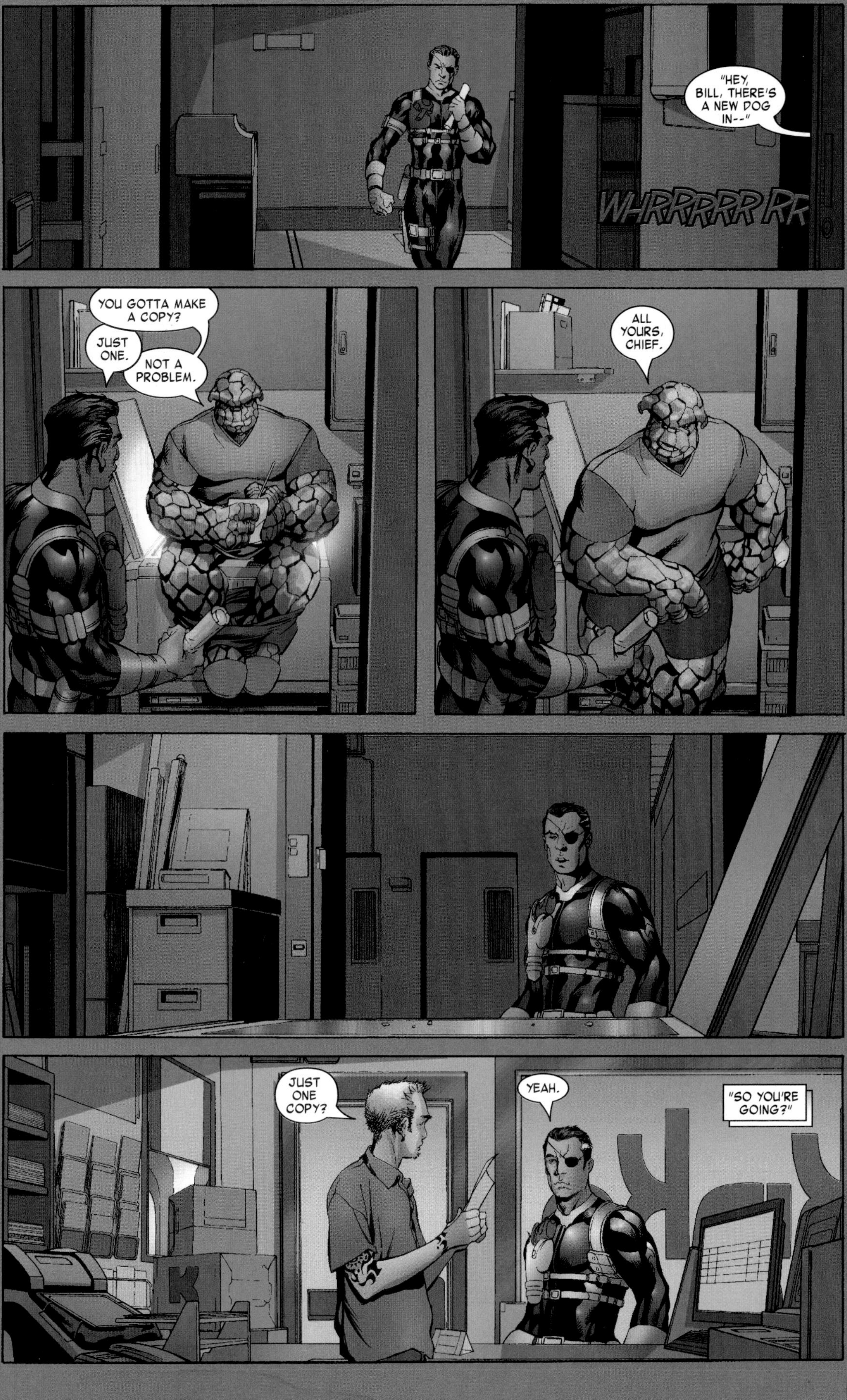
"HEY, BILL, THERE'S A NEW DOG IN--"
WHRRRRRR RR
YOU GOTTA MAKE A COPY?
JUST ONE.
NOT A PROBLEM.
ALL YOURS, CHIEF.
JUST ONE COPY?
YEAH.
"SO YOU'RE GOING?"

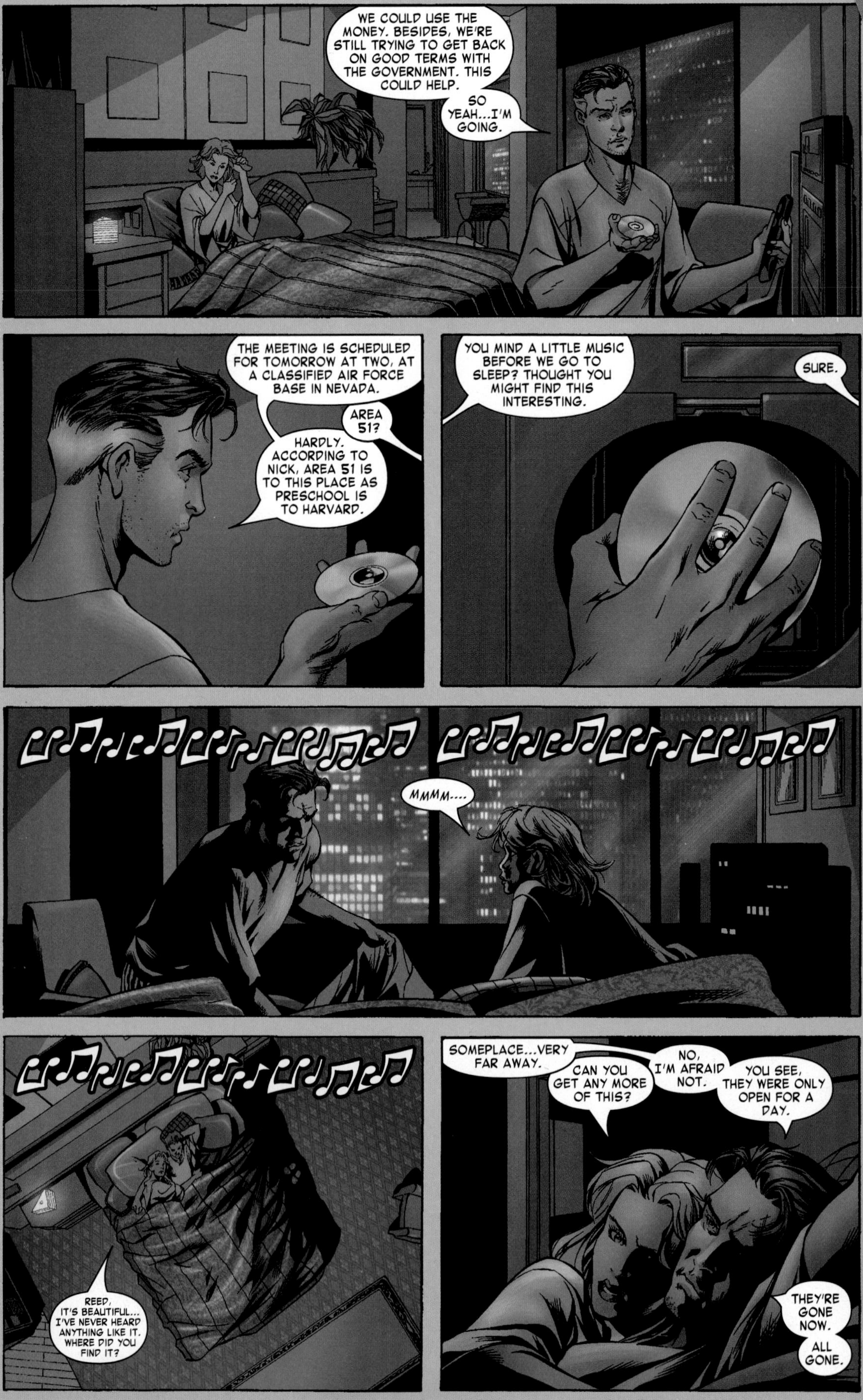
WE COULD USE THE MONEY. BESIDES, WE'RE STILL TRYING TO GET BACK ON GOOD TERMS WITH THE GOVERNMENT. THIS COULD HELP.
SO YEAH...I'M GOING.
THE MEETING IS SCHEDULED FOR TOMORROW AT TWO, AT A CLASSIFIED AIR FORCE BASE IN NEVADA.
AREA 51?
HARDLY. ACCORDING TO NICK, AREA 51 IS TO THIS PLACE AS PRESCHOOL IS TO HARVARD.
YOU MIND A LITTLE MUSIC BEFORE WE GO TO SLEEP? THOUGHT YOU MIGHT FIND THIS INTERESTING.
SURE.
MMMM....
REED, IT'S BEAUTIFUL... I'VE NEVER HEARD ANYTHING LIKE IT. WHERE DID YOU FIND IT?
SOMEPLACE...VERY FAR AWAY.
CAN YOU GET ANY MORE OF THIS?
NO, I'M AFRAID NOT.
YOU SEE, THEY WERE ONLY OPEN FOR A DAY.
THEY'RE GONE NOW.
ALL GONE.

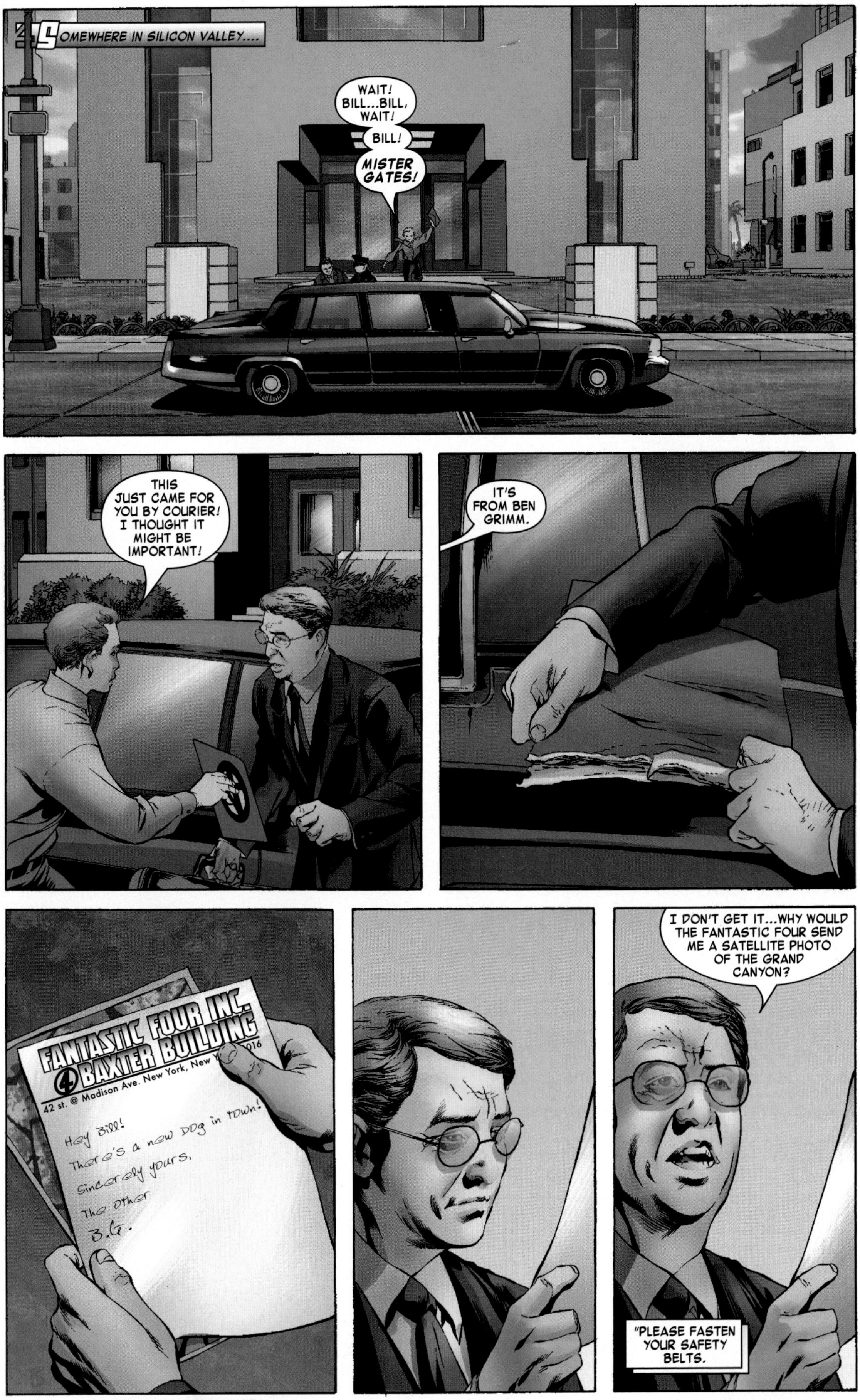
SOMEWHERE IN SILICON VALLEY....
WAIT! BILL...BILL, WAIT!
BILL!
MISTER GATES!
THIS JUST CAME FOR YOU BY COURIER! I THOUGHT IT MIGHT BE IMPORTANT!
IT'S FROM BEN GRIMM.
FANTASTIC FOUR INC.
BAXTER BUILDING
42 st. @ Madison Ave. New York, New Y 016
Hey Bill!
There's a new DOg in town!
Sincerely yours,
The other
B.G.
I DON'T GET IT...WHY WOULD THE FANTASTIC FOUR SEND ME A SATELLITE PHOTO OF THE GRAND CANYON?
"PLEASE FASTEN YOUR SAFETY BELTS.

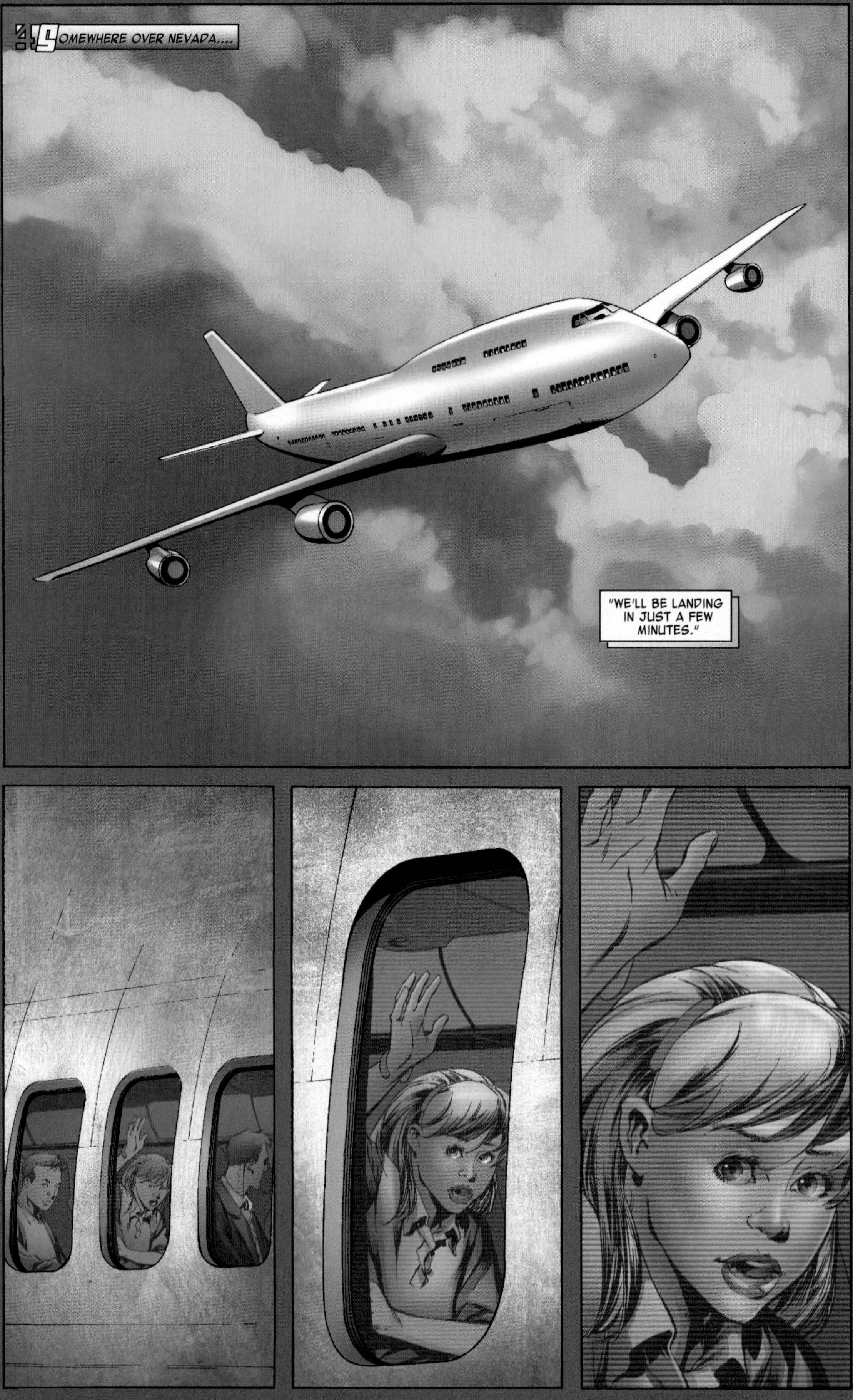
SOMEWHERE OVER NEVADA....
"WE'LL BE LANDING IN JUST A FEW MINUTES."

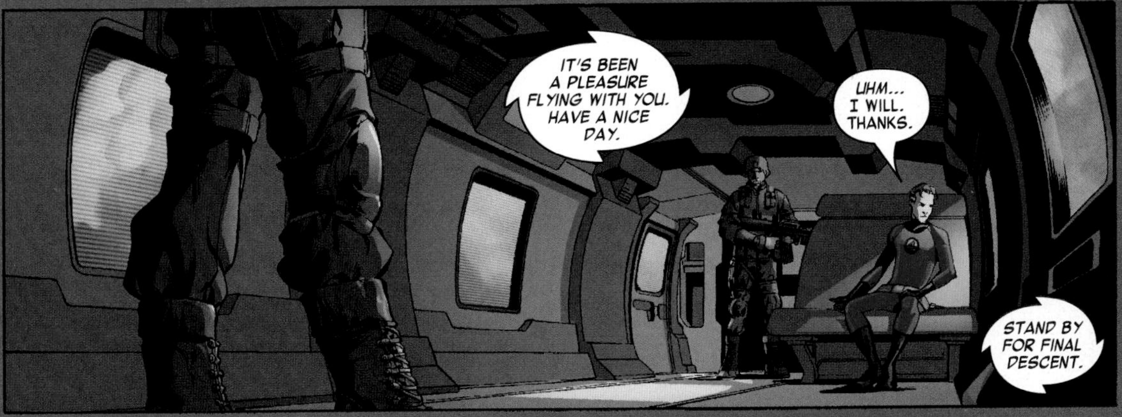
IT'S BEEN A PLEASURE FLYING WITH YOU. HAVE A NICE DAY.
UHM... I WILL. THANKS.
STAND BY FOR FINAL DESCENT.

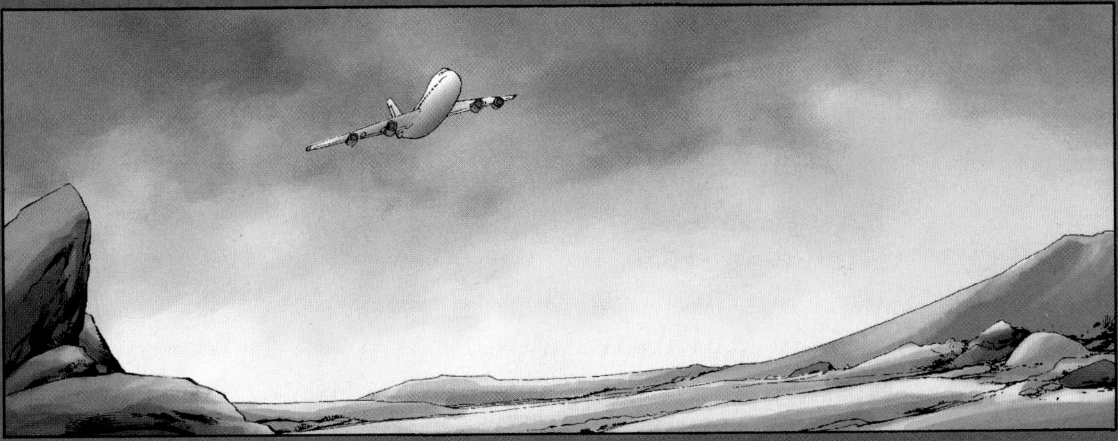

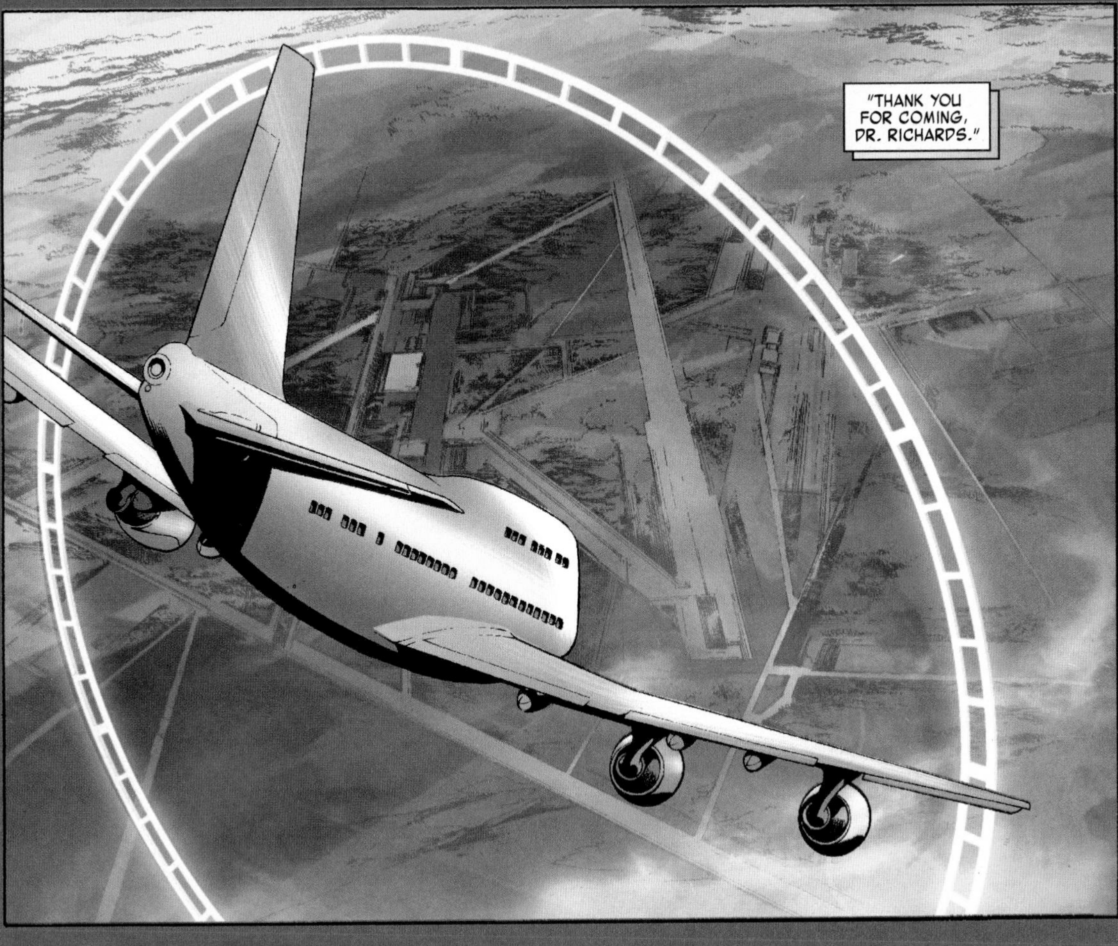
"THANK YOU FOR COMING, DR. RICHARDS."

IT'S REED, AND YOU'RE WELCOME. IT'S QUITE A SET-UP YOU'VE GOT HERE.

IT SHOULD BE. IT COST THE GOVERNMENT SOMETHING LIKE TWO BILLION DOLLARS JUST IN CONSTRUCTION, BEFORE WE BOUGHT A SINGLE PIECE OF EQUIPMENT.

I CAN IMAGINE SOME FOLKS IN CONGRESS WEREN'T TOO HAPPY ABOUT THAT.

NOT INITIALLY, NO--

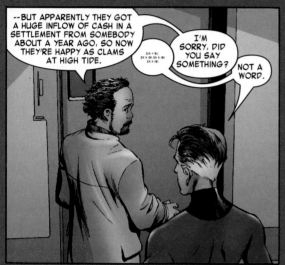

--BUT APPARENTLY THEY GOT A HUGE INFLOW OF CASH IN A SETTLEMENT FROM SOMEBODY ABOUT A YEAR AGO, SO NOW THEY'RE HAPPY AS CLAMS AT HIGH TIDE.

I'M SORRY, DID YOU SAY SOMETHING?

NOT A WORD.

THIS IS THE PLACE. HOLD ONTO YOUR SOCKS, YOU'LL LIKE THIS.

NICE. VERY NICE.

I'LL TAKE TWO.

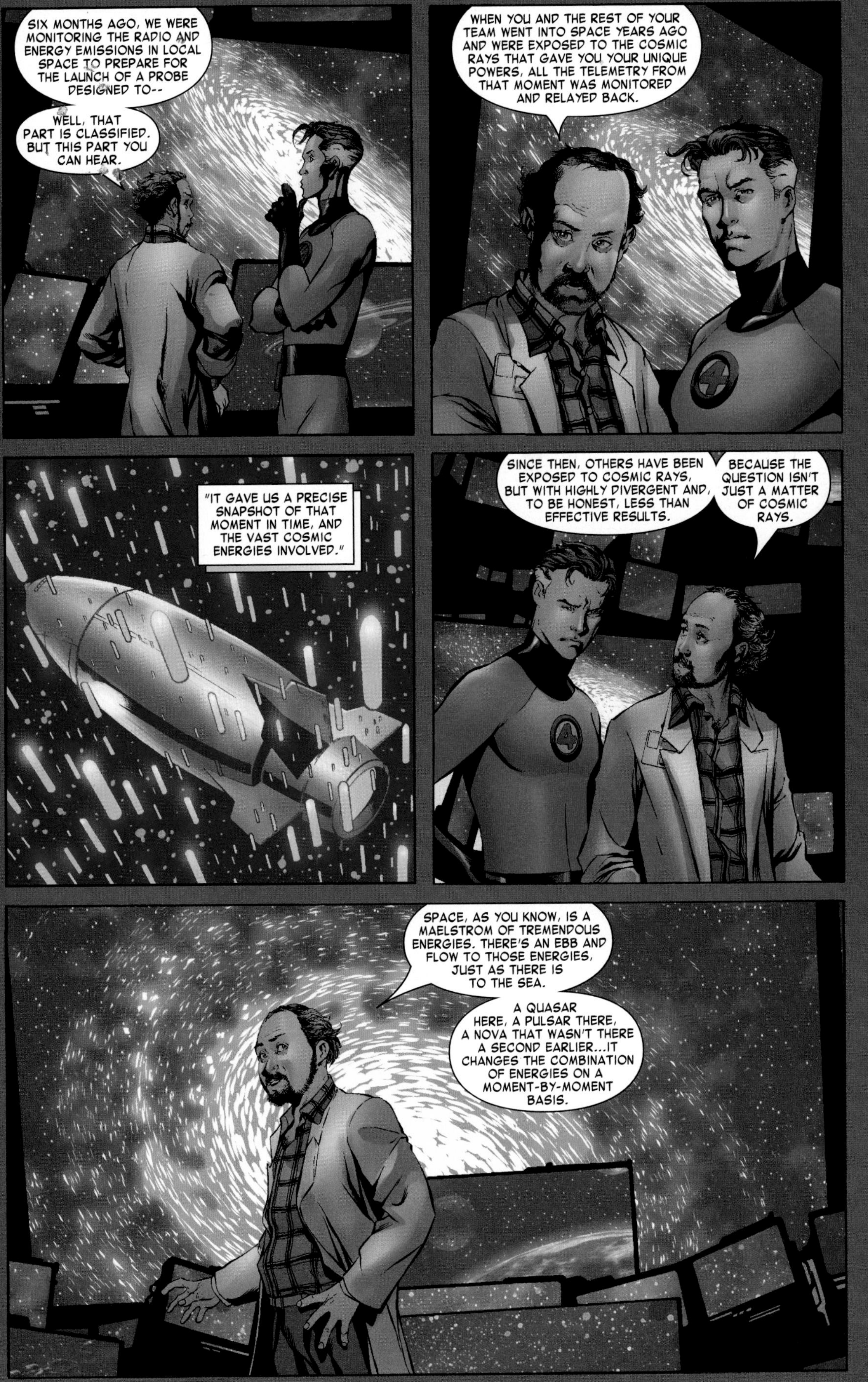
SIX MONTHS AGO, WE WERE MONITORING THE RADIO AND ENERGY EMISSIONS IN LOCAL SPACE TO PREPARE FOR THE LAUNCH OF A PROBE DESIGNED TO--
WELL, THAT PART IS CLASSIFIED. BUT THIS PART YOU CAN HEAR.
WHEN YOU AND THE REST OF YOUR TEAM WENT INTO SPACE YEARS AGO AND WERE EXPOSED TO THE COSMIC RAYS THAT GAVE YOU YOUR UNIQUE POWERS, ALL THE TELEMETRY FROM THAT MOMENT WAS MONITORED AND RELAYED BACK.
"IT GAVE US A PRECISE SNAPSHOT OF THAT MOMENT IN TIME, AND THE VAST COSMIC ENERGIES INVOLVED."
SINCE THEN, OTHERS HAVE BEEN EXPOSED TO COSMIC RAYS, BUT WITH HIGHLY DIVERGENT AND, TO BE HONEST, LESS THAN EFFECTIVE RESULTS.
BECAUSE THE QUESTION ISN'T JUST A MATTER OF COSMIC RAYS.
SPACE, AS YOU KNOW, IS A MAELSTROM OF TREMENDOUS ENERGIES. THERE'S AN EBB AND FLOW TO THOSE ENERGIES, JUST AS THERE IS TO THE SEA.
A QUASAR HERE, A PULSAR THERE, A NOVA THAT WASN'T THERE A SECOND EARLIER...IT CHANGES THE COMBINATION OF ENERGIES ON A MOMENT-BY-MOMENT BASIS.

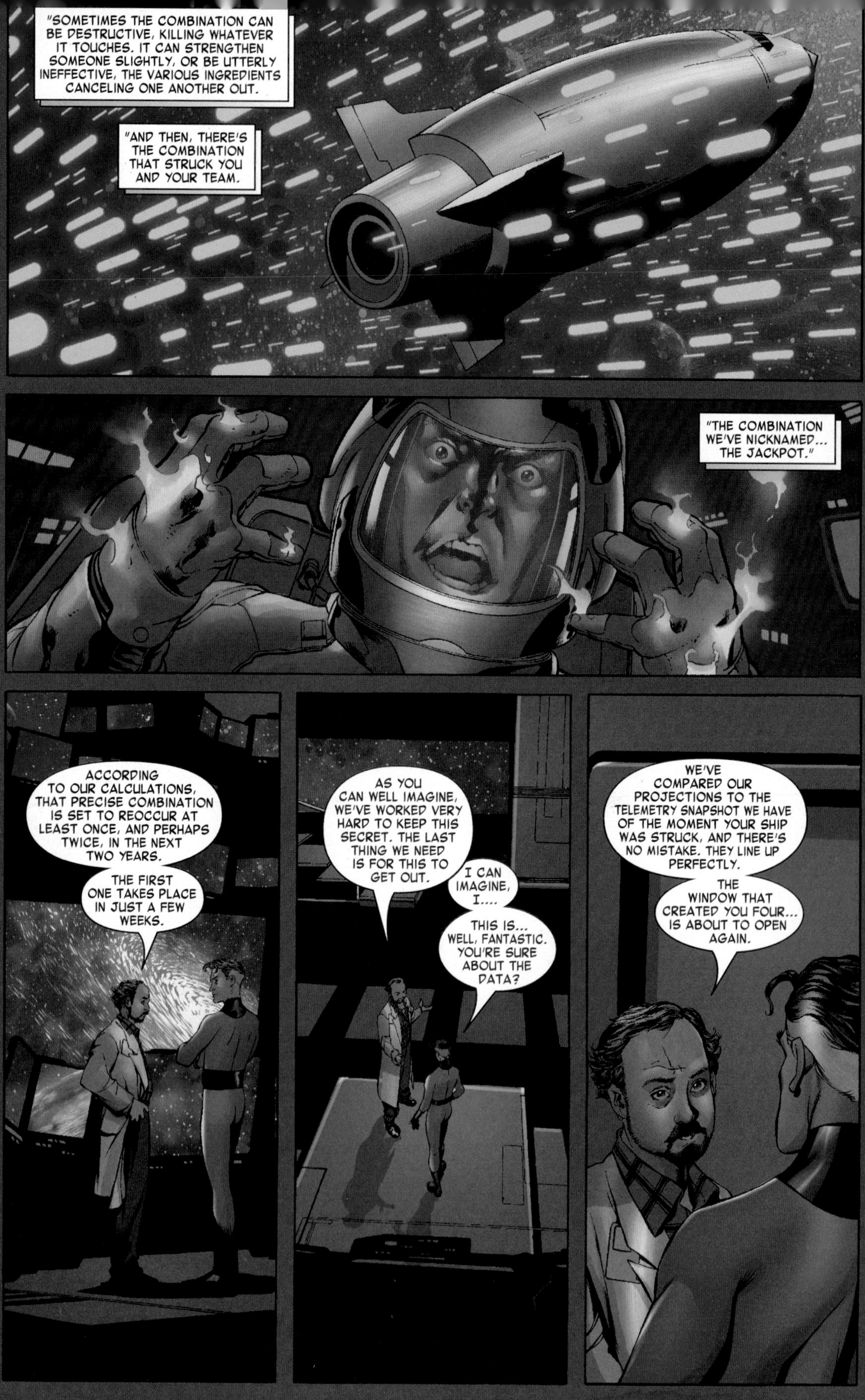
"SOMETIMES THE COMBINATION CAN BE DESTRUCTIVE, KILLING WHATEVER IT TOUCHES. IT CAN STRENGTHEN SOMEONE SLIGHTLY, OR BE UTTERLY INEFFECTIVE, THE VARIOUS INGREDIENTS CANCELING ONE ANOTHER OUT.
"AND THEN, THERE'S THE COMBINATION THAT STRUCK YOU AND YOUR TEAM.
"THE COMBINATION WE'VE NICKNAMED... THE JACKPOT."
ACCORDING TO OUR CALCULATIONS, THAT PRECISE COMBINATION IS SET TO REOCCUR AT LEAST ONCE, AND PERHAPS TWICE, IN THE NEXT TWO YEARS.
THE FIRST ONE TAKES PLACE IN JUST A FEW WEEKS.
AS YOU CAN WELL IMAGINE, WE'VE WORKED VERY HARD TO KEEP THIS SECRET. THE LAST THING WE NEED IS FOR THIS TO GET OUT.
I CAN IMAGINE, I....
THIS IS... WELL, FANTASTIC. YOU'RE SURE ABOUT THE DATA?
WE'VE COMPARED OUR PROJECTIONS TO THE TELEMETRY SNAPSHOT WE HAVE OF THE MOMENT YOUR SHIP WAS STRUCK, AND THERE'S NO MISTAKE. THEY LINE UP PERFECTLY.
THE WINDOW THAT CREATED YOU FOUR... IS ABOUT TO OPEN AGAIN.

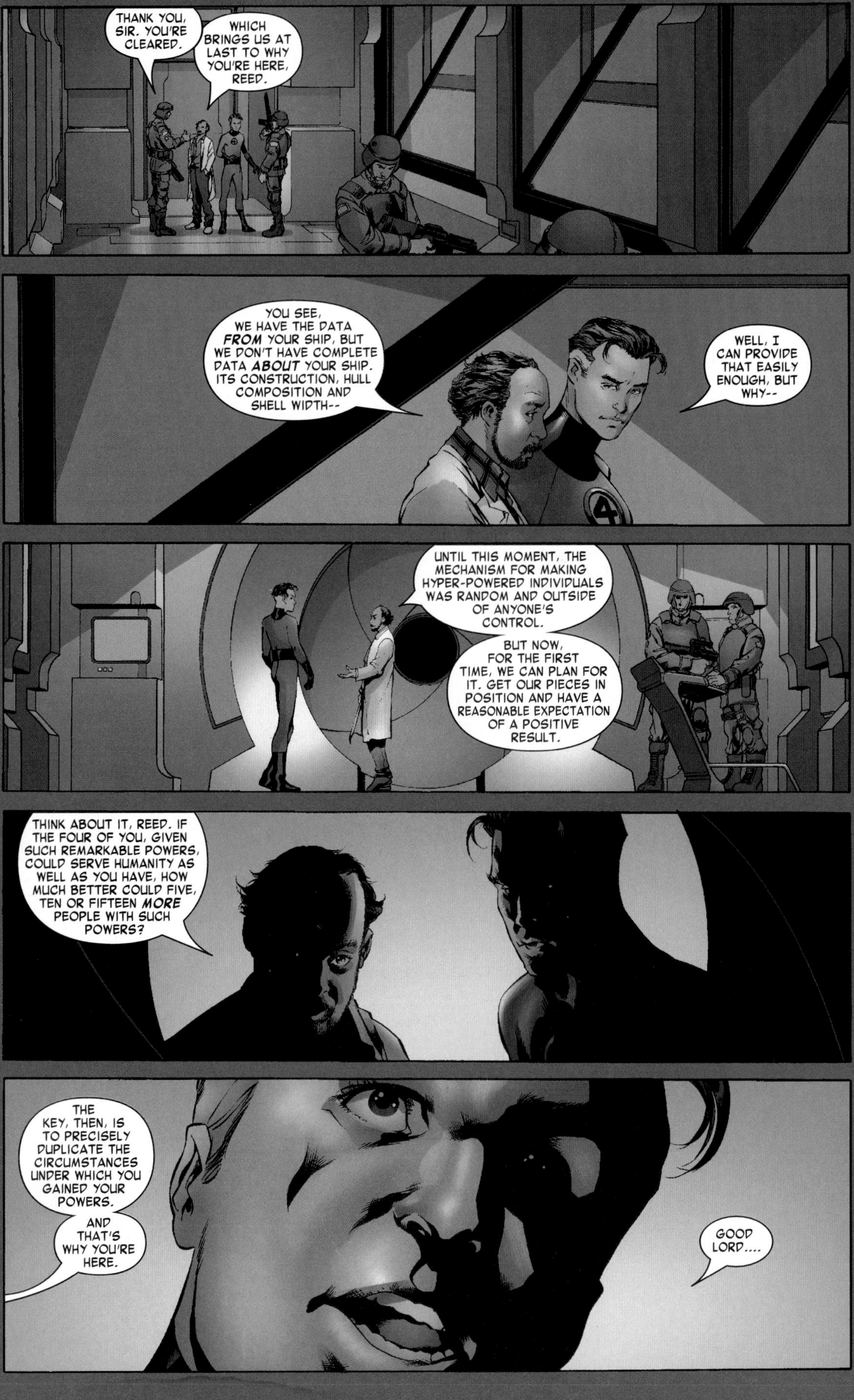
THANK YOU, SIR. YOU'RE CLEARED.
WHICH BRINGS US AT LAST TO WHY YOU'RE HERE, REED.
YOU SEE, WE HAVE THE DATA FROM YOUR SHIP, BUT WE DON'T HAVE COMPLETE DATA ABOUT YOUR SHIP. ITS CONSTRUCTION, HULL COMPOSITION AND SHELL WIDTH--
WELL, I CAN PROVIDE THAT EASILY ENOUGH, BUT WHY--
UNTIL THIS MOMENT, THE MECHANISM FOR MAKING HYPER-POWERED INDIVIDUALS WAS RANDOM AND OUTSIDE OF ANYONE'S CONTROL.
BUT NOW, FOR THE FIRST TIME, WE CAN PLAN FOR IT. GET OUR PIECES IN POSITION AND HAVE A REASONABLE EXPECTATION OF A POSITIVE RESULT.
THINK ABOUT IT, REED. IF THE FOUR OF YOU, GIVEN SUCH REMARKABLE POWERS, COULD SERVE HUMANITY AS WELL AS YOU HAVE, HOW MUCH BETTER COULD FIVE, TEN OR FIFTEEN MORE PEOPLE WITH SUCH POWERS?
THE KEY, THEN, IS TO PRECISELY DUPLICATE THE CIRCUMSTANCES UNDER WHICH YOU GAINED YOUR POWERS.
AND THAT'S WHY YOU'RE HERE.
GOOD LORD....

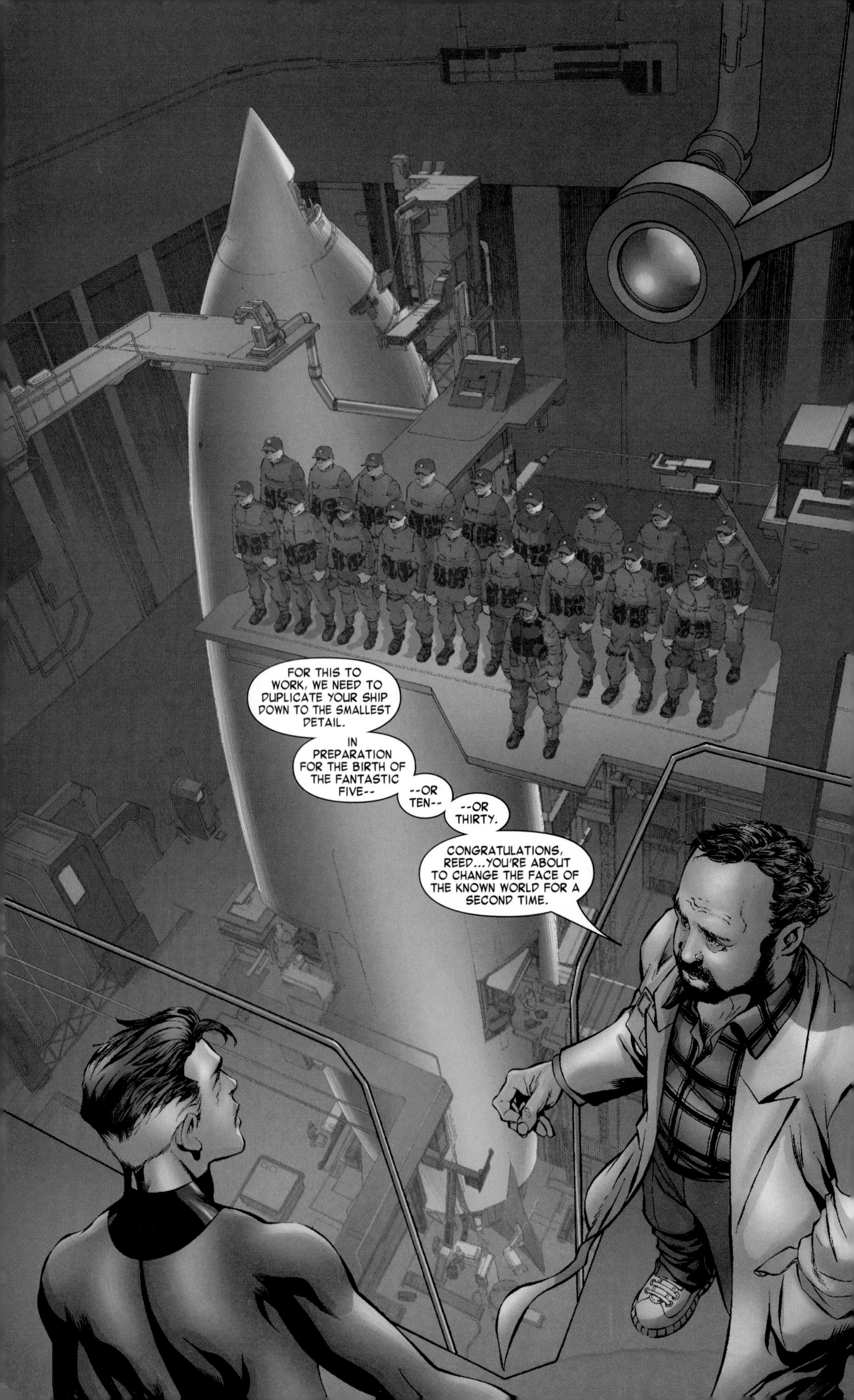
FOR THIS TO WORK, WE NEED TO DUPLICATE YOUR SHIP DOWN TO THE SMALLEST DETAIL.
IN PREPARATION FOR THE BIRTH OF THE FANTASTIC FIVE--
--OR TEN--
--OR THIRTY.
CONGRATULATIONS, REED...YOU'RE ABOUT TO CHANGE THE FACE OF THE KNOWN WORLD FOR A SECOND TIME.

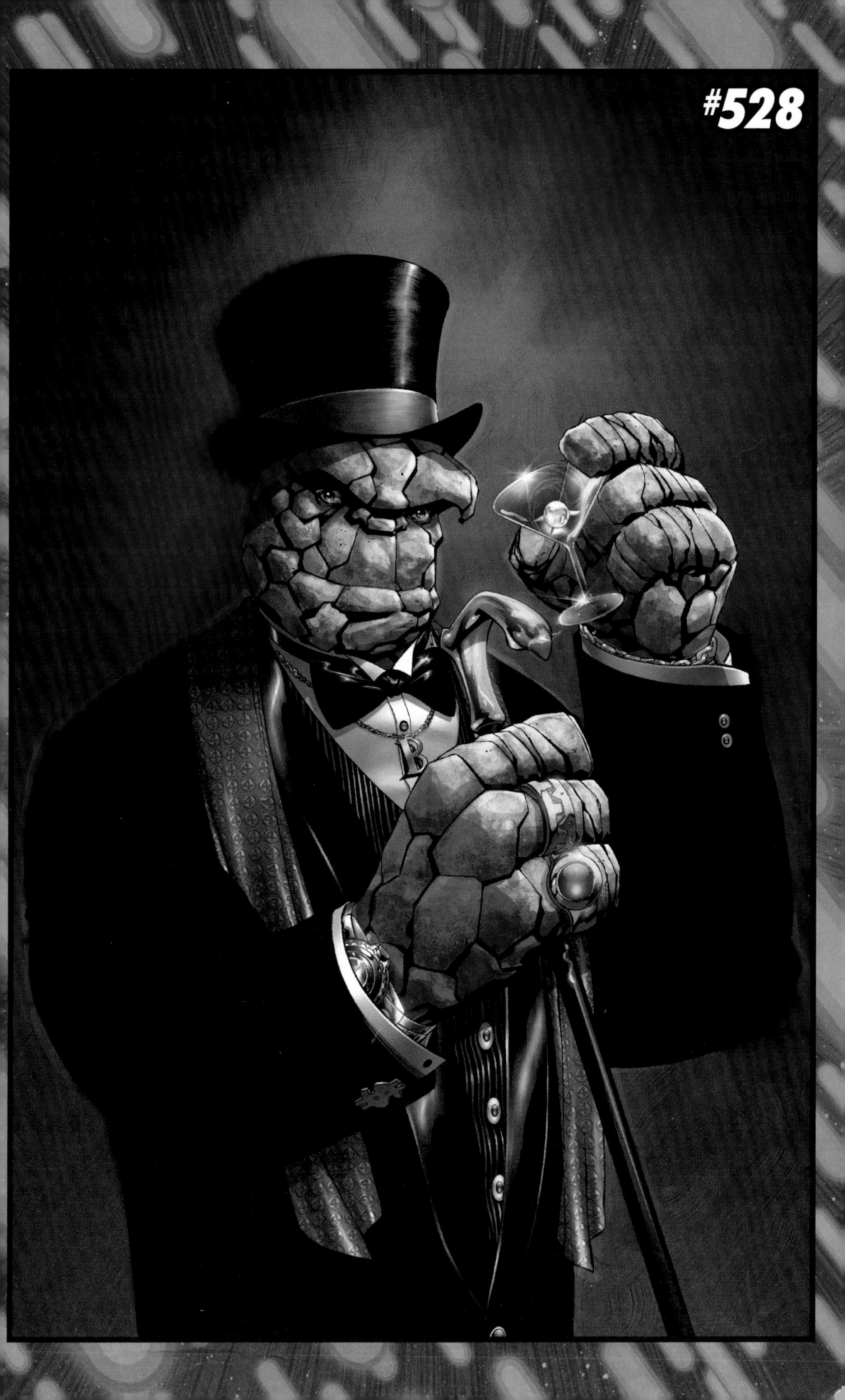

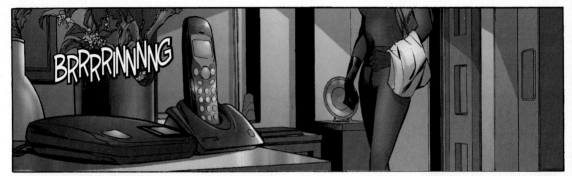

BRRRRINNNNG

HELLO?

SUE... HI.

REED? WELL, THIS IS A SURPRISE. GIVEN HOW SECRET THE GOVERNMENT WAS BEING ABOUT THIS ASSIGNMENT, I DIDN'T THINK I'D HEAR FROM YOU UNTIL YOU LEFT THE BASE.

NEITHER DID I.

BUT THEY SAID I COULD CALL IF I USED ACS, THE ALL-CLEAR SYSTEM. IT'S AN INTELLIGENT PROGRAM THAT USES A TWO-SECOND DELAY WHILE IT LISTENS FOR KEY WORDS OR PHRASES THAT CONTAIN CLASSIFIED REFERENCES--

UH-HUH--

--AND REPLACES THEM WITH WHITE NOISE THAT CANCELS OUT WHAT'S BEING SAID. THIS WAY ONLY THE NONCLASSIFIED PARTS CAN BE HEARD.

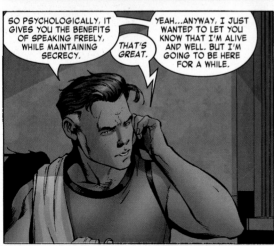

SO PSYCHOLOGICALLY, IT GIVES YOU THE BENEFITS OF SPEAKING FREELY, WHILE MAINTAINING SECRECY.

THAT'S GREAT.

YEAH...ANYWAY, I JUST WANTED TO LET YOU KNOW THAT I'M ALIVE AND WELL. BUT I'M GOING TO BE HERE FOR A WHILE.

I WAS TALKING TO   AND HE SAID MAYBE TWO, THREE WEEKS UNTIL THE   HAS BEEN PREPPED AND THE LAST OF THE   DESIGN WORK DONE. HE SEEMS LIKE A NICE GUY.

WHO DOES?

DOCTOR   . HE'S   OF THE PROJECT.

THEY THINK THE COMPOSITION OF COSMIC RAYS IN A FEW WEEKS WILL GIVE THEM THE CHANCE TO REPLICATE THE SITUATION THAT GAVE US OUR ABILITIES, ALLOWING THEM TO PRODUCE DOZENS OF OTHERS WITH SIMILAR POWERS.

UHM, REED, I--

ONCE WE FINISH MODIFYING THE SHIP SO IT'S EXACTLY THE SAME AS THE ONE WE USED, THEY'LL BE READY FOR LAUNCH.

AFTER THAT

SO, HOW ARE YOU?

I...FINE, REED. WE'RE ALL GOOD.

"BEN'S OUT SHOPPING, ENJOYING THE FACT THAT HE HAS MORE MONEY THAN HE CAN EVER SPEND IN A LIFETIME. HE TOOK JOHNNY WITH HIM."

"BEN SAID IT WAS TO HAVE ANOTHER PAIR OF EYES ALONG, BUT I THINK HE JUST WANTS TO LORD THE MONEY THING OVER JOHNNY FOR A BIT."

SO, DO YA THINK IT'S ME?

TELL THE TRUTH: I LOOK HOT, DON'T I?

YEAH...IT'S SWELL...

...IF WE CHANGE OUR NAME TO THE FANTASTIC THREE AND THEIR PIMP.

WATCH IT, MATCHSTICK. THIS IS A CLASS JOINT. YA CAN'T EVEN GET IN HERE WITHOUT RESERVATIONS.

DON'T WORRY, WITH YOU DRESSED LIKE THAT, I'VE GOT ENOUGH RESERVATIONS FOR BOTH OF US.

SO, HOW MUCH FOR THE WHOLE OUTFIT?

WELL, WE'LL HAVE TO TAILOR IT TO FIT, WHICH WILL ADD QUITE A BIT, BUT...TEN THOUSAND FOR THIS ENSEMBLE.

TEN G'S, HUH?

OKAY, I'LL TAKE IT. IN FACT, I'LL TAKE ALL OF THEM.

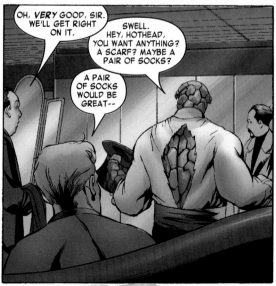

OH, VERY GOOD, SIR. WE'LL GET RIGHT ON IT.

SWELL. HEY, HOTHEAD, YOU WANT ANYTHING? A SCARF? MAYBE A PAIR OF SOCKS?

A PAIR OF SOCKS WOULD BE GREAT--

--FILLED WITH PLASTIQUE AND A FUSE.

"I'M SURE I'LL HEAR ALL ABOUT IT WHEN THEY GET HOME."

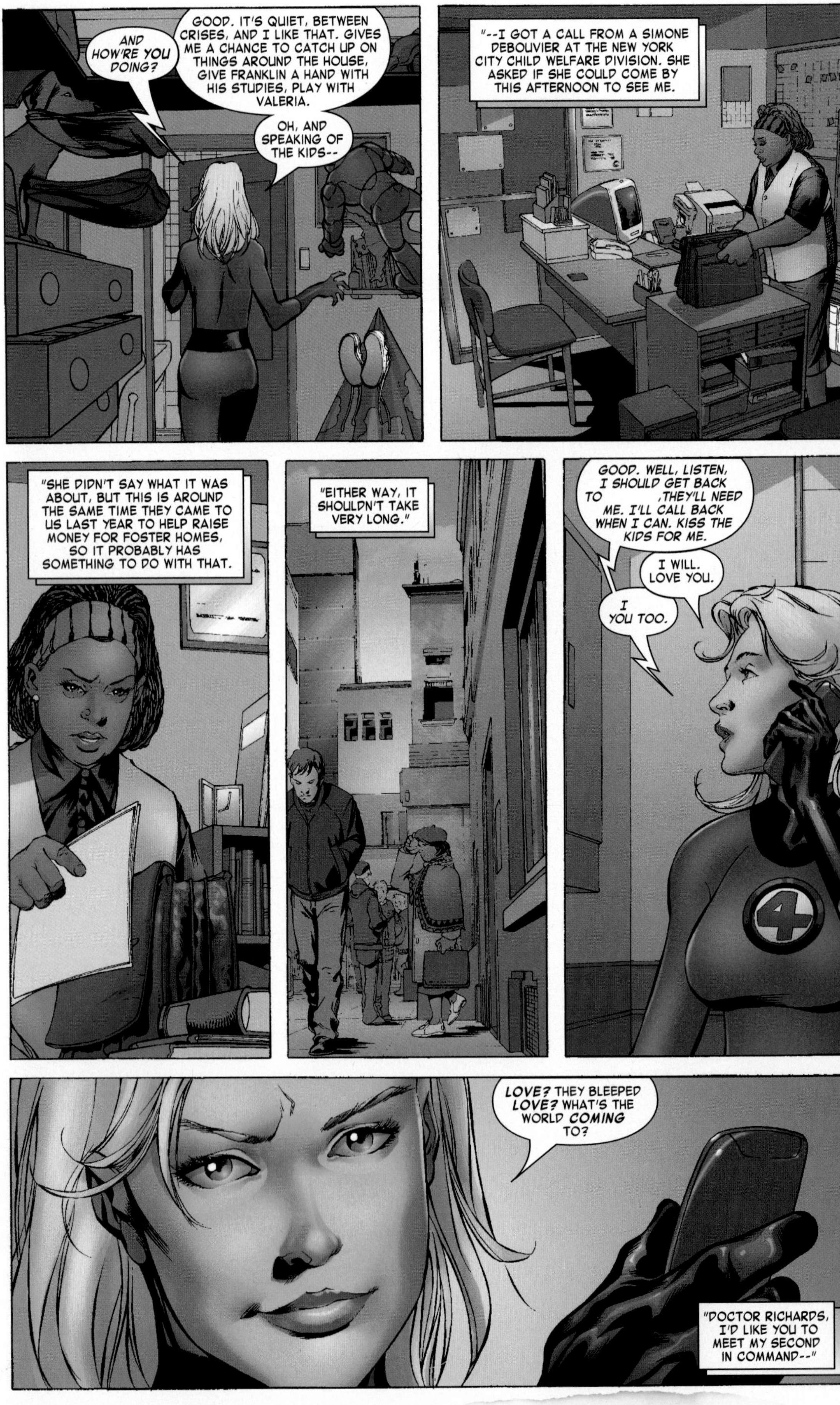
AND HOW'RE YOU DOING?
GOOD. IT'S QUIET, BETWEEN CRISES, AND I LIKE THAT. GIVES ME A CHANCE TO CATCH UP ON THINGS AROUND THE HOUSE, GIVE FRANKLIN A HAND WITH HIS STUDIES, PLAY WITH VALERIA.
OH, AND SPEAKING OF THE KIDS--
"--I GOT A CALL FROM A SIMONE DEBOUVIER AT THE NEW YORK CITY CHILD WELFARE DIVISION. SHE ASKED IF SHE COULD COME BY THIS AFTERNOON TO SEE ME.
"SHE DIDN'T SAY WHAT IT WAS ABOUT, BUT THIS IS AROUND THE SAME TIME THEY CAME TO US LAST YEAR TO HELP RAISE MONEY FOR FOSTER HOMES, SO IT PROBABLY HAS SOMETHING TO DO WITH THAT.
"EITHER WAY, IT SHOULDN'T TAKE VERY LONG."
GOOD. WELL, LISTEN, I SHOULD GET BACK TO ,THEY'LL NEED ME. I'LL CALL BACK WHEN I CAN. KISS THE KIDS FOR ME.
I WILL. LOVE YOU.
I YOU TOO.
LOVE? THEY BLEEPED LOVE? WHAT'S THE WORLD COMING TO?
"DOCTOR RICHARDS, I'D LIKE YOU TO MEET MY SECOND IN COMMAND--"

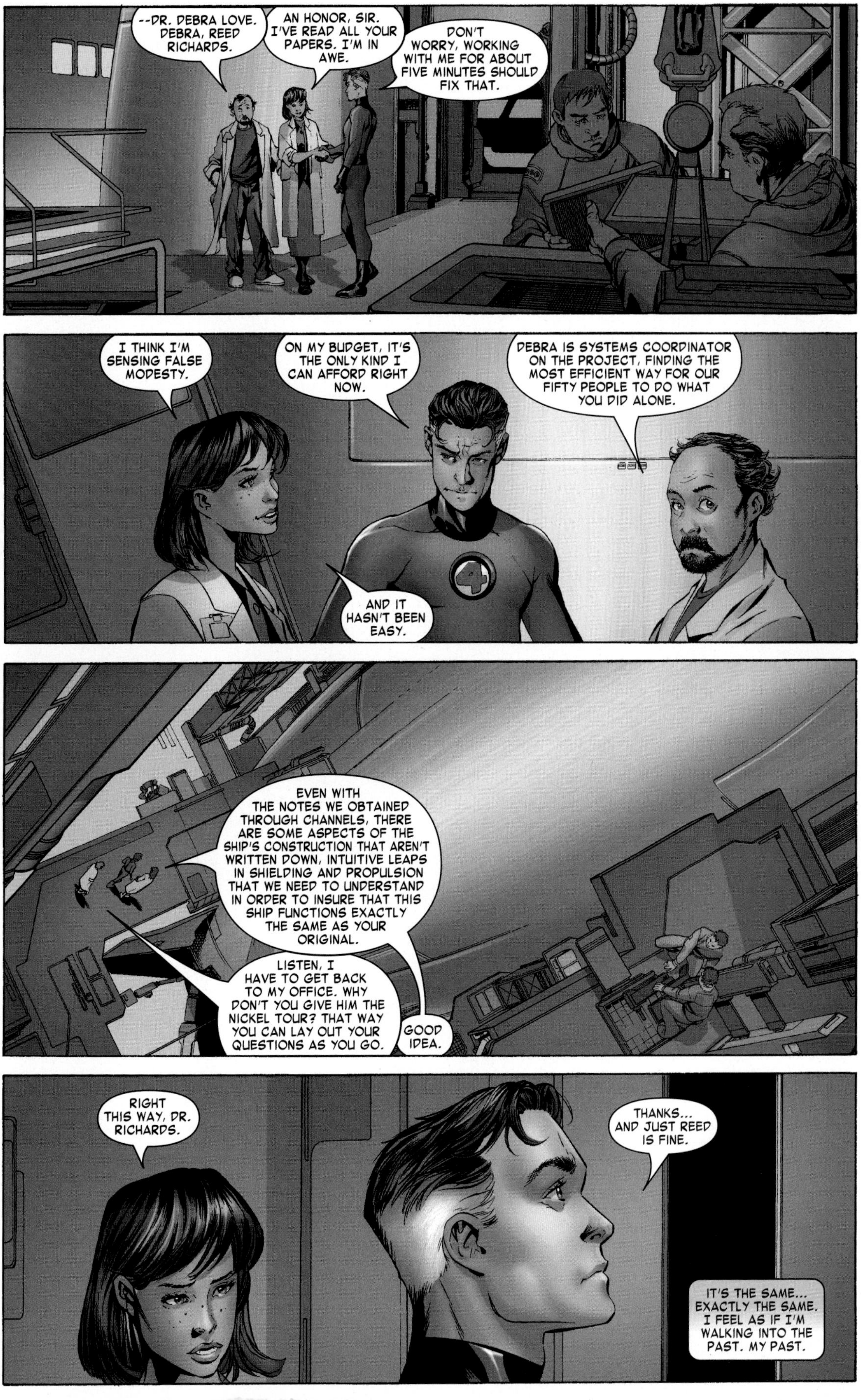
--DR. DEBRA LOVE. DEBRA, REED RICHARDS.
AN HONOR, SIR. I'VE READ ALL YOUR PAPERS. I'M IN AWE.
DON'T WORRY, WORKING WITH ME FOR ABOUT FIVE MINUTES SHOULD FIX THAT.
I THINK I'M SENSING FALSE MODESTY.
ON MY BUDGET, IT'S THE ONLY KIND I CAN AFFORD RIGHT NOW.
AND IT HASN'T BEEN EASY.
DEBRA IS SYSTEMS COORDINATOR ON THE PROJECT, FINDING THE MOST EFFICIENT WAY FOR OUR FIFTY PEOPLE TO DO WHAT YOU DID ALONE.
EVEN WITH THE NOTES WE OBTAINED THROUGH CHANNELS, THERE ARE SOME ASPECTS OF THE SHIP'S CONSTRUCTION THAT AREN'T WRITTEN DOWN, INTUITIVE LEAPS IN SHIELDING AND PROPULSION THAT WE NEED TO UNDERSTAND IN ORDER TO INSURE THAT THIS SHIP FUNCTIONS EXACTLY THE SAME AS YOUR ORIGINAL.
LISTEN, I HAVE TO GET BACK TO MY OFFICE. WHY DON'T YOU GIVE HIM THE NICKEL TOUR? THAT WAY YOU CAN LAY OUT YOUR QUESTIONS AS YOU GO.
GOOD IDEA.
RIGHT THIS WAY, DR. RICHARDS.
THANKS... AND JUST REED IS FINE.
IT'S THE SAME... EXACTLY THE SAME. I FEEL AS IF I'M WALKING INTO THE PAST. MY PAST.

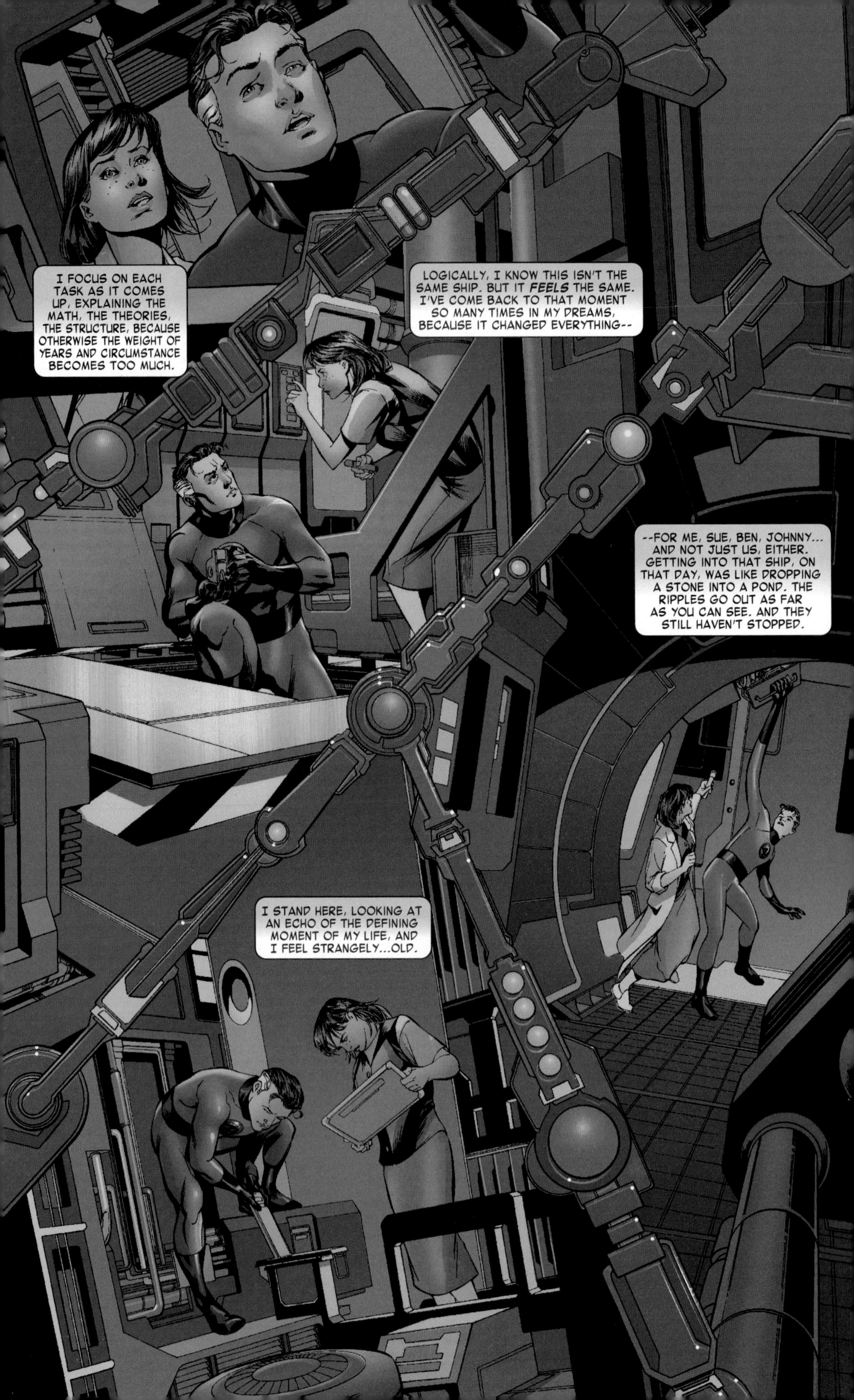
I FOCUS ON EACH TASK AS IT COMES UP, EXPLAINING THE MATH, THE THEORIES, THE STRUCTURE, BECAUSE OTHERWISE THE WEIGHT OF YEARS AND CIRCUMSTANCE BECOMES TOO MUCH.
LOGICALLY, I KNOW THIS ISN'T THE SAME SHIP. BUT IT *FEELS* THE SAME. I'VE COME BACK TO THAT MOMENT SO MANY TIMES IN MY DREAMS, BECAUSE IT CHANGED EVERYTHING--
--FOR ME, SUE, BEN, JOHNNY... AND NOT JUST US, EITHER. GETTING INTO THAT SHIP, ON THAT DAY, WAS LIKE DROPPING A STONE INTO A POND. THE RIPPLES GO OUT AS FAR AS YOU CAN SEE. AND THEY STILL HAVEN'T STOPPED.
I STAND HERE, LOOKING AT AN ECHO OF THE DEFINING MOMENT OF MY LIFE, AND I FEEL STRANGELY...OLD.

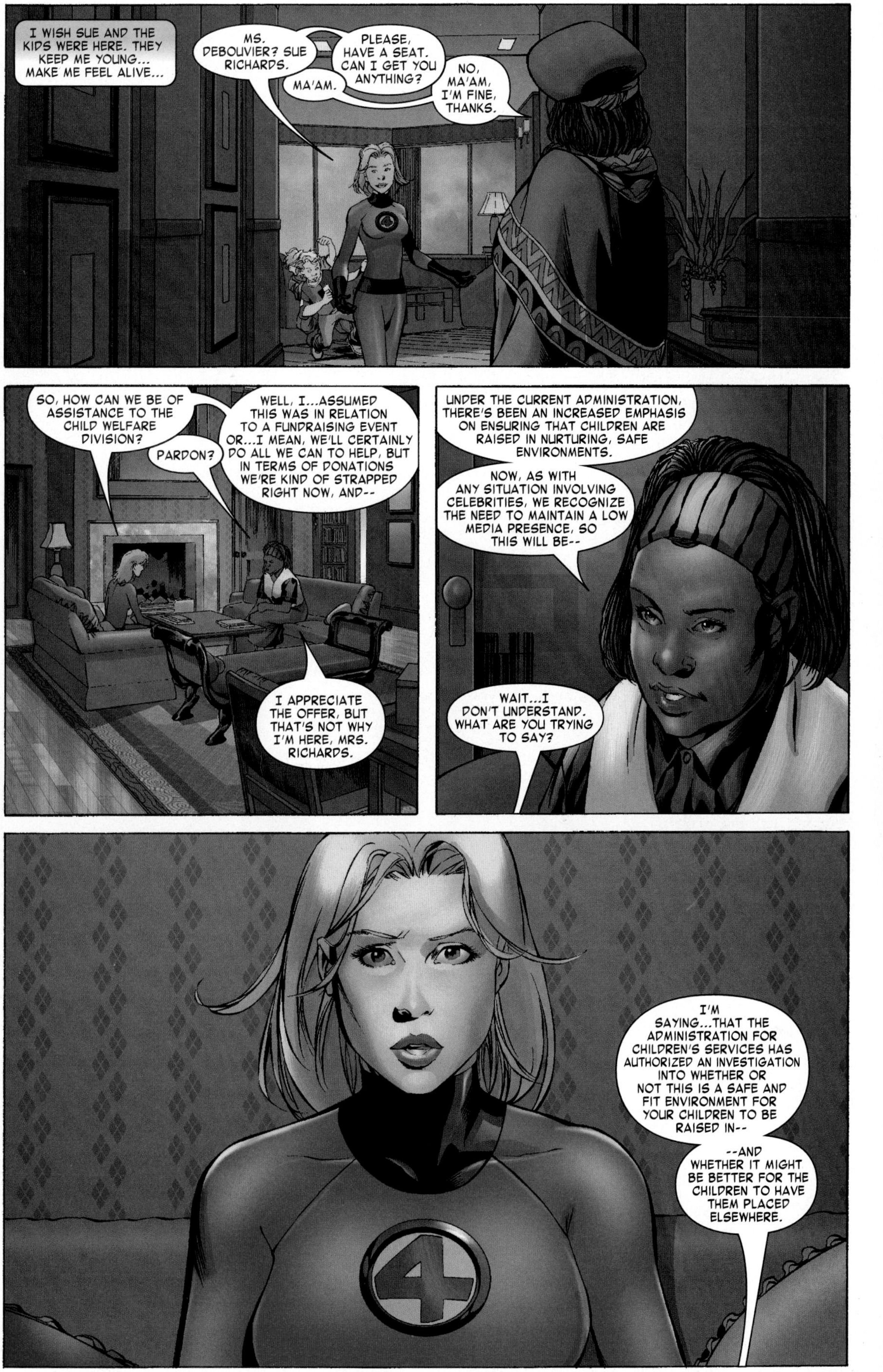
I WISH SUE AND THE KIDS WERE HERE. THEY KEEP ME YOUNG... MAKE ME FEEL ALIVE...
MS. DEBOUVIER? SUE RICHARDS.
MA'AM.
PLEASE, HAVE A SEAT. CAN I GET YOU ANYTHING?
NO, MA'AM, I'M FINE, THANKS.
SO, HOW CAN WE BE OF ASSISTANCE TO THE CHILD WELFARE DIVISION?
PARDON?
WELL, I...ASSUMED THIS WAS IN RELATION TO A FUNDRAISING EVENT OR...I MEAN, WE'LL CERTAINLY DO ALL WE CAN TO HELP, BUT IN TERMS OF DONATIONS WE'RE KIND OF STRAPPED RIGHT NOW, AND--
I APPRECIATE THE OFFER, BUT THAT'S NOT WHY I'M HERE, MRS. RICHARDS.
UNDER THE CURRENT ADMINISTRATION, THERE'S BEEN AN INCREASED EMPHASIS ON ENSURING THAT CHILDREN ARE RAISED IN NURTURING, SAFE ENVIRONMENTS.
NOW, AS WITH ANY SITUATION INVOLVING CELEBRITIES, WE RECOGNIZE THE NEED TO MAINTAIN A LOW MEDIA PRESENCE, SO THIS WILL BE--
WAIT...I DON'T UNDERSTAND. WHAT ARE YOU TRYING TO SAY?
I'M SAYING...THAT THE ADMINISTRATION FOR CHILDREN'S SERVICES HAS AUTHORIZED AN INVESTIGATION INTO WHETHER OR NOT THIS IS A SAFE AND FIT ENVIRONMENT FOR YOUR CHILDREN TO BE RAISED IN--
--AND WHETHER IT MIGHT BE BETTER FOR THE CHILDREN TO HAVE THEM PLACED ELSEWHERE.

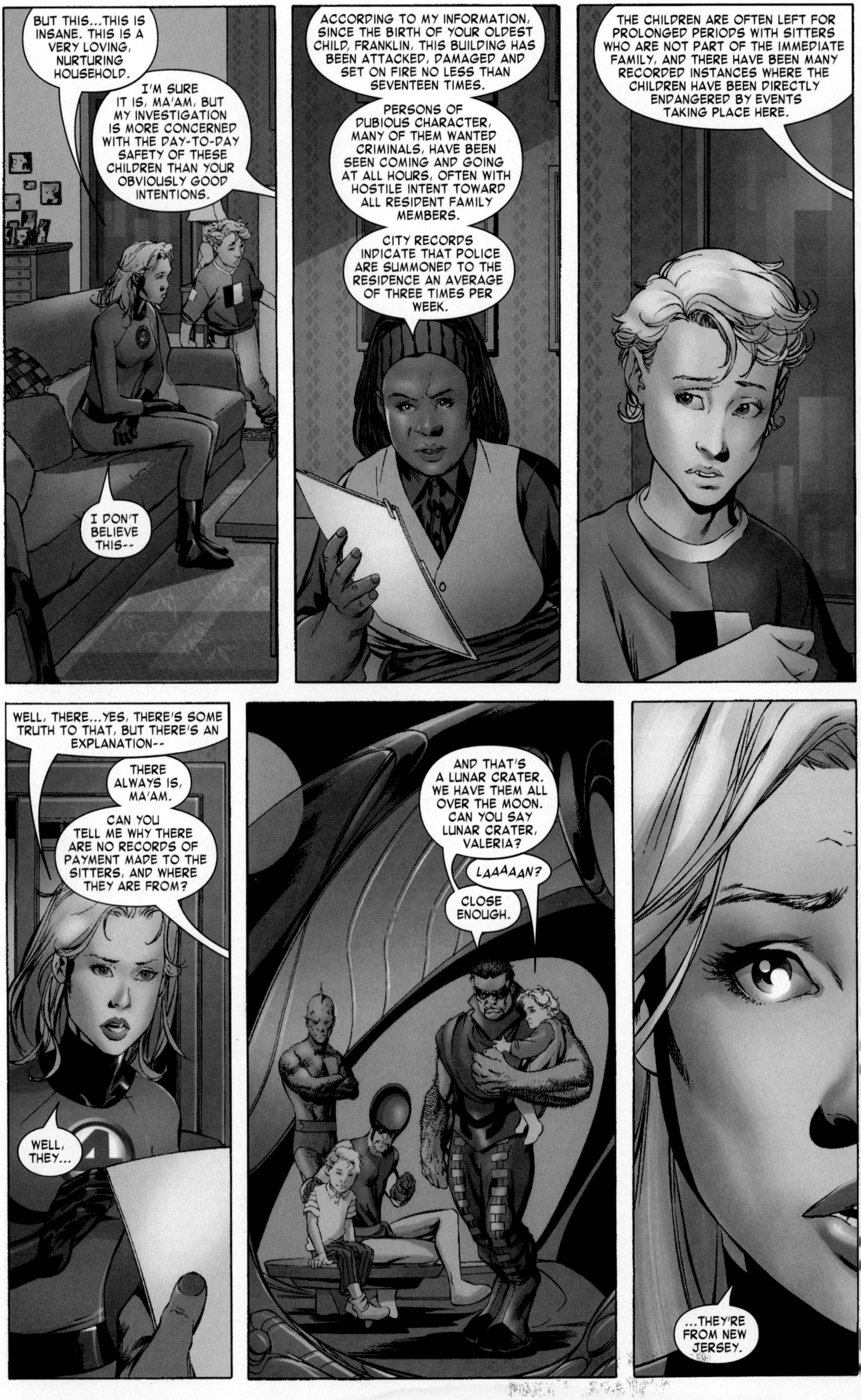
BUT THIS...THIS IS INSANE. THIS IS A VERY LOVING, NURTURING HOUSEHOLD.
I'M SURE IT IS, MA'AM, BUT MY INVESTIGATION IS MORE CONCERNED WITH THE DAY-TO-DAY SAFETY OF THESE CHILDREN THAN YOUR OBVIOUSLY GOOD INTENTIONS.
I DON'T BELIEVE THIS--
ACCORDING TO MY INFORMATION, SINCE THE BIRTH OF YOUR OLDEST CHILD, FRANKLIN, THIS BUILDING HAS BEEN ATTACKED, DAMAGED AND SET ON FIRE NO LESS THAN SEVENTEEN TIMES.
PERSONS OF DUBIOUS CHARACTER, MANY OF THEM WANTED CRIMINALS, HAVE BEEN SEEN COMING AND GOING AT ALL HOURS, OFTEN WITH HOSTILE INTENT TOWARD ALL RESIDENT FAMILY MEMBERS.
CITY RECORDS INDICATE THAT POLICE ARE SUMMONED TO THE RESIDENCE AN AVERAGE OF THREE TIMES PER WEEK.
THE CHILDREN ARE OFTEN LEFT FOR PROLONGED PERIODS WITH SITTERS WHO ARE NOT PART OF THE IMMEDIATE FAMILY, AND THERE HAVE BEEN MANY RECORDED INSTANCES WHERE THE CHILDREN HAVE BEEN DIRECTLY ENDANGERED BY EVENTS TAKING PLACE HERE.
WELL, THERE...YES, THERE'S SOME TRUTH TO THAT, BUT THERE'S AN EXPLANATION--
THERE ALWAYS IS, MA'AM.
CAN YOU TELL ME WHY THERE ARE NO RECORDS OF PAYMENT MADE TO THE SITTERS, AND WHERE THEY ARE FROM?
WELL, THEY...
AND THAT'S A LUNAR CRATER. WE HAVE THEM ALL OVER THE MOON. CAN YOU SAY LUNAR CRATER, VALERIA?
LAAAAAN?
CLOSE ENOUGH.
...THEY'RE FROM NEW JERSEY.

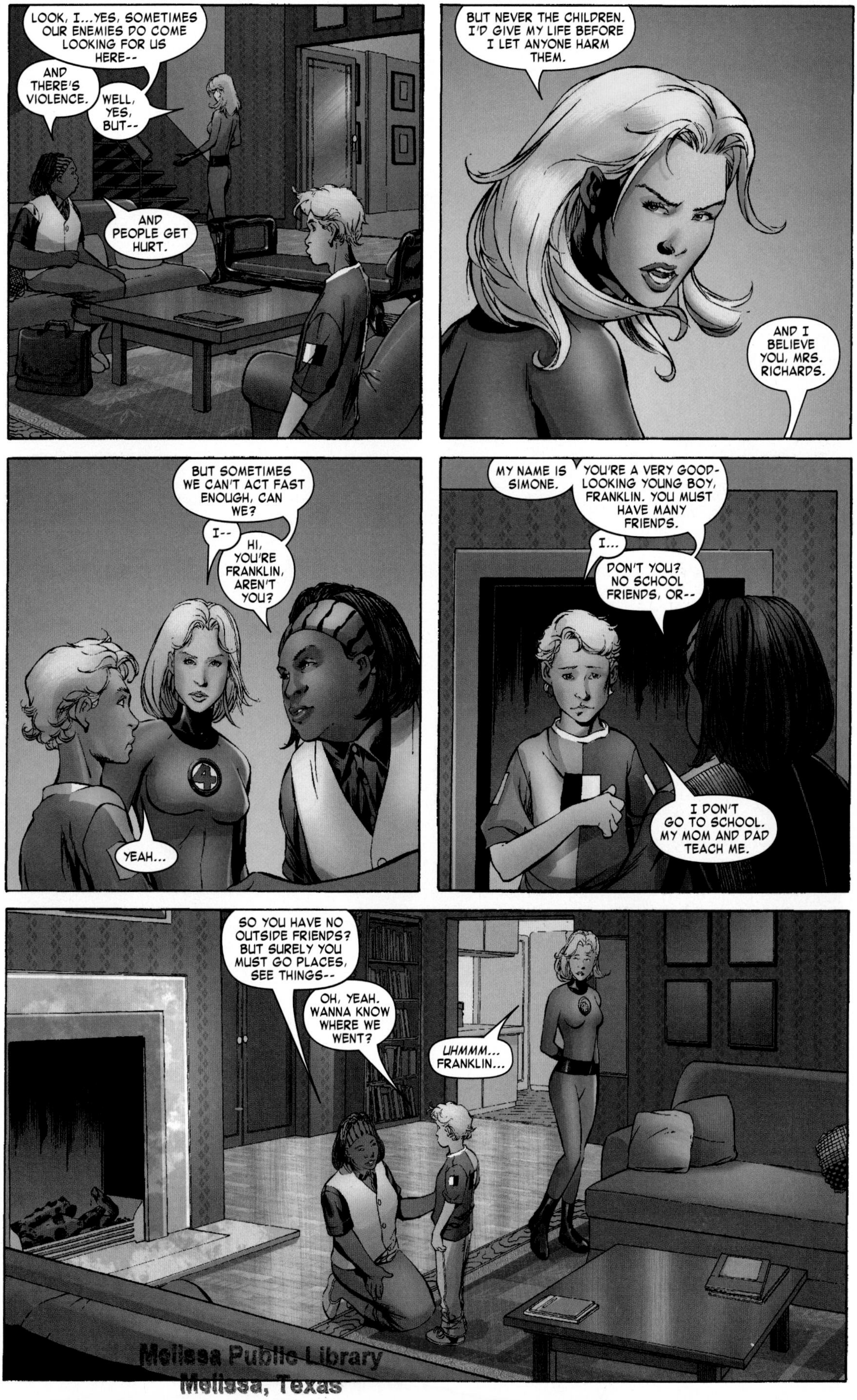
LOOK, I...YES, SOMETIMES OUR ENEMIES DO COME LOOKING FOR US HERE--
AND THERE'S VIOLENCE.
WELL, YES, BUT--
AND PEOPLE GET HURT.
BUT NEVER THE CHILDREN. I'D GIVE MY LIFE BEFORE I LET ANYONE HARM THEM.
AND I BELIEVE YOU, MRS. RICHARDS.
BUT SOMETIMES WE CAN'T ACT FAST ENOUGH, CAN WE?
I--
HI, YOU'RE FRANKLIN, AREN'T YOU?
YEAH...
MY NAME IS SIMONE.
YOU'RE A VERY GOOD-LOOKING YOUNG BOY, FRANKLIN. YOU MUST HAVE MANY FRIENDS.
I...
DON'T YOU? NO SCHOOL FRIENDS, OR--
I DON'T GO TO SCHOOL. MY MOM AND DAD TEACH ME.
SO YOU HAVE NO OUTSIDE FRIENDS? BUT SURELY YOU MUST GO PLACES, SEE THINGS--
OH, YEAH. WANNA KNOW WHERE WE WENT?
UHMMM... FRANKLIN...

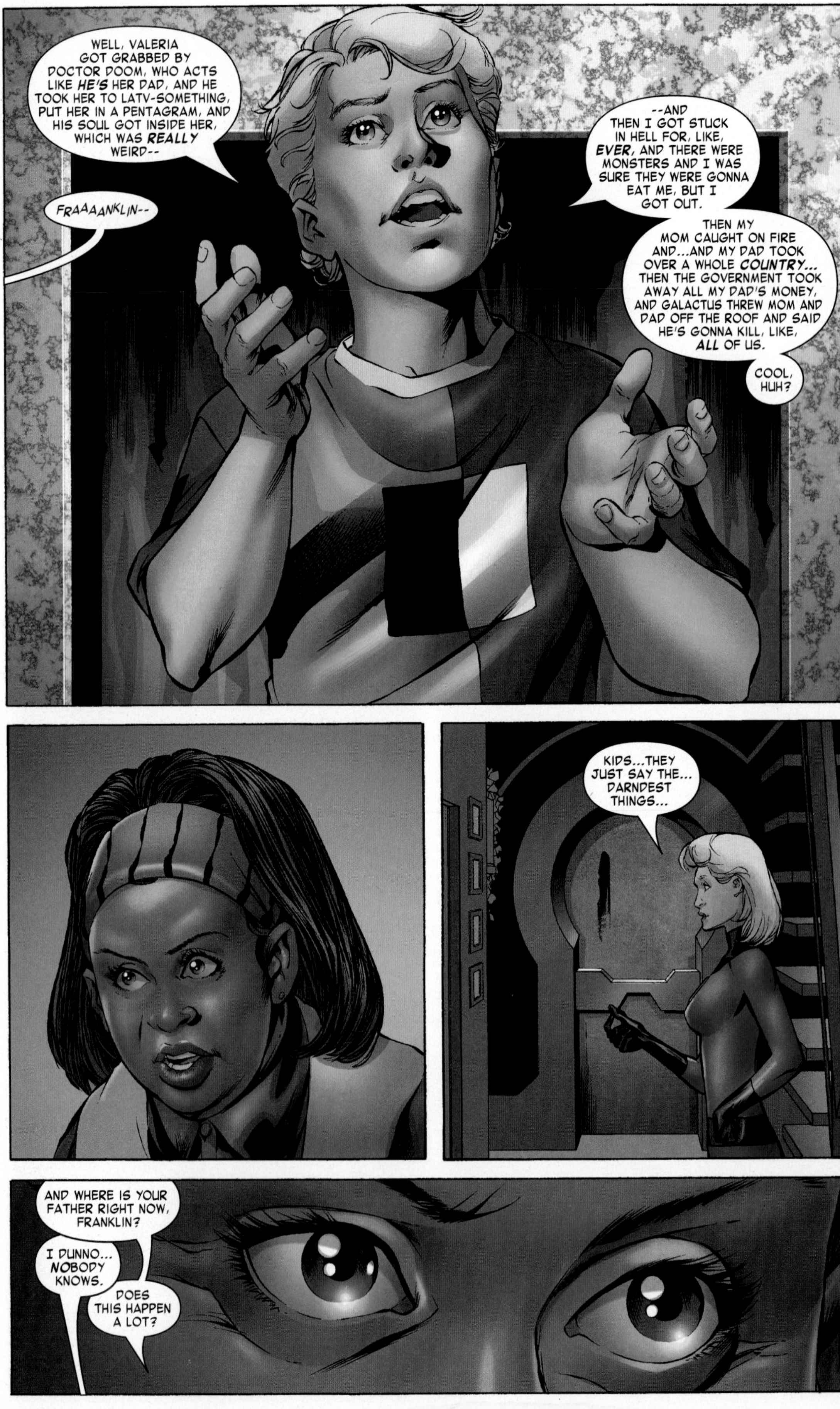
WELL, VALERIA GOT GRABBED BY DOCTOR DOOM, WHO ACTS LIKE HE'S HER DAD, AND HE TOOK HER TO LATV-SOMETHING, PUT HER IN A PENTAGRAM, AND HIS SOUL GOT INSIDE HER, WHICH WAS REALLY WEIRD--
FRAAAANKLIN--
--AND THEN I GOT STUCK IN HELL FOR, LIKE, EVER, AND THERE WERE MONSTERS AND I WAS SURE THEY WERE GONNA EAT ME, BUT I GOT OUT.
THEN MY MOM CAUGHT ON FIRE AND...AND MY DAD TOOK OVER A WHOLE COUNTRY... THEN THE GOVERNMENT TOOK AWAY ALL MY DAD'S MONEY, AND GALACTUS THREW MOM AND DAD OFF THE ROOF AND SAID HE'S GONNA KILL, LIKE, ALL OF US.
COOL, HUH?
KIDS...THEY JUST SAY THE... DARNDEST THINGS...
AND WHERE IS YOUR FATHER RIGHT NOW, FRANKLIN?
I DUNNO... NOBODY KNOWS.
DOES THIS HAPPEN A LOT?

"OH, YEAH, ALL THE TIME."

SO WHAT DO YOU THINK OF OUR FINE DINING ACCOMMODATIONS?

IT'S FINE. I'M USED TO IT, GIVEN THE KIND OF HOURS I'M USED TO KEEPING. IT'S HARD TO SET ASIDE TIME FOR REGULAR MEALS.

MUST BE TOUGH ON YOUR FAMILY.

YES...YES, IT IS. I KEEP MEANING TO WORK ON THAT, BUT--

THERE'S NEVER TIME.

THERE'S NEVER TIME.

WELL, FOR WHAT IT'S WORTH, GIVEN HOW QUICKLY WE'VE BEEN BLASTING THROUGH EVERYTHING, I THINK WE CAN PROBABLY WRAP THIS UP FASTER THAN EXPECTED. LET YOU GET BACK TO YOUR FAMILY A LITTLE EARLY.

THERE ARE JUST SO MANY VARIABLES TO CONSIDER...NOT COUNTING THE BIG ONE.

WHICH BIG ONE IS THAT?

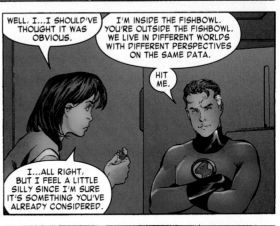

WELL, I...I SHOULD'VE THOUGHT IT WAS OBVIOUS.

I'M INSIDE THE FISHBOWL. YOU'RE OUTSIDE THE FISHBOWL. WE LIVE IN DIFFERENT WORLDS WITH DIFFERENT PERSPECTIVES ON THE SAME DATA.

HIT ME.

I...ALL RIGHT, BUT I FEEL A LITTLE SILLY SINCE I'M SURE IT'S SOMETHING YOU'VE ALREADY CONSIDERED.

IF I WERE TO FLOOD THIS ROOM WITH RADIATION, OR TOXIC CHEMICALS, THE *DEGREE* TO WHICH WE WOULD BE AFFECTED WOULD VARY, PERSON TO PERSON, BUT THE EFFECTS *THEMSELVES* WOULD BE IDENTICAL.

BARRING NATURAL IMMUNITIES, A GIVEN SUBSTANCE WILL HAVE CONSISTENT AND PREDICTABLE EFFECTS ON MEMBERS OF THE SAME SPECIES WHEN ADMINISTERED UNDER UNIFORM CONDITIONS.

THE FOUR OF YOU WERE IN THE SAME SHIP, EATING THE SAME FOOD, BREATHING THE SAME AIR, SHIELDED BY THE SAME MATERIAL, AND HIT BY THE SAME COSMIC RAYS THAT BATHED YOUR SHIP UNIFORMLY FROM END TO END.

THE PETRI DISH WAS THE SAME, THE INGREDIENTS WERE THE SAME, THE CONDITIONS WERE THE SAME. THE OUTCOME SHOULD HAVE BEEN UNIFORM.

SO WHY WERE THE EFFECTS SO RADICALLY DIFFERENT FOR EACH OF YOU? NOT JUST IN DEGREE, BUT IN FORM?

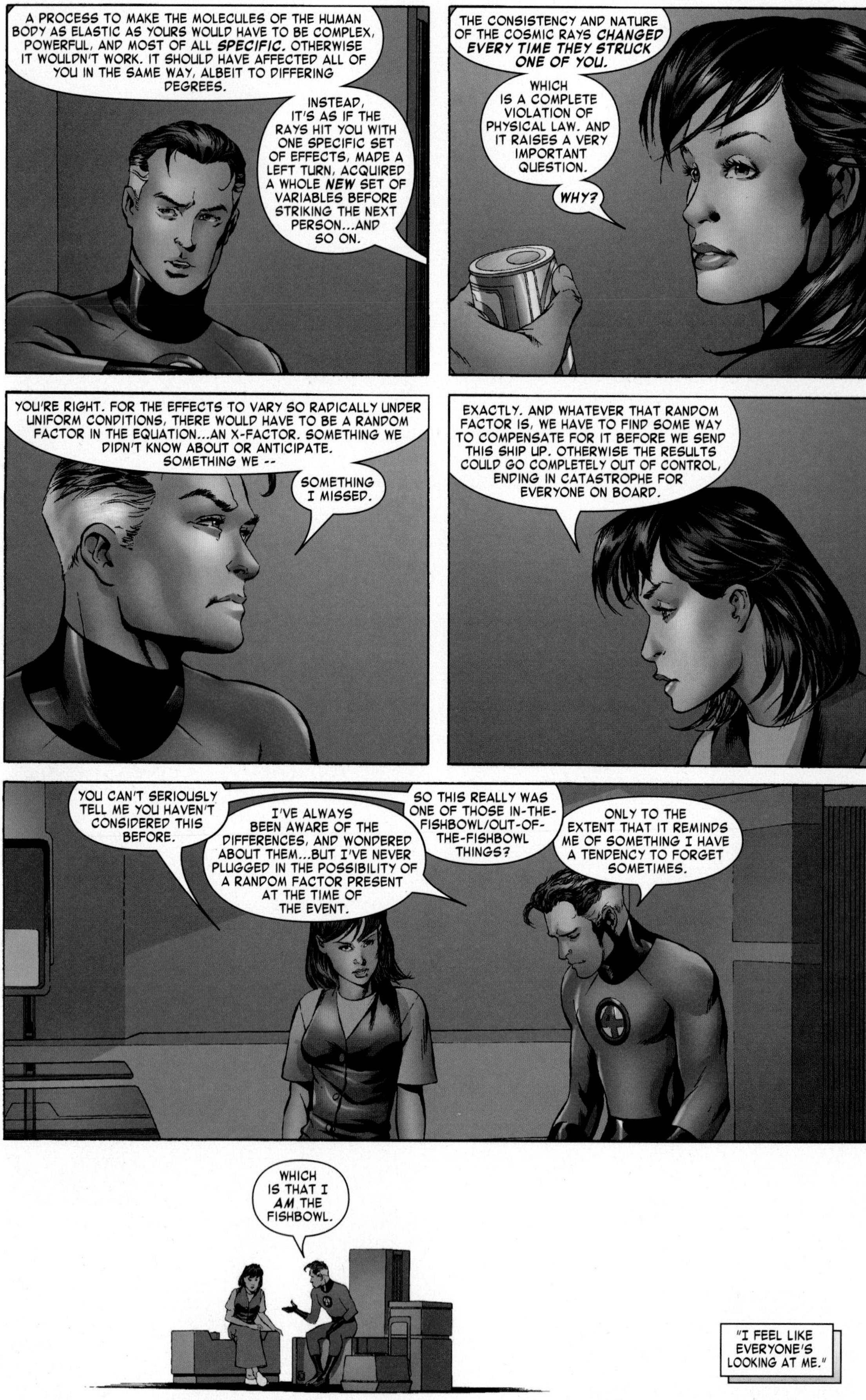
A PROCESS TO MAKE THE MOLECULES OF THE HUMAN BODY AS ELASTIC AS YOURS WOULD HAVE TO BE COMPLEX, POWERFUL, AND MOST OF ALL SPECIFIC. OTHERWISE IT WOULDN'T WORK. IT SHOULD HAVE AFFECTED ALL OF YOU IN THE SAME WAY, ALBEIT TO DIFFERING DEGREES.
INSTEAD, IT'S AS IF THE RAYS HIT YOU WITH ONE SPECIFIC SET OF EFFECTS, MADE A LEFT TURN, ACQUIRED A WHOLE NEW SET OF VARIABLES BEFORE STRIKING THE NEXT PERSON...AND SO ON.
THE CONSISTENCY AND NATURE OF THE COSMIC RAYS CHANGED EVERY TIME THEY STRUCK ONE OF YOU.
WHICH IS A COMPLETE VIOLATION OF PHYSICAL LAW. AND IT RAISES A VERY IMPORTANT QUESTION.
WHY?
YOU'RE RIGHT. FOR THE EFFECTS TO VARY SO RADICALLY UNDER UNIFORM CONDITIONS, THERE WOULD HAVE TO BE A RANDOM FACTOR IN THE EQUATION...AN X-FACTOR. SOMETHING WE DIDN'T KNOW ABOUT OR ANTICIPATE. SOMETHING WE --
SOMETHING I MISSED.
EXACTLY. AND WHATEVER THAT RANDOM FACTOR IS, WE HAVE TO FIND SOME WAY TO COMPENSATE FOR IT BEFORE WE SEND THIS SHIP UP. OTHERWISE THE RESULTS COULD GO COMPLETELY OUT OF CONTROL, ENDING IN CATASTROPHE FOR EVERYONE ON BOARD.
YOU CAN'T SERIOUSLY TELL ME YOU HAVEN'T CONSIDERED THIS BEFORE.
I'VE ALWAYS BEEN AWARE OF THE DIFFERENCES, AND WONDERED ABOUT THEM...BUT I'VE NEVER PLUGGED IN THE POSSIBILITY OF A RANDOM FACTOR PRESENT AT THE TIME OF THE EVENT.
SO THIS REALLY WAS ONE OF THOSE IN-THE-FISHBOWL/OUT-OF-THE-FISHBOWL THINGS?
ONLY TO THE EXTENT THAT IT REMINDS ME OF SOMETHING I HAVE A TENDENCY TO FORGET SOMETIMES.
WHICH IS THAT I AM THE FISHBOWL.
"I FEEL LIKE EVERYONE'S LOOKING AT ME."

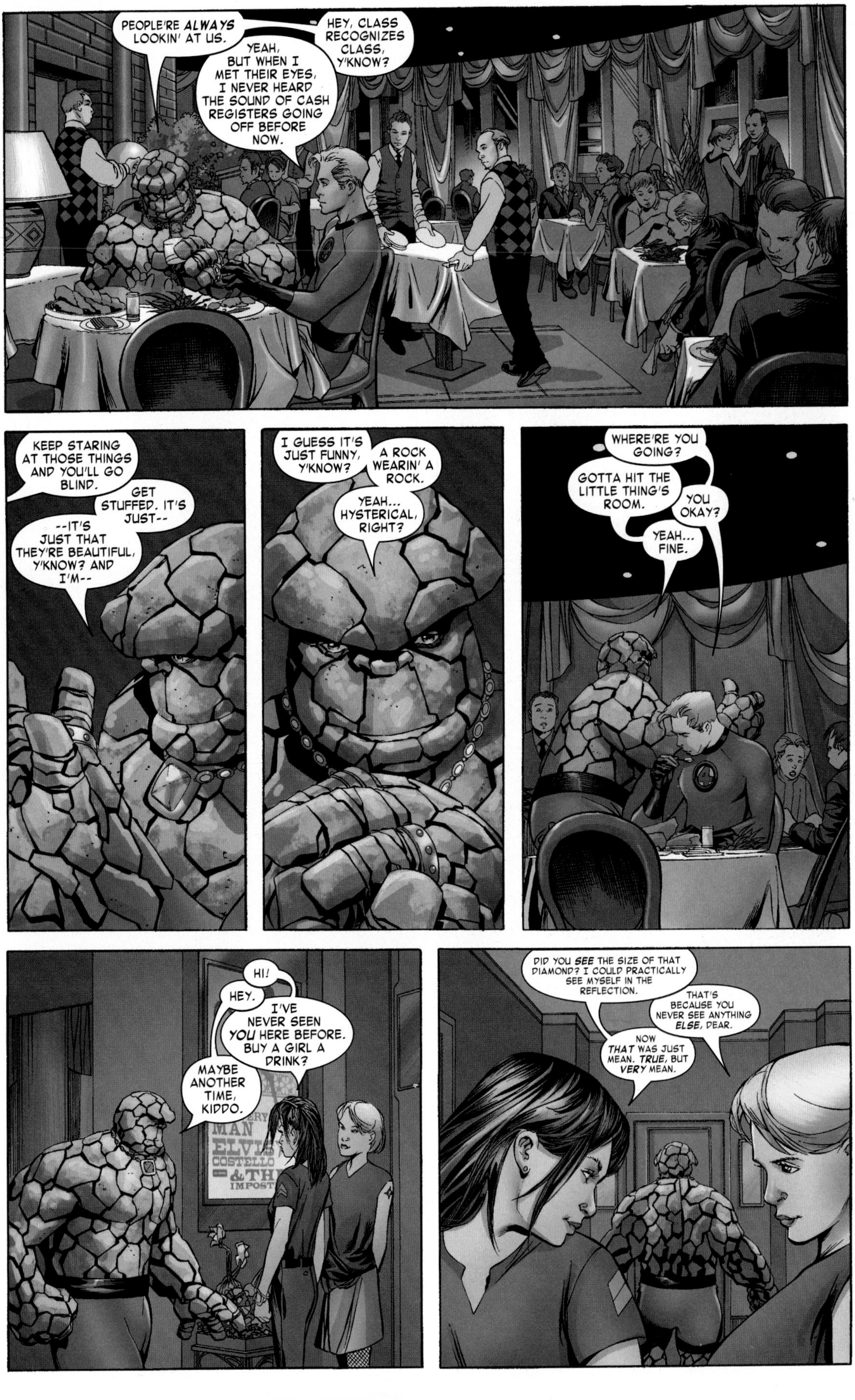
PEOPLE'RE ALWAYS LOOKIN' AT US.
HEY, CLASS RECOGNIZES CLASS, Y'KNOW?
YEAH, BUT WHEN I MET THEIR EYES, I NEVER HEARD THE SOUND OF CASH REGISTERS GOING OFF BEFORE NOW.
KEEP STARING AT THOSE THINGS AND YOU'LL GO BLIND.
GET STUFFED. IT'S JUST--
--IT'S JUST THAT THEY'RE BEAUTIFUL, Y'KNOW? AND I'M--
I GUESS IT'S JUST FUNNY, Y'KNOW?
A ROCK WEARIN' A ROCK.
YEAH... HYSTERICAL, RIGHT?
WHERE'RE YOU GOING?
GOTTA HIT THE LITTLE THING'S ROOM.
YOU OKAY?
YEAH... FINE.
HI!
HEY.
I'VE NEVER SEEN YOU HERE BEFORE. BUY A GIRL A DRINK?
MAYBE ANOTHER TIME, KIDDO.
MAN
ELVIS
COSTELLO
&TH
IMPOST
DID YOU SEE THE SIZE OF THAT DIAMOND? I COULD PRACTICALLY SEE MYSELF IN THE REFLECTION.
THAT'S BECAUSE YOU NEVER SEE ANYTHING ELSE, DEAR.
NOW THAT WAS JUST MEAN. TRUE, BUT VERY MEAN.

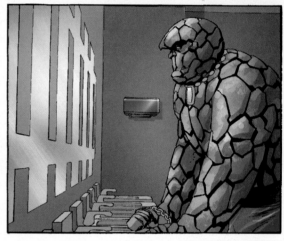

I KNOW WHAT YOU'RE THINKING.

YOU'RE THINKING, IF I WASN'T WEARING ENOUGH ICE TO STUN A POLICE DOG, THAT WOMAN WOULDN'T HAVE SAID BOO TO US. IF ANYTHING, SHE WOULD'A RUN THE OTHER WAY. RIGHT?

RIGHT.

OF COURSE RIGHT. I MEAN, WHO KNOWS US BETTER THAN US, RIGHT? SO HERE'S THE QUESTION.

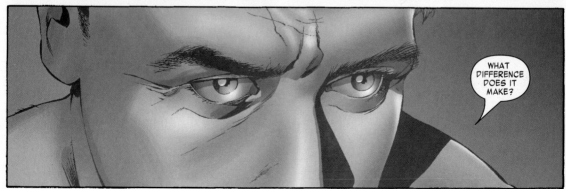

WHAT DIFFERENCE DOES IT MAKE?

OF COURSE WE DO. NEVER SAID OTHERWISE, PAL. WE'RE HERS AND SHE'S OURS.

BUT EVEN SO....

DIFFERENCE IS... I LOVE ALICIA.

...EVEN SO...WHEN A BEAUTIFUL WOMAN LOOKS AT YOU, AND SMILES...IT MAKES YOU STAND A LITTLE STRAIGHTER...MAKES YOU FEEL A LITTLE TALLER IN YOUR SHOES.

IS THERE ANYTHING IN THE WORLD WRONG WITH THAT? WITH FEELING ATTRACTIVE?

MAYBE. DEPENDS.

I KNOW, I KNOW...YOU'RE WORRIED ABOUT LOOKING LIKE THIS....

OF COURSE I DIDN'T MARRY HIM FOR HIS MONEY. DON'T BE RIDICULOUS. EVEN AT NINETY HE'S A SEXUAL DYNAMO.

NOW COME ON, HONEY, IT'S TIME FOR YOUR NAP WHILE BERNARDO AND I GO SHOPPING FOR... WHATEVER.

LIKE I SAID, I UNDERSTAND. DON'T FORGET, THIS IS ME YOU'RE TALKING TO. THE ME YOU SEE IN YOUR DREAMS, EVERY NIGHT...THE ME YOU SEE IN YOUR HEAD EVERY MORNING RIGHT BEFORE YOU TURN ON THE LIGHTS AND LOOK IN THE MIRROR....

THE ME THAT'S STILL THERE UNDERNEATH ALL THAT BRICKWORK.

THE ME...THE YOU...THAT WOULD JUST LIKE TO FEEL APPRECIATED ONCE IN AWHILE...WOULD LIKE TO FEEL ATTRACTIVE FOR A WHILE, EVEN IF WE KNOW IT'S NOT REAL, THAT IT WON'T LAST.

BECAUSE NOTHING EVER LASTS, DOES IT?

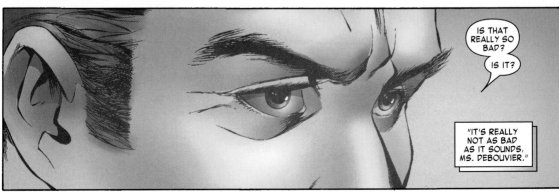

IS THAT REALLY SO BAD?

IS IT?

"IT'S REALLY NOT AS BAD AS IT SOUNDS, MS. DEBOUVIER."

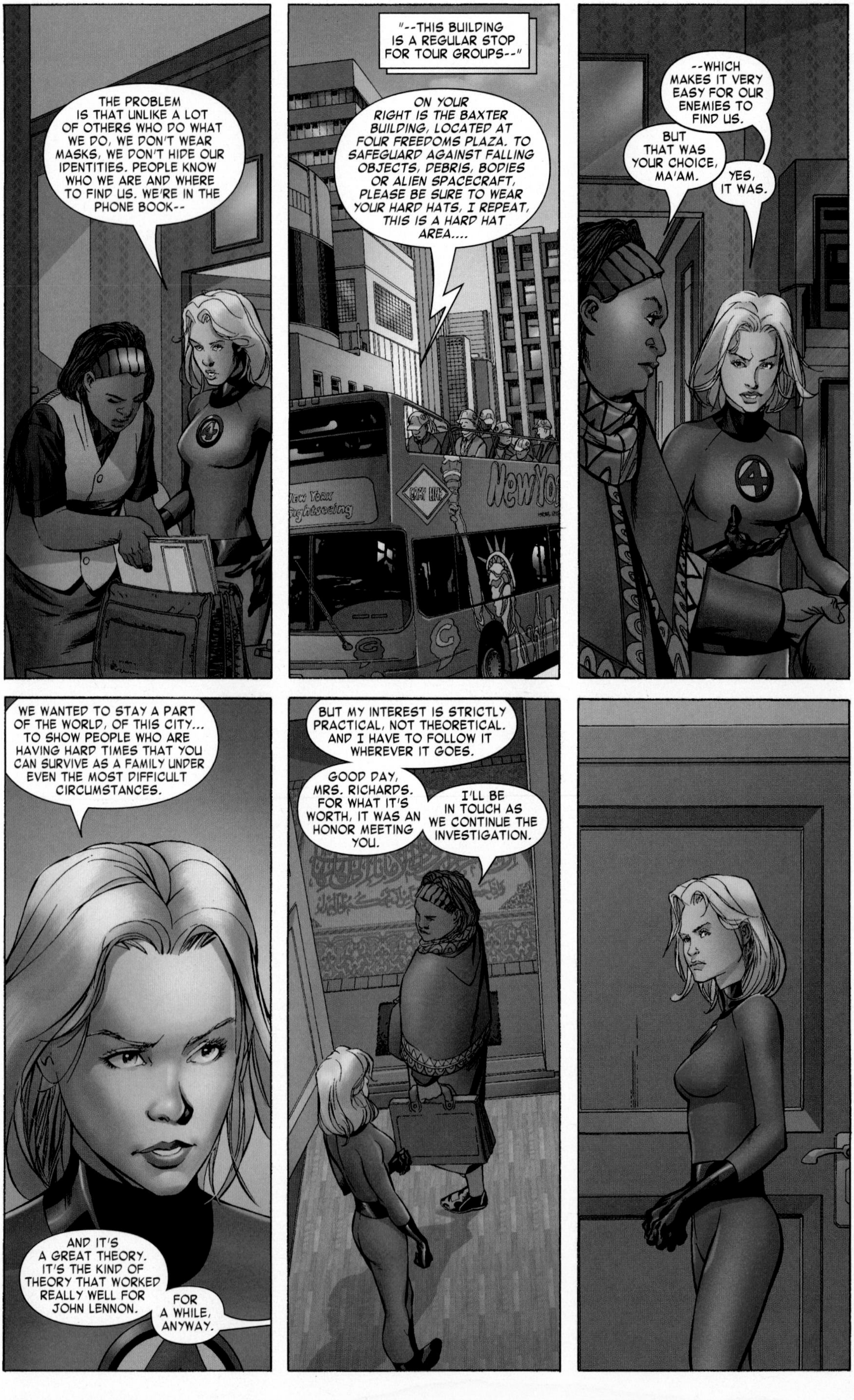
THE PROBLEM IS THAT UNLIKE A LOT OF OTHERS WHO DO WHAT WE DO, WE DON'T WEAR MASKS, WE DON'T HIDE OUR IDENTITIES. PEOPLE KNOW WHO WE ARE AND WHERE TO FIND US. WE'RE IN THE PHONE BOOK--
"--THIS BUILDING IS A REGULAR STOP FOR TOUR GROUPS--"
ON YOUR RIGHT IS THE BAXTER BUILDING, LOCATED AT FOUR FREEDOMS PLAZA. TO SAFEGUARD AGAINST FALLING OBJECTS, DEBRIS, BODIES OR ALIEN SPACECRAFT, PLEASE BE SURE TO WEAR YOUR HARD HATS, I REPEAT, THIS IS A HARD HAT AREA....
New York Sightseeing
New York
--WHICH MAKES IT VERY EASY FOR OUR ENEMIES TO FIND US.
BUT THAT WAS YOUR CHOICE, MA'AM.
YES, IT WAS.
WE WANTED TO STAY A PART OF THE WORLD, OF THIS CITY... TO SHOW PEOPLE WHO ARE HAVING HARD TIMES THAT YOU CAN SURVIVE AS A FAMILY UNDER EVEN THE MOST DIFFICULT CIRCUMSTANCES.
AND IT'S A GREAT THEORY. IT'S THE KIND OF THEORY THAT WORKED REALLY WELL FOR JOHN LENNON.
FOR A WHILE, ANYWAY.
BUT MY INTEREST IS STRICTLY PRACTICAL, NOT THEORETICAL. AND I HAVE TO FOLLOW IT WHEREVER IT GOES.
GOOD DAY, MRS. RICHARDS. FOR WHAT IT'S WORTH, IT WAS AN HONOR MEETING YOU.
I'LL BE IN TOUCH AS WE CONTINUE THE INVESTIGATION.

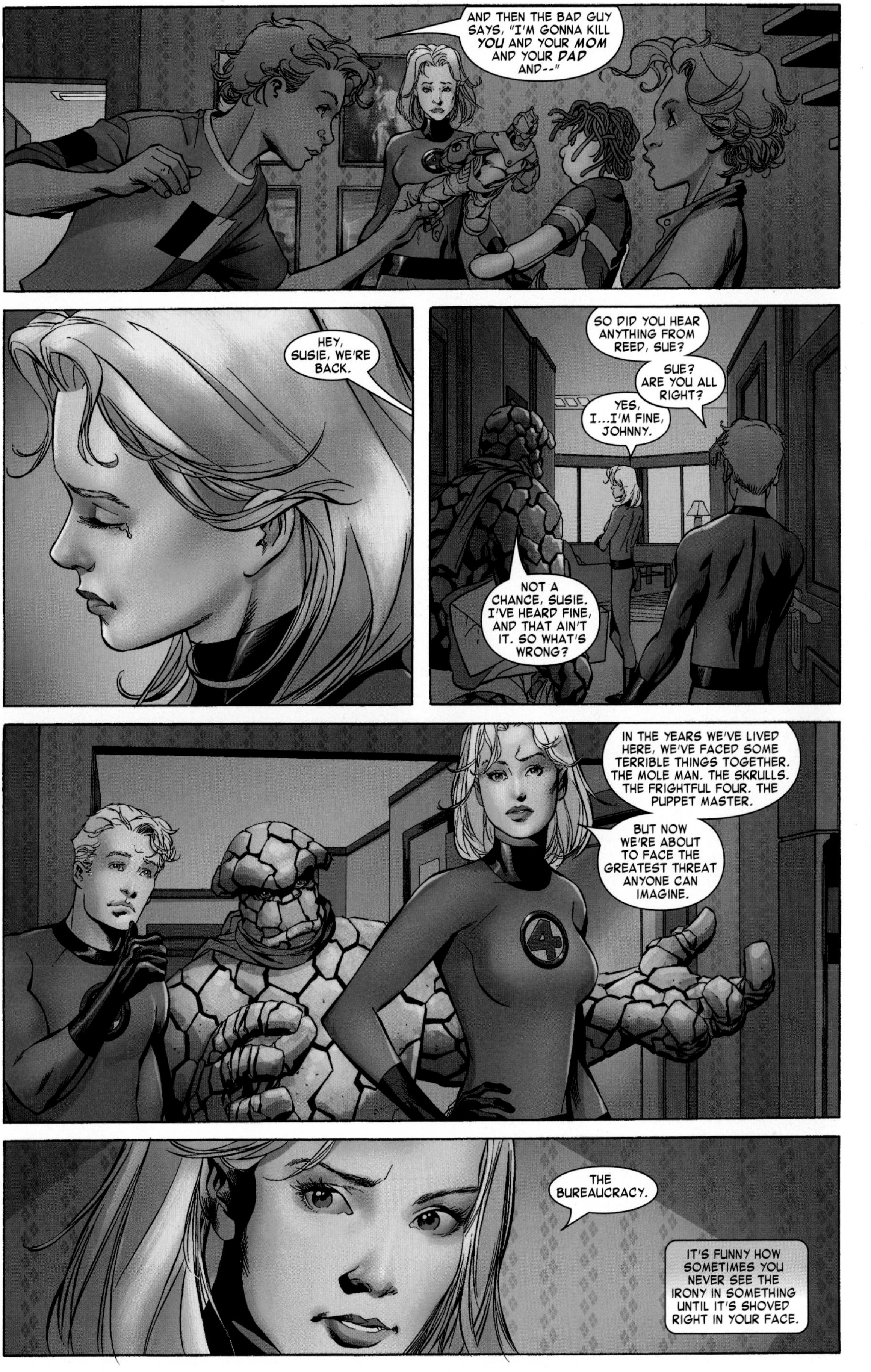
AND THEN THE BAD GUY SAYS, "I'M GONNA KILL *YOU* AND YOUR *MOM* AND YOUR *DAD* AND--"
HEY, SUSIE, WE'RE BACK.
SO DID YOU HEAR ANYTHING FROM REED, SUE?
SUE? ARE YOU ALL RIGHT?
YES, I...I'M FINE, JOHNNY.
NOT A CHANCE, SUSIE. I'VE HEARD FINE, AND THAT AIN'T IT. SO WHAT'S WRONG?
IN THE YEARS WE'VE LIVED HERE, WE'VE FACED SOME TERRIBLE THINGS TOGETHER. THE MOLE MAN. THE SKRULLS. THE FRIGHTFUL FOUR. THE PUPPET MASTER.
BUT NOW WE'RE ABOUT TO FACE THE GREATEST THREAT ANYONE CAN IMAGINE.
THE BUREAUCRACY.
IT'S FUNNY HOW SOMETIMES YOU NEVER SEE THE IRONY IN SOMETHING UNTIL IT'S SHOVED RIGHT IN YOUR FACE.

I'VE ALWAYS BEEN AWARE OF THE DIFFERENCES BETWEEN OUR POWERS AFTER WE WERE HIT BY THE COSMIC RAYS, AND HOW THEY ECHOED OUR PERSONALITIES, BUT I NEVER DROPPED ANCHOR TOO DEEPLY INTO THAT LINE OF THOUGHT.

BUT THE PARALLELS ARE OBVIOUS.

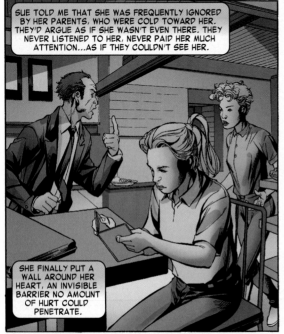

SUE TOLD ME THAT SHE WAS FREQUENTLY IGNORED BY HER PARENTS, WHO WERE COLD TOWARD HER. THEY'D ARGUE AS IF SHE WASN'T EVEN THERE. THEY NEVER LISTENED TO HER, NEVER PAID HER MUCH ATTENTION...AS IF THEY COULDN'T SEE HER.

SHE FINALLY PUT A WALL AROUND HER HEART, AN INVISIBLE BARRIER NO AMOUNT OF HURT COULD PENETRATE.

AND THEN...

JOHNNY WAS ALWAYS A HOTHEAD...FOND OF FAST CARS AND FAST LIVING. A FIERY TEMPERAMENT THAT UNLESS TEMPERED AND FOCUSED LIKE A LASER WOULD HAVE ONE DAY LED HIM TO DISASTER.

AND THEN...

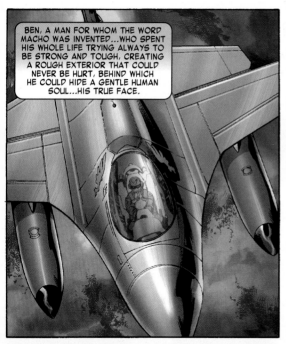

BEN, A MAN FOR WHOM THE WORD MACHO WAS INVENTED...WHO SPENT HIS WHOLE LIFE TRYING ALWAYS TO BE STRONG AND TOUGH, CREATING A ROUGH EXTERIOR THAT COULD NEVER BE HURT, BEHIND WHICH HE COULD HIDE A GENTLE HUMAN SOUL...HIS TRUE FACE.

AND THEN...

AND THEN...

GO AHEAD, REED...TURN THAT SPOTLIGHT ON YOURSELF FOR A MINUTE.

A MAN STRETCHED THIN BY WORK, GOING FROM GRANT TO GRANT, PROJECT TO PROJECT, BETWEEN THE RIGORS OF SCIENCE AND THE LOVE HE THOUGHT HE'D NEVER HAVE TIME FOR... ALWAYS BEING PULLED BETWEEN HIS HEART AND HIS HEAD...STRETCHED SO THIN HE THOUGHT SOONER OR LATER HE'D SNAP.

THAT SOUND ABOUT RIGHT?

YEAH...YEAH, IT DOES.

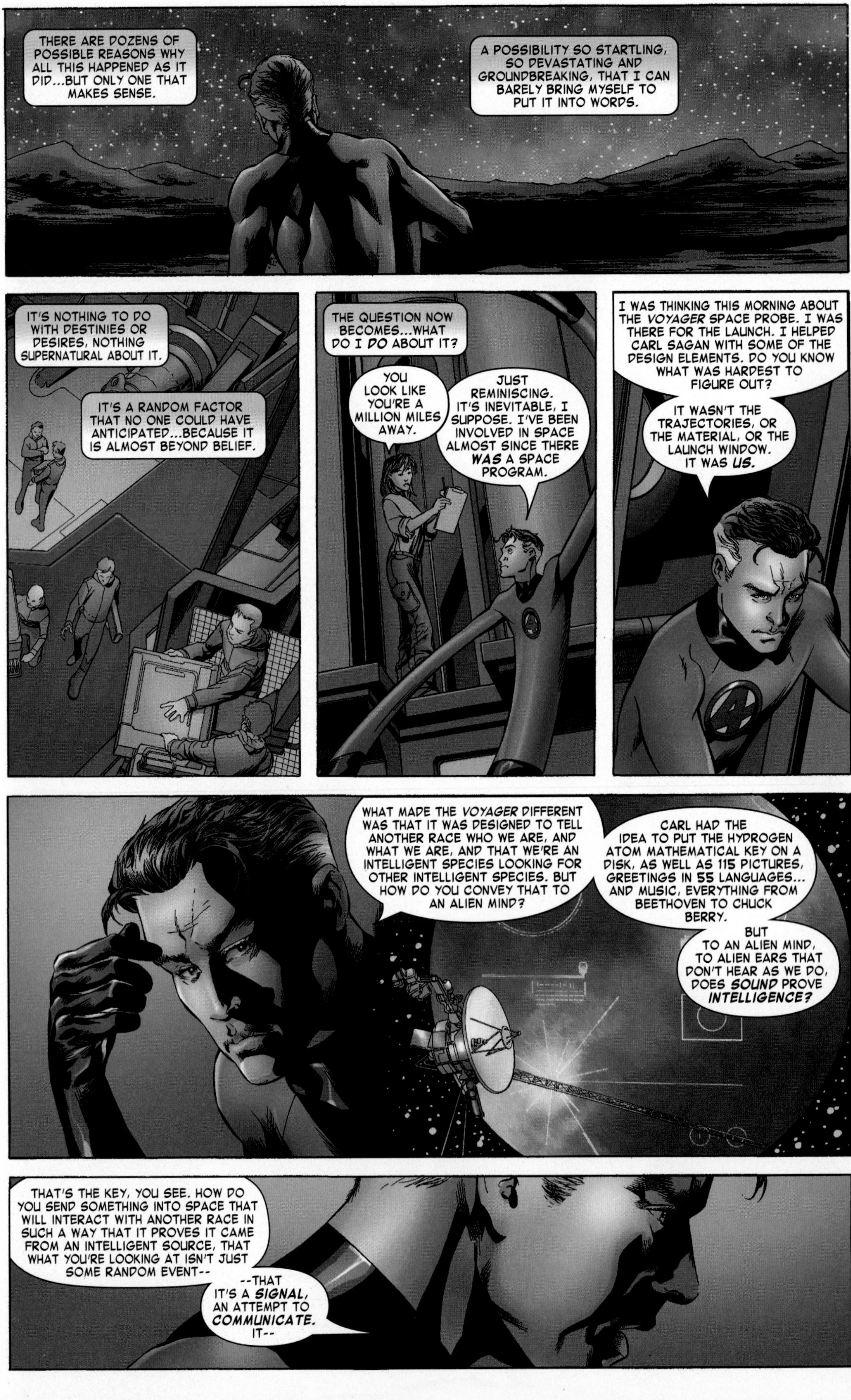
THERE ARE DOZENS OF POSSIBLE REASONS WHY ALL THIS HAPPENED AS IT DID...BUT ONLY ONE THAT MAKES SENSE.
A POSSIBILITY SO STARTLING, SO DEVASTATING AND GROUNDBREAKING, THAT I CAN BARELY BRING MYSELF TO PUT IT INTO WORDS.
IT'S NOTHING TO DO WITH DESTINIES OR DESIRES, NOTHING SUPERNATURAL ABOUT IT.
IT'S A RANDOM FACTOR THAT NO ONE COULD HAVE ANTICIPATED...BECAUSE IT IS ALMOST BEYOND BELIEF.
THE QUESTION NOW BECOMES...WHAT DO I DO ABOUT IT?
YOU LOOK LIKE YOU'RE A MILLION MILES AWAY.
JUST REMINISCING. IT'S INEVITABLE, I SUPPOSE. I'VE BEEN INVOLVED IN SPACE ALMOST SINCE THERE WAS A SPACE PROGRAM.
I WAS THINKING THIS MORNING ABOUT THE VOYAGER SPACE PROBE. I WAS THERE FOR THE LAUNCH. I HELPED CARL SAGAN WITH SOME OF THE DESIGN ELEMENTS. DO YOU KNOW WHAT WAS HARDEST TO FIGURE OUT?
IT WASN'T THE TRAJECTORIES, OR THE MATERIAL, OR THE LAUNCH WINDOW. IT WAS US.
WHAT MADE THE VOYAGER DIFFERENT WAS THAT IT WAS DESIGNED TO TELL ANOTHER RACE WHO WE ARE, AND WHAT WE ARE, AND THAT WE'RE AN INTELLIGENT SPECIES LOOKING FOR OTHER INTELLIGENT SPECIES. BUT HOW DO YOU CONVEY THAT TO AN ALIEN MIND?
CARL HAD THE IDEA TO PUT THE HYDROGEN ATOM MATHEMATICAL KEY ON A DISK, AS WELL AS 115 PICTURES, GREETINGS IN 55 LANGUAGES... AND MUSIC, EVERYTHING FROM BEETHOVEN TO CHUCK BERRY.
BUT TO AN ALIEN MIND, TO ALIEN EARS THAT DON'T HEAR AS WE DO, DOES SOUND PROVE INTELLIGENCE?
THAT'S THE KEY, YOU SEE. HOW DO YOU SEND SOMETHING INTO SPACE THAT WILL INTERACT WITH ANOTHER RACE IN SUCH A WAY THAT IT PROVES IT CAME FROM AN INTELLIGENT SOURCE, THAT WHAT YOU'RE LOOKING AT ISN'T JUST SOME RANDOM EVENT--
--THAT IT'S A SIGNAL, AN ATTEMPT TO COMMUNICATE. IT--

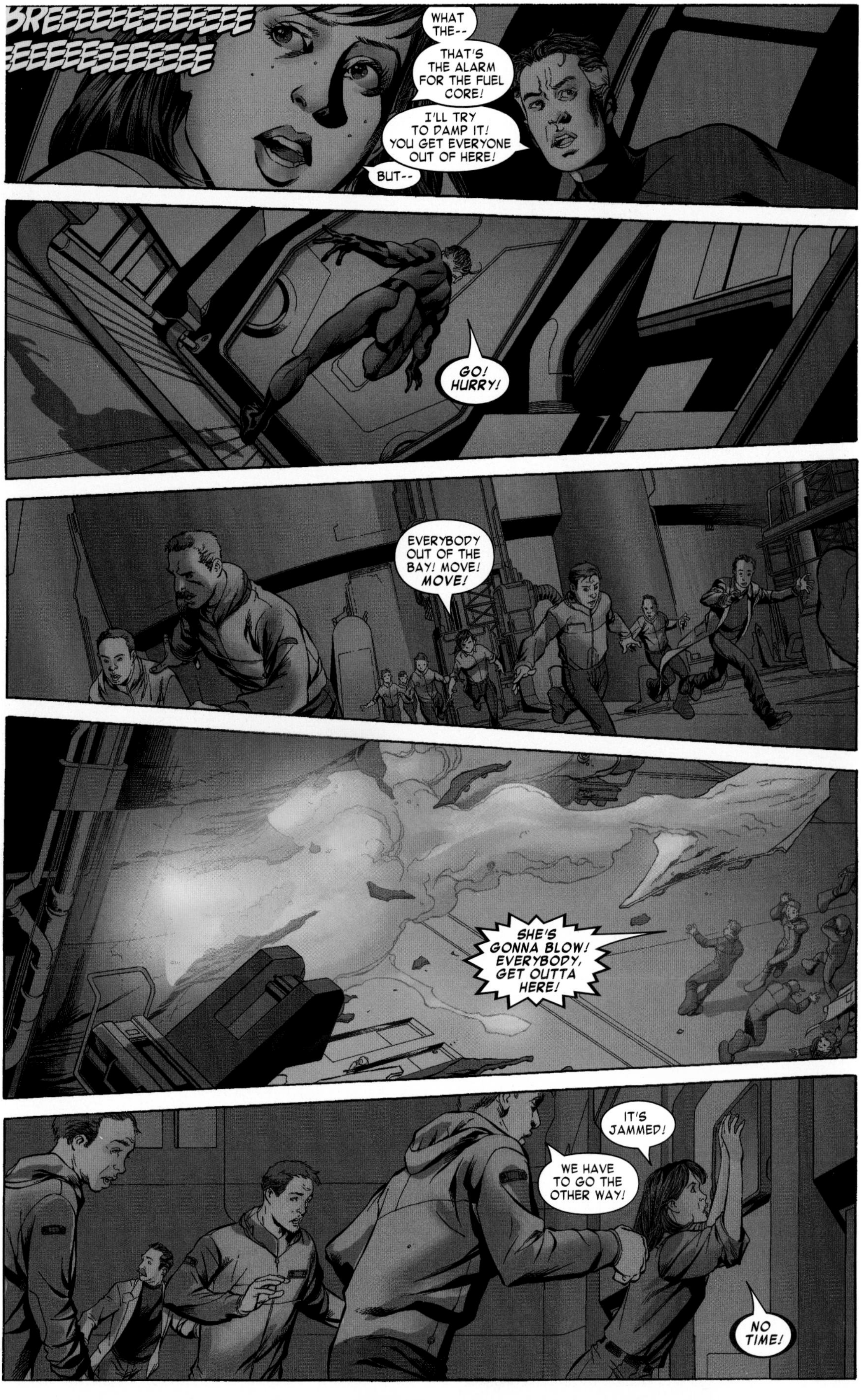
BREEEEEEEEEEEEE
EEEEEEEEEEEEE
WHAT THE--
THAT'S THE ALARM FOR THE FUEL CORE!
I'LL TRY TO DAMP IT! YOU GET EVERYONE OUT OF HERE!
BUT--
GO! HURRY!
EVERYBODY OUT OF THE BAY! MOVE! MOVE!
SHE'S GONNA BLOW! EVERYBODY, GET OUTTA HERE!
IT'S JAMMED!
WE HAVE TO GO THE OTHER WAY!
NO TIME!

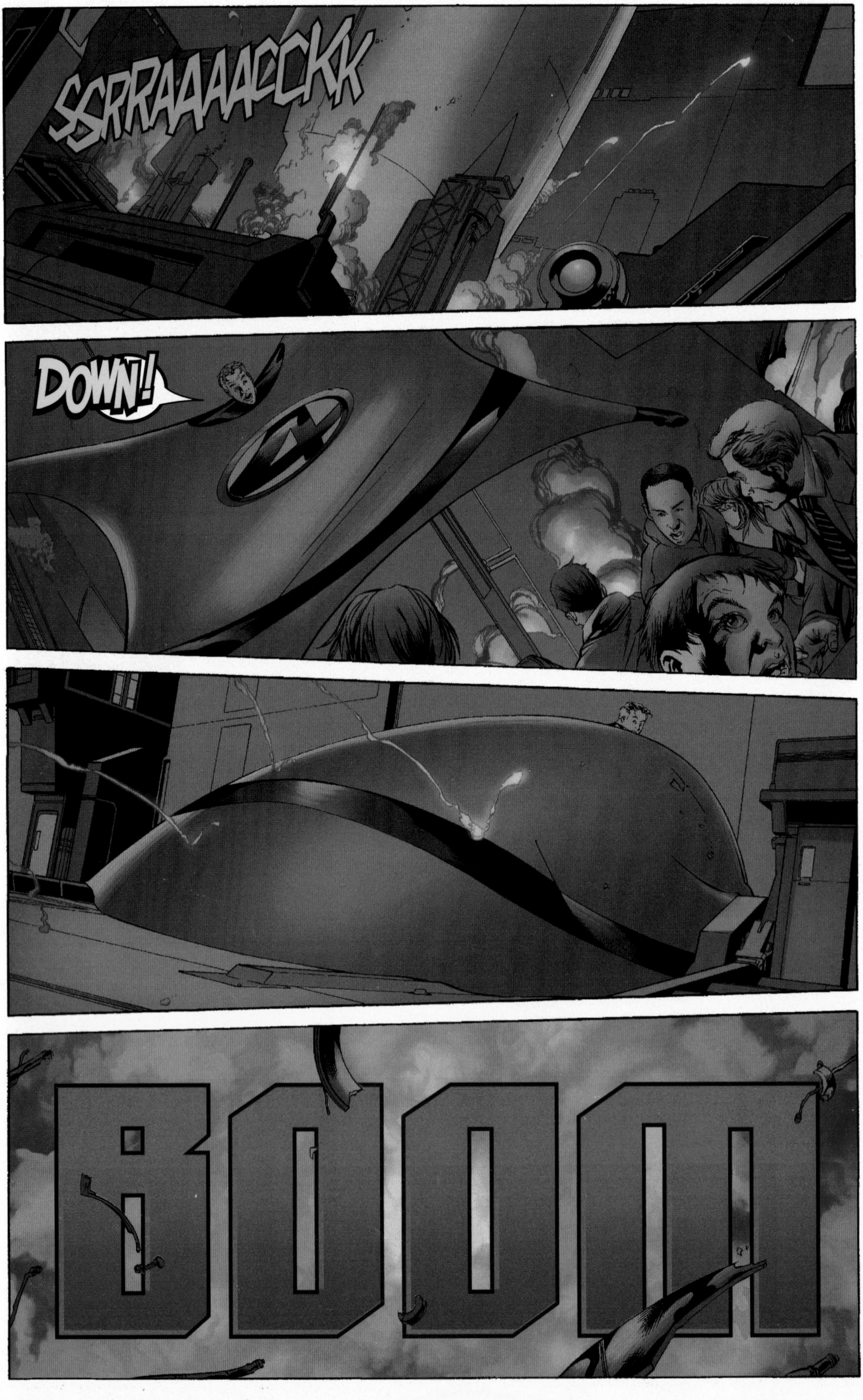
SSRRAAAACCKK
DOWN!!
BOOM

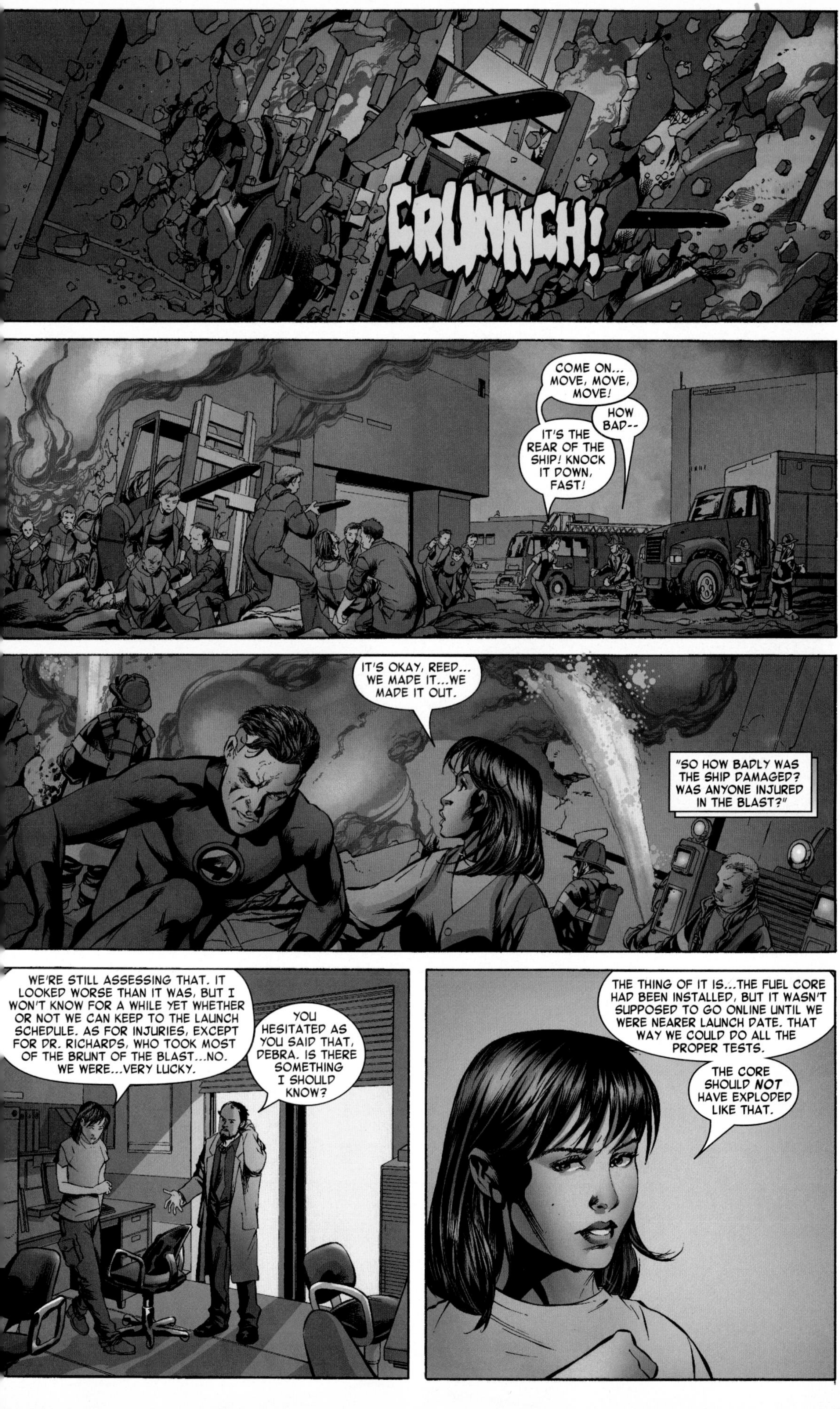
CRUNNCH!
COME ON... MOVE, MOVE, MOVE!
HOW BAD--
IT'S THE REAR OF THE SHIP! KNOCK IT DOWN, FAST!
IT'S OKAY, REED... WE MADE IT...WE MADE IT OUT.
"SO HOW BADLY WAS THE SHIP DAMAGED? WAS ANYONE INJURED IN THE BLAST?"
WE'RE STILL ASSESSING THAT. IT LOOKED WORSE THAN IT WAS, BUT I WON'T KNOW FOR A WHILE YET WHETHER OR NOT WE CAN KEEP TO THE LAUNCH SCHEDULE. AS FOR INJURIES, EXCEPT FOR DR. RICHARDS, WHO TOOK MOST OF THE BRUNT OF THE BLAST...NO. WE WERE...VERY LUCKY.
YOU HESITATED AS YOU SAID THAT, DEBRA. IS THERE SOMETHING I SHOULD KNOW?
THE THING OF IT IS...THE FUEL CORE HAD BEEN INSTALLED, BUT IT WASN'T SUPPOSED TO GO ONLINE UNTIL WE WERE NEARER LAUNCH DATE. THAT WAY WE COULD DO ALL THE PROPER TESTS.
THE CORE SHOULD NOT HAVE EXPLODED LIKE THAT.

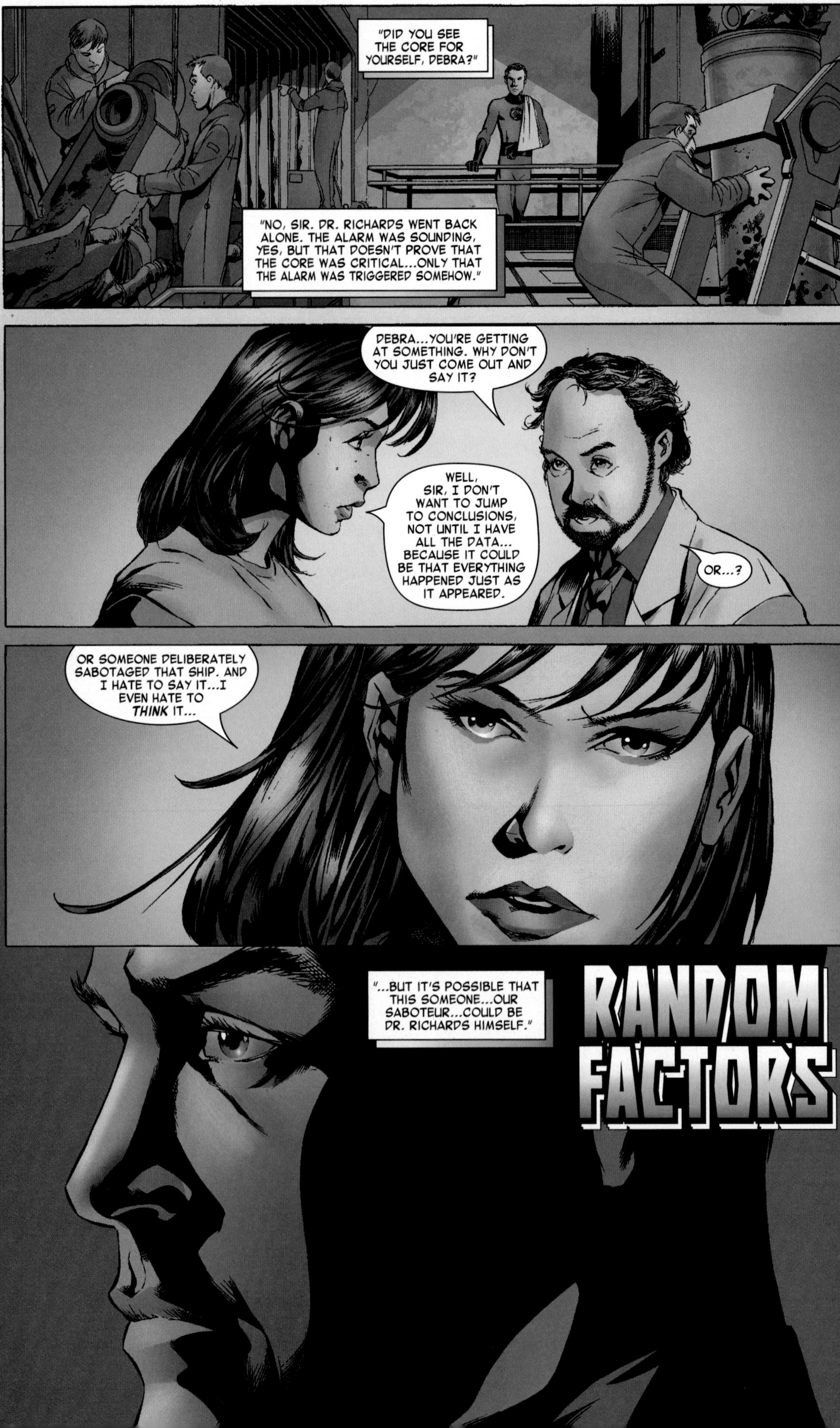
"DID YOU SEE THE CORE FOR YOURSELF, DEBRA?"
"NO, SIR. DR. RICHARDS WENT BACK ALONE. THE ALARM WAS SOUNDING, YES, BUT THAT DOESN'T PROVE THAT THE CORE WAS CRITICAL...ONLY THAT THE ALARM WAS TRIGGERED SOMEHOW."
DEBRA...YOU'RE GETTING AT SOMETHING. WHY DON'T YOU JUST COME OUT AND SAY IT?
WELL, SIR, I DON'T WANT TO JUMP TO CONCLUSIONS, NOT UNTIL I HAVE ALL THE DATA... BECAUSE IT COULD BE THAT EVERYTHING HAPPENED JUST AS IT APPEARED.
OR...?
OR SOMEONE DELIBERATELY SABOTAGED THAT SHIP. AND I HATE TO SAY IT...I EVEN HATE TO *THINK* IT...
"...BUT IT'S POSSIBLE THAT THIS SOMEONE...OUR SABOTEUR...COULD BE DR. RICHARDS HIMSELF."
RANDOM FACTORS

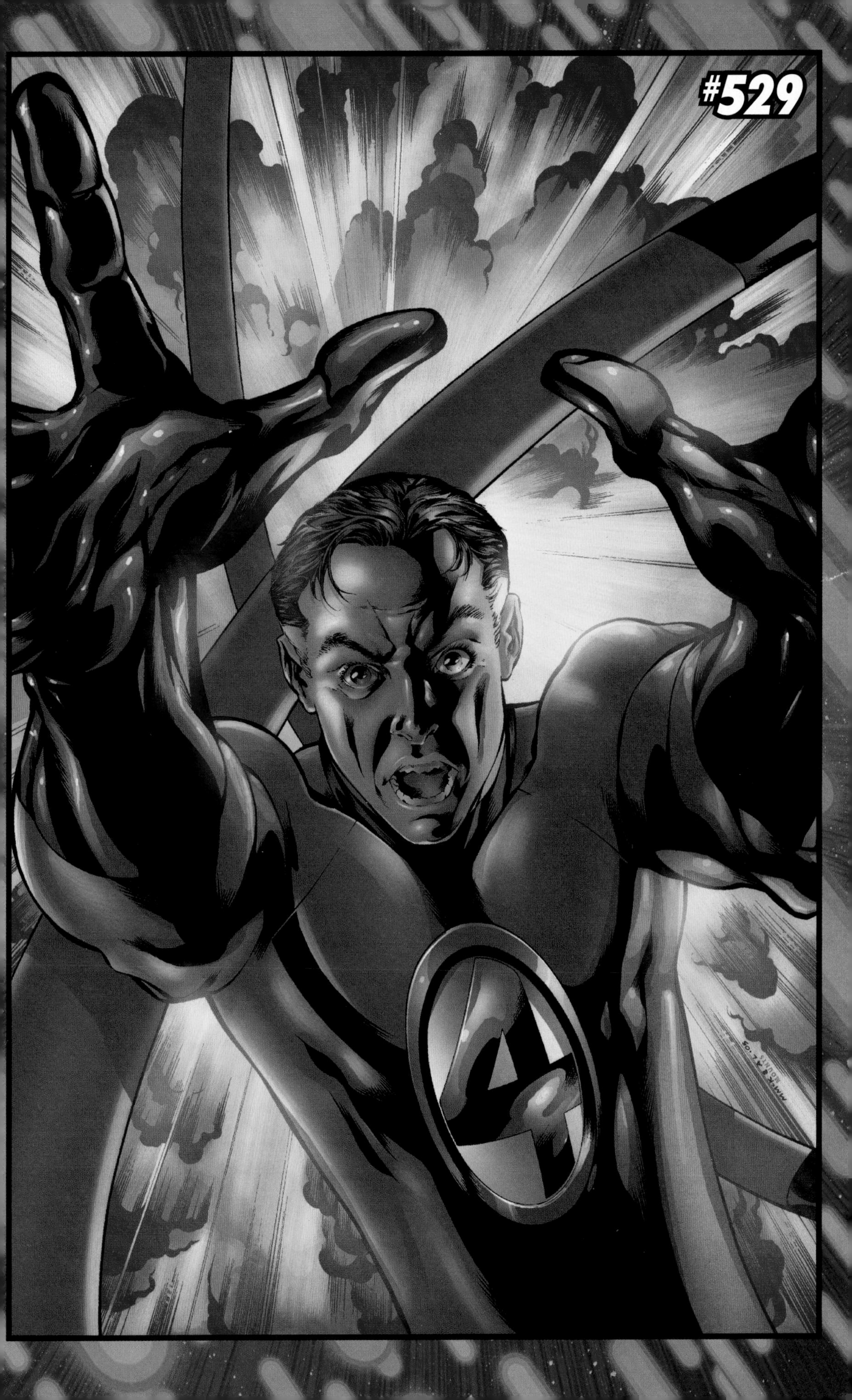
#529

"AND YOU'RE SURE THERE'S NOTHING WE CAN DO TO GET THIS SHIP OFF THE GROUND, DEBRA?"

NO, SIR. THE DAMAGE TO THE ELECTRICAL AND ENVIRONMENTAL SYSTEMS WAS TOO EXTENSIVE TO BE REPAIRED IN THE WINDOW WE HAVE TO WORK WITH.

THE EXACT COSMIC RAY CONFIGURATION THAT CREATED THE FANTASTIC FOUR WILL OCCUR IN 24 HOURS, AND THERE'S NO WAY ON GOD'S GREEN EARTH THAT WE CAN GET THIS THING FIXED IN TIME.

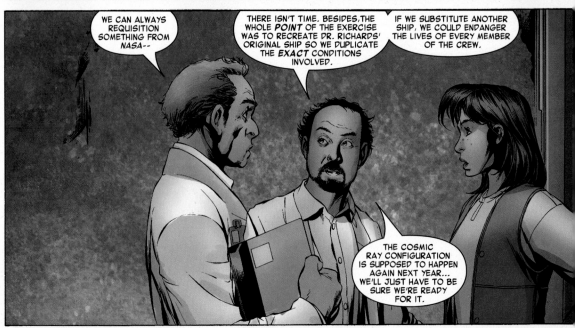

WE CAN ALWAYS REQUISITION SOMETHING FROM NASA--

THERE ISN'T TIME. BESIDES, THE WHOLE *POINT* OF THE EXERCISE WAS TO RECREATE DR. RICHARDS' ORIGINAL SHIP SO WE DUPLICATE THE *EXACT* CONDITIONS INVOLVED.

IF WE SUBSTITUTE ANOTHER SHIP, WE COULD ENDANGER THE LIVES OF EVERY MEMBER OF THE CREW.

THE COSMIC RAY CONFIGURATION IS SUPPOSED TO HAPPEN AGAIN NEXT YEAR... WE'LL JUST HAVE TO BE SURE WE'RE READY FOR IT.

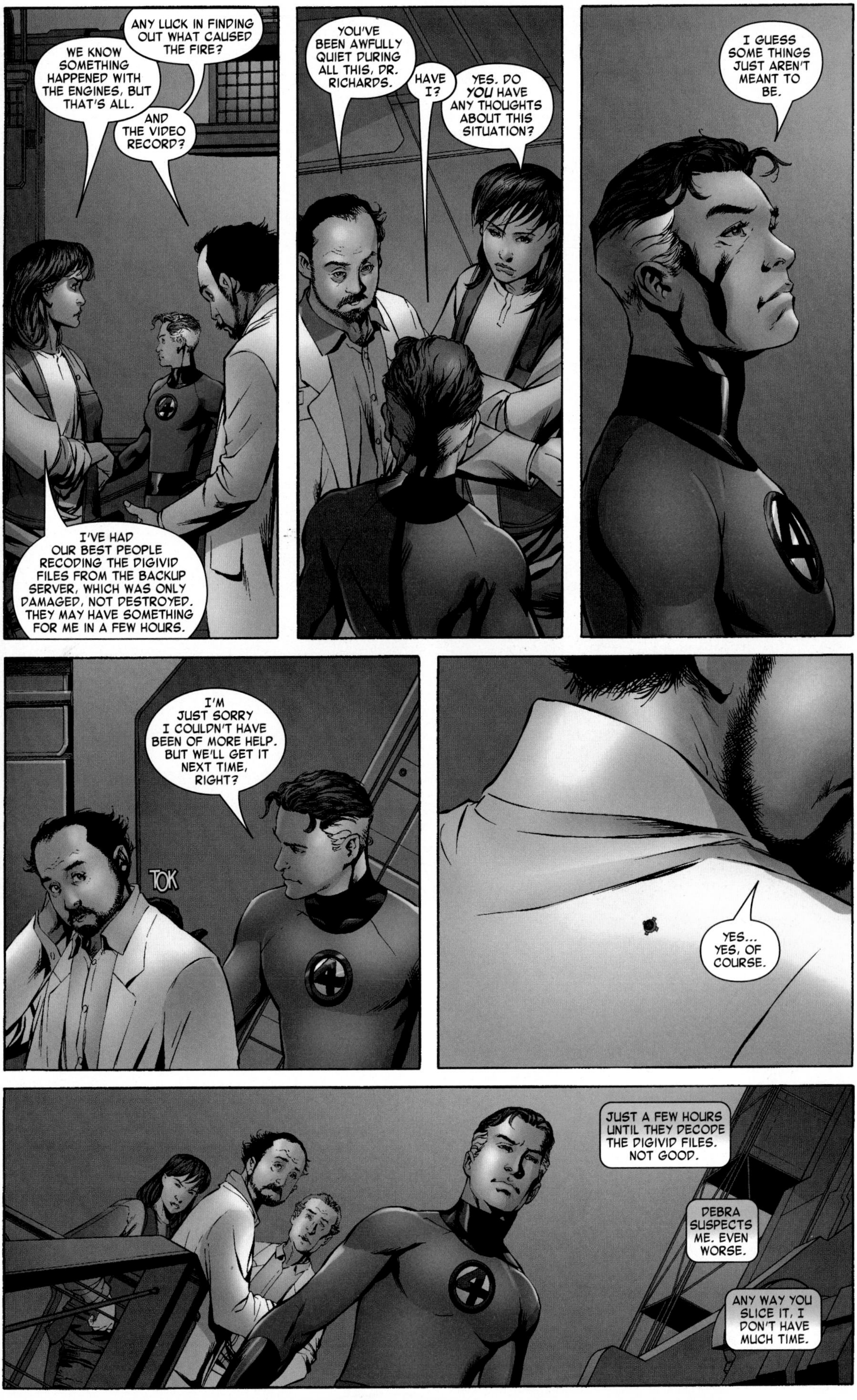
WE KNOW SOMETHING HAPPENED WITH THE ENGINES, BUT THAT'S ALL.
ANY LUCK IN FINDING OUT WHAT CAUSED THE FIRE?
AND THE VIDEO RECORD?
I'VE HAD OUR BEST PEOPLE RECODING THE DIGIVID FILES FROM THE BACKUP SERVER, WHICH WAS ONLY DAMAGED, NOT DESTROYED. THEY MAY HAVE SOMETHING FOR ME IN A FEW HOURS.
YOU'VE BEEN AWFULLY QUIET DURING ALL THIS, DR. RICHARDS.
HAVE I?
YES. DO YOU HAVE ANY THOUGHTS ABOUT THIS SITUATION?
I GUESS SOME THINGS JUST AREN'T MEANT TO BE.
I'M JUST SORRY I COULDN'T HAVE BEEN OF MORE HELP. BUT WE'LL GET IT NEXT TIME, RIGHT?
TOK
YES... YES, OF COURSE.
JUST A FEW HOURS UNTIL THEY DECODE THE DIGIVID FILES. NOT GOOD.
DEBRA SUSPECTS ME. EVEN WORSE.
ANY WAY YOU SLICE IT, I DON'T HAVE MUCH TIME.

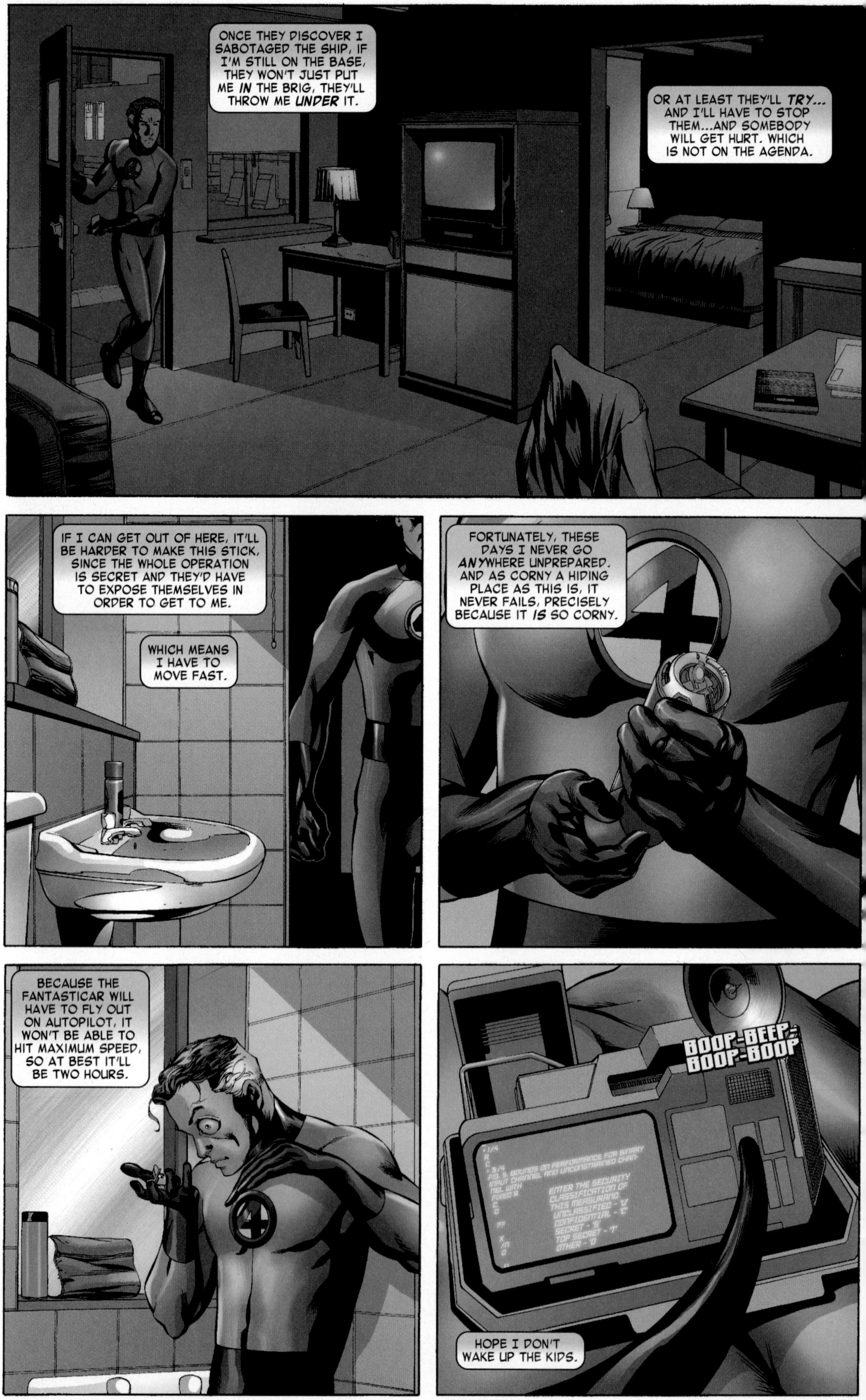
ONCE THEY DISCOVER I SABOTAGED THE SHIP, IF I'M STILL ON THE BASE, THEY WON'T JUST PUT ME *IN* THE BRIG, THEY'LL THROW ME *UNDER* IT.
OR AT LEAST THEY'LL *TRY*... AND I'LL HAVE TO STOP THEM...AND SOMEBODY WILL GET HURT. WHICH IS NOT ON THE AGENDA.
IF I CAN GET OUT OF HERE, IT'LL BE HARDER TO MAKE THIS STICK, SINCE THE WHOLE OPERATION IS SECRET AND THEY'D HAVE TO EXPOSE THEMSELVES IN ORDER TO GET TO ME.
WHICH MEANS I HAVE TO MOVE FAST.
FORTUNATELY, THESE DAYS I NEVER GO *ANY*WHERE UNPREPARED. AND AS CORNY A HIDING PLACE AS THIS IS, IT NEVER FAILS, PRECISELY BECAUSE IT *IS* SO CORNY.
BECAUSE THE FANTASTICAR WILL HAVE TO FLY OUT ON AUTOPILOT, IT WON'T BE ABLE TO HIT MAXIMUM SPEED, SO AT BEST IT'LL BE TWO HOURS.
BOOP-BEEP-BOOP-BOOP
HOPE I DON'T WAKE UP THE KIDS.

SKWISH-SKWISH-
SKWISH-SKWISH

RRRRRRRRRRR

HRMPH?

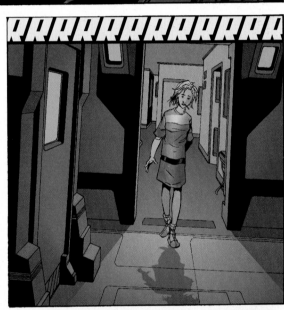

RRRRRRRRRRRR

RRRRRRRRRRR

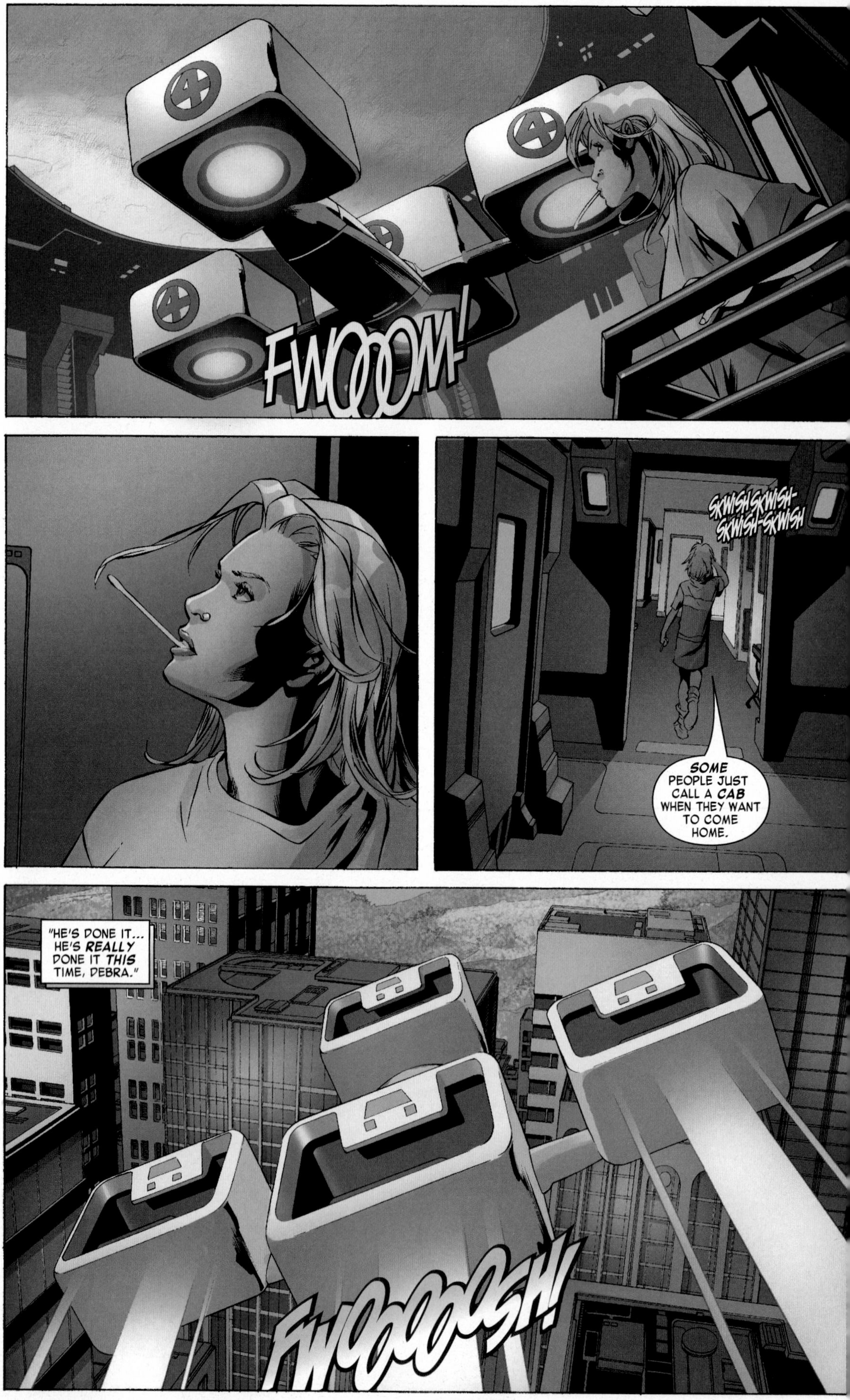
FWOOOM!
SKWISH-SKWISH-SKWISH-SKWISH
SOME PEOPLE JUST CALL A CAB WHEN THEY WANT TO COME HOME.
"HE'S DONE IT... HE'S REALLY DONE IT THIS TIME, DEBRA."
FWOOOOSH!

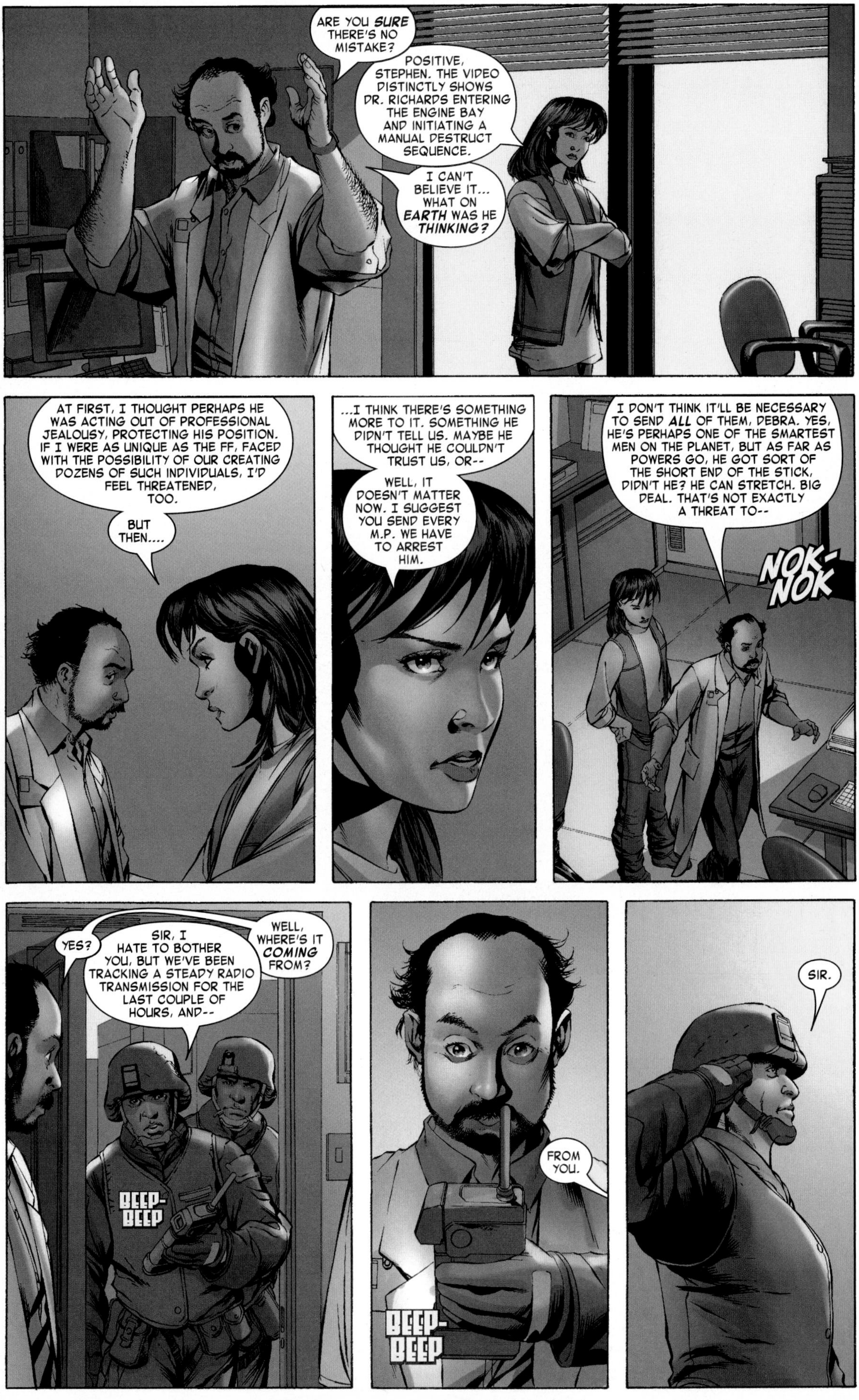
ARE YOU SURE THERE'S NO MISTAKE?
POSITIVE, STEPHEN. THE VIDEO DISTINCTLY SHOWS DR. RICHARDS ENTERING THE ENGINE BAY AND INITIATING A MANUAL DESTRUCT SEQUENCE.
I CAN'T BELIEVE IT... WHAT ON EARTH WAS HE THINKING?
AT FIRST, I THOUGHT PERHAPS HE WAS ACTING OUT OF PROFESSIONAL JEALOUSY, PROTECTING HIS POSITION. IF I WERE AS UNIQUE AS THE FF, FACED WITH THE POSSIBILITY OF OUR CREATING DOZENS OF SUCH INDIVIDUALS, I'D FEEL THREATENED, TOO.
BUT THEN....
...I THINK THERE'S SOMETHING MORE TO IT. SOMETHING HE DIDN'T TELL US. MAYBE HE THOUGHT HE COULDN'T TRUST US, OR--
WELL, IT DOESN'T MATTER NOW. I SUGGEST YOU SEND EVERY M.P. WE HAVE TO ARREST HIM.
I DON'T THINK IT'LL BE NECESSARY TO SEND ALL OF THEM, DEBRA. YES, HE'S PERHAPS ONE OF THE SMARTEST MEN ON THE PLANET, BUT AS FAR AS POWERS GO, HE GOT SORT OF THE SHORT END OF THE STICK, DIDN'T HE? HE CAN STRETCH. BIG DEAL. THAT'S NOT EXACTLY A THREAT TO--
NOK-NOK
YES?
SIR, I HATE TO BOTHER YOU, BUT WE'VE BEEN TRACKING A STEADY RADIO TRANSMISSION FOR THE LAST COUPLE OF HOURS, AND--
WELL, WHERE'S IT COMING FROM?
BEEP-BEEP
FROM YOU.
BEEP-BEEP
SIR.

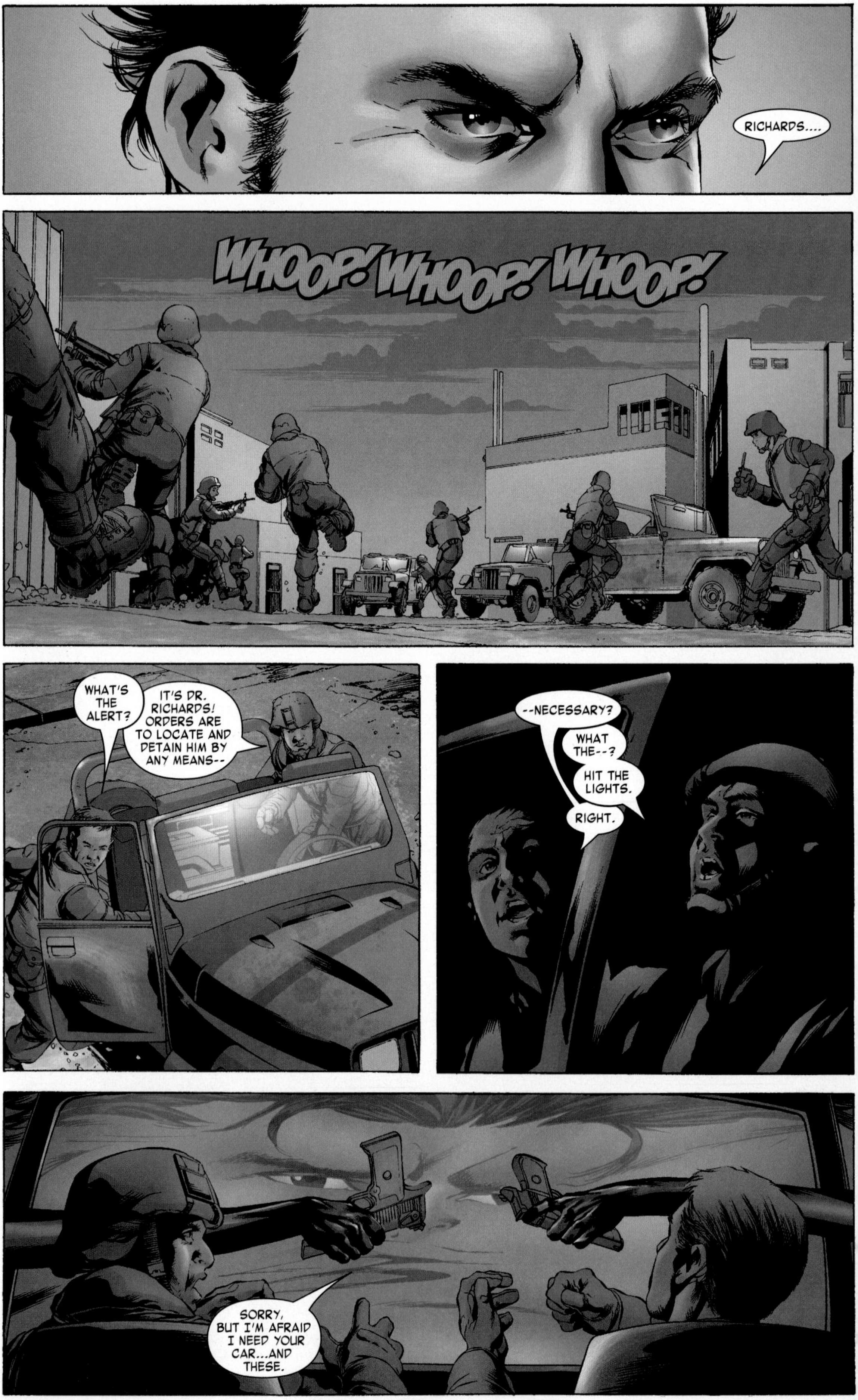
RICHARDS....
WHOOP! WHOOP! WHOOP!
WHAT'S THE ALERT?
IT'S DR. RICHARDS! ORDERS ARE TO LOCATE AND DETAIN HIM BY ANY MEANS--
--NECESSARY?
WHAT THE--?
HIT THE LIGHTS.
RIGHT.
SORRY, BUT I'M AFRAID I NEED YOUR CAR...AND THESE.

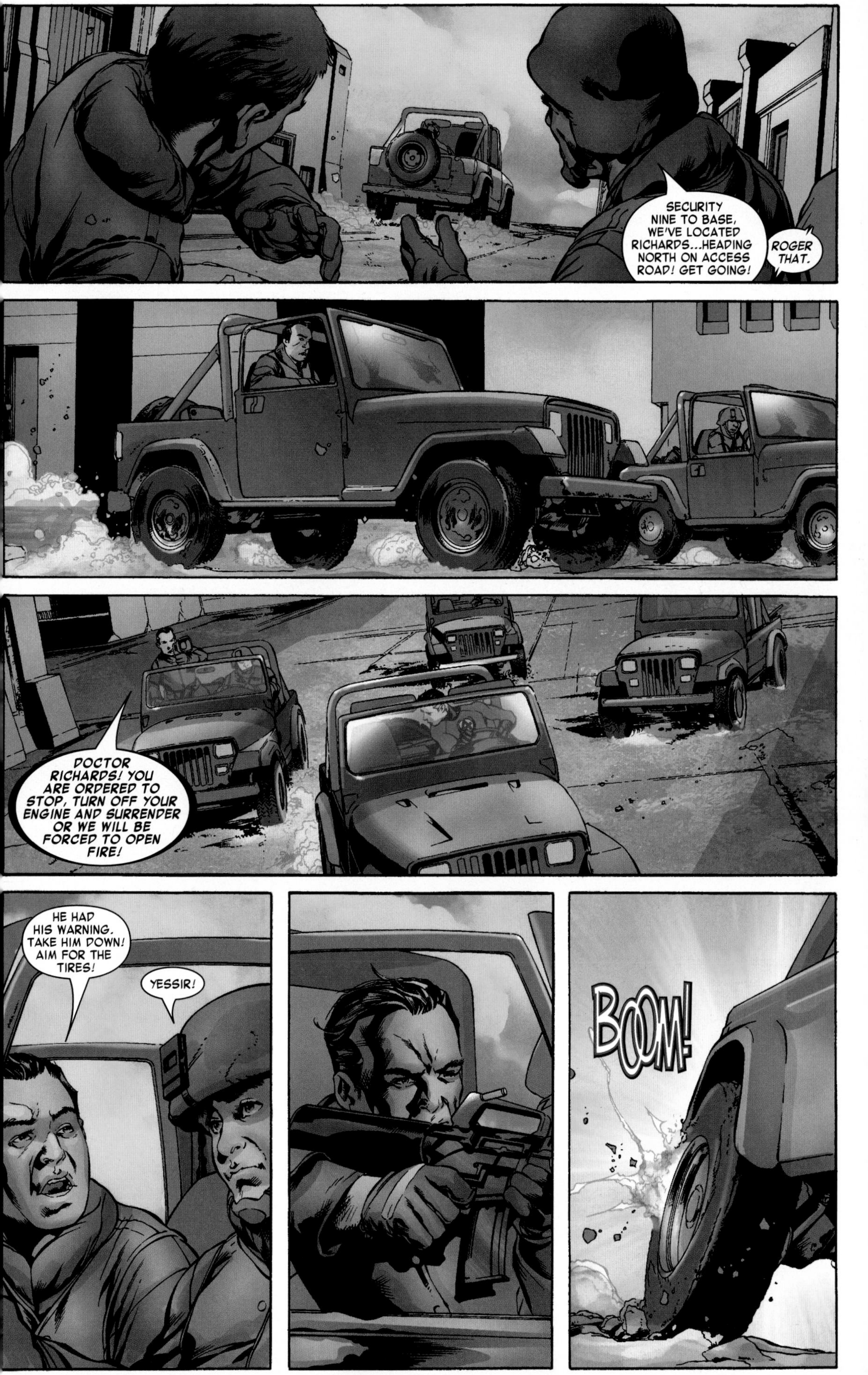
SECURITY NINE TO BASE, WE'VE LOCATED RICHARDS...HEADING NORTH ON ACCESS ROAD! GET GOING!
ROGER THAT.
DOCTOR RICHARDS! YOU ARE ORDERED TO STOP, TURN OFF YOUR ENGINE AND SURRENDER OR WE WILL BE FORCED TO OPEN FIRE!
HE HAD HIS WARNING. TAKE HIM DOWN! AIM FOR THE TIRES!
YESSIR!
BOOM!

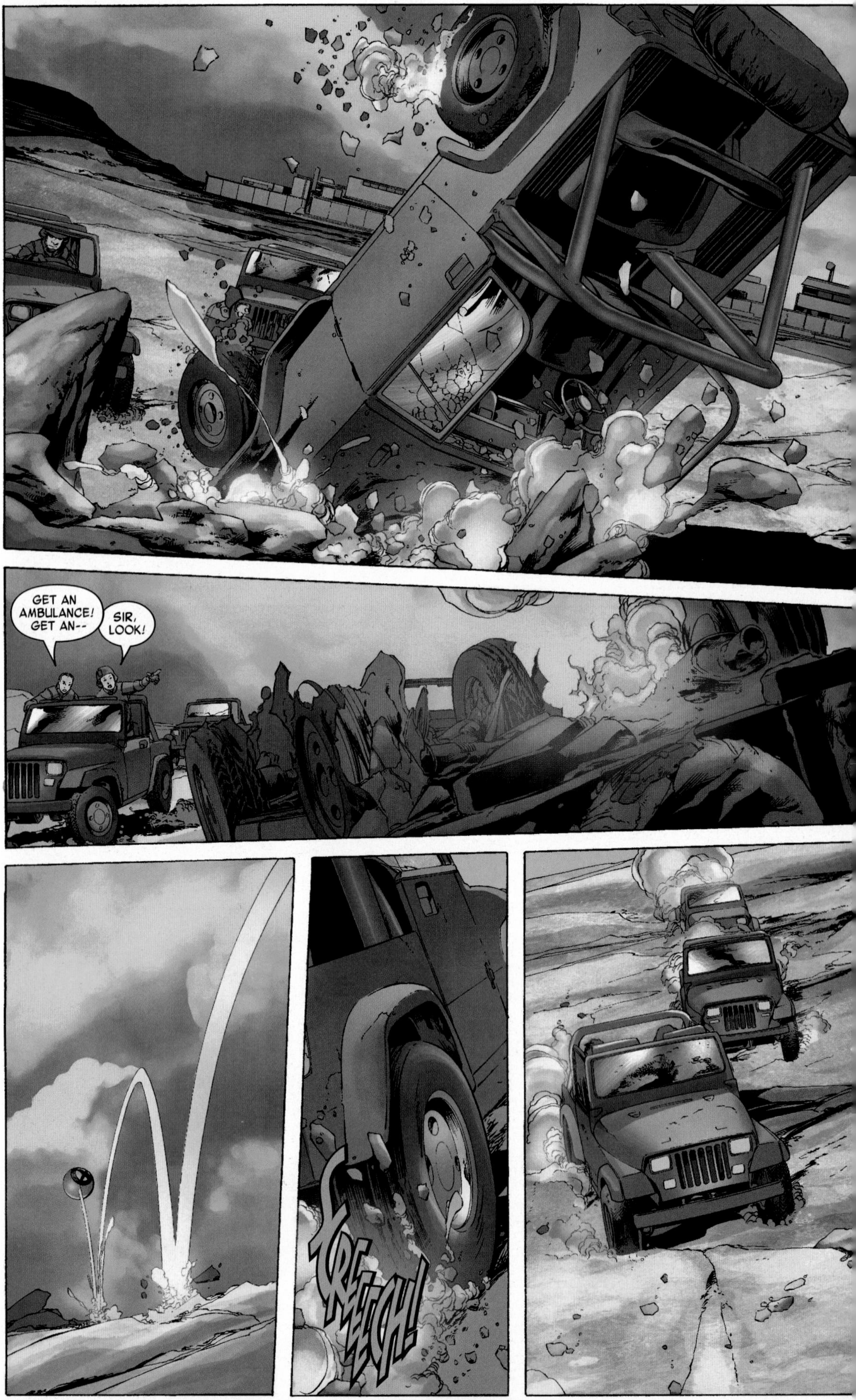
GET AN AMBULANCE! GET AN--
SIR, LOOK!
SKREEEEECH!

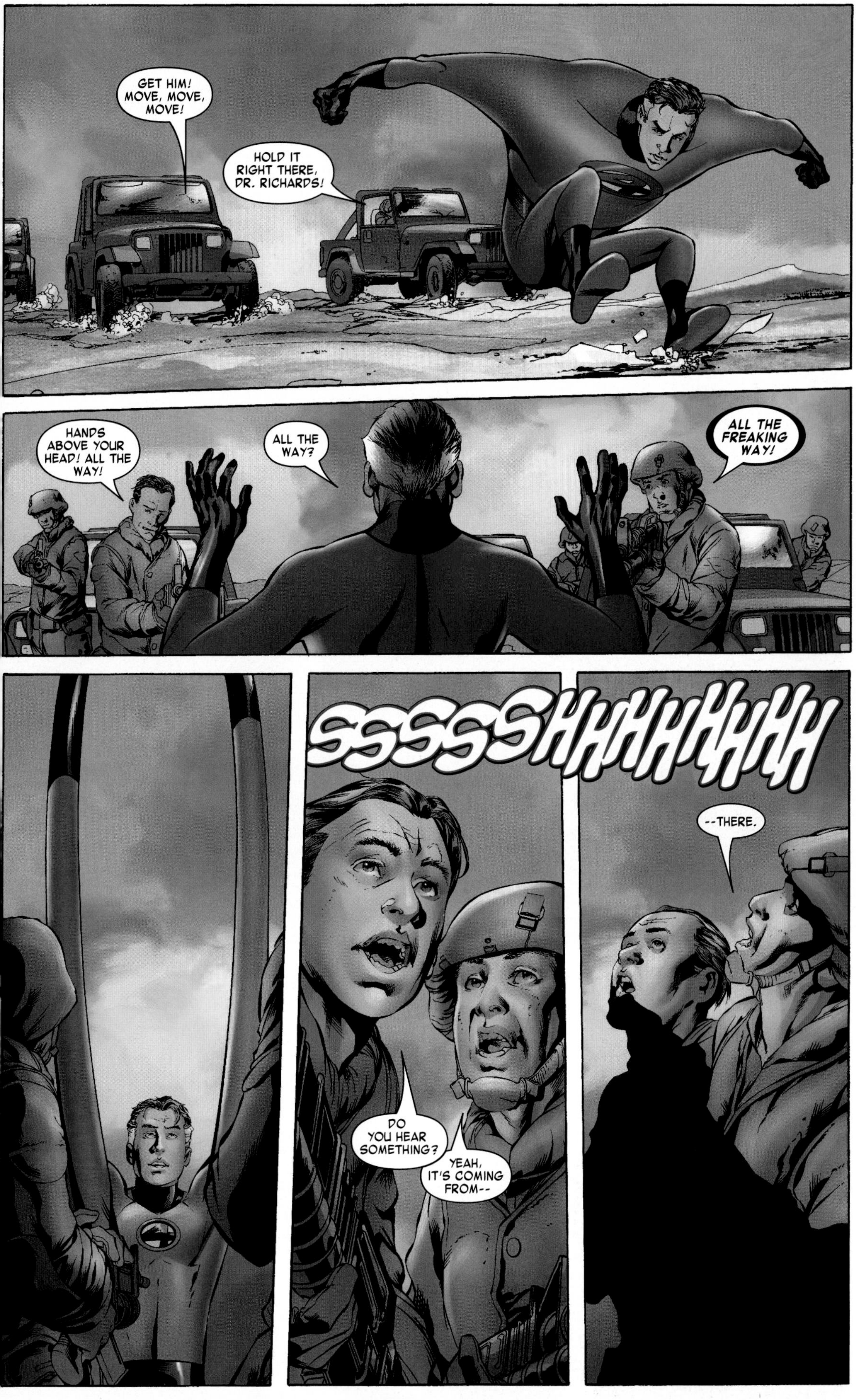
GET HIM! MOVE, MOVE, MOVE!
HOLD IT RIGHT THERE, DR. RICHARDS!
HANDS ABOVE YOUR HEAD! ALL THE WAY!
ALL THE WAY?
ALL THE FREAKING WAY!
SSSSSHHHHHHHH
DO YOU HEAR SOMETHING?
YEAH, IT'S COMING FROM--
--THERE.

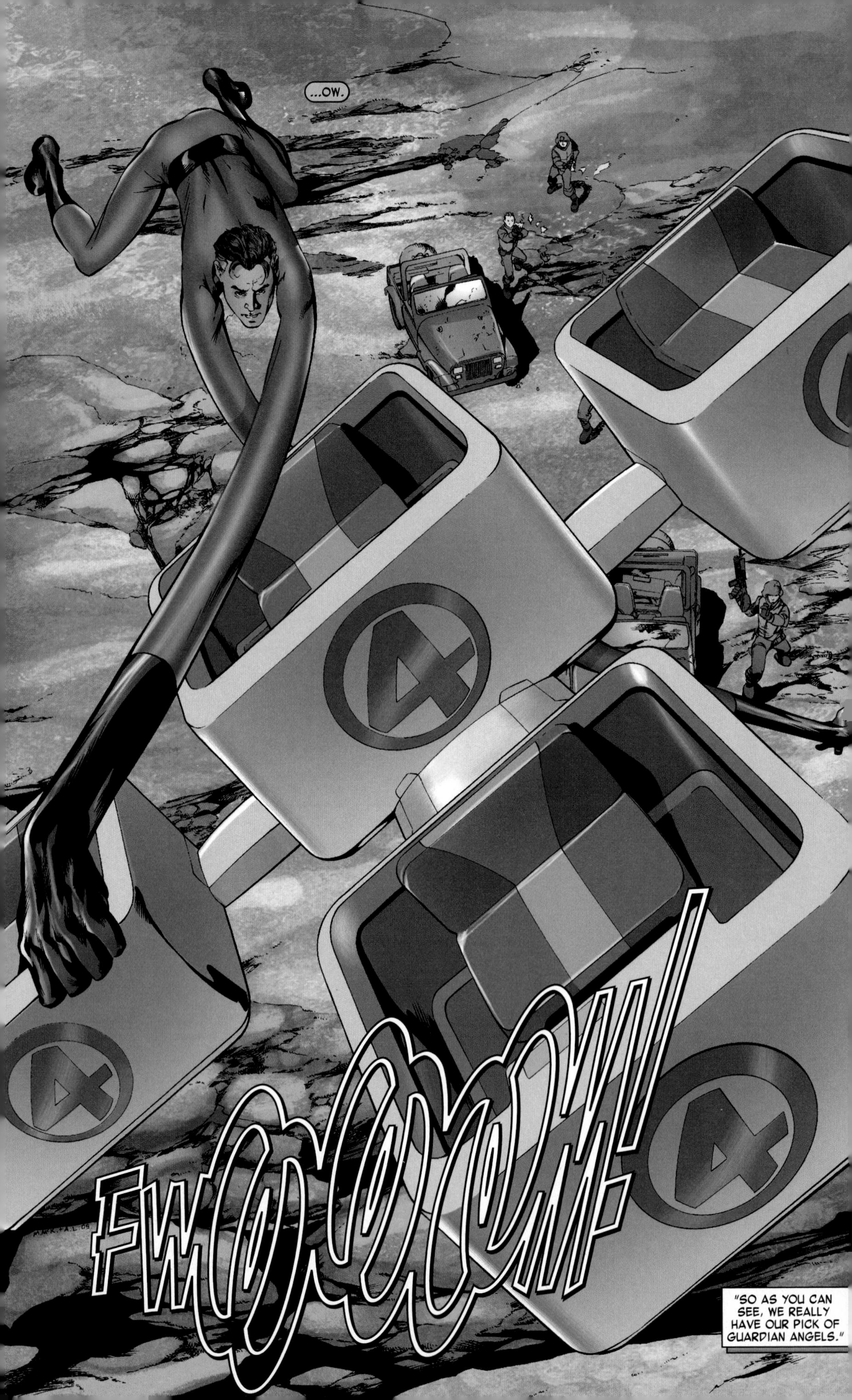
...OW.
FWOOOOM!
"SO AS YOU CAN SEE, WE REALLY HAVE OUR PICK OF GUARDIAN ANGELS."

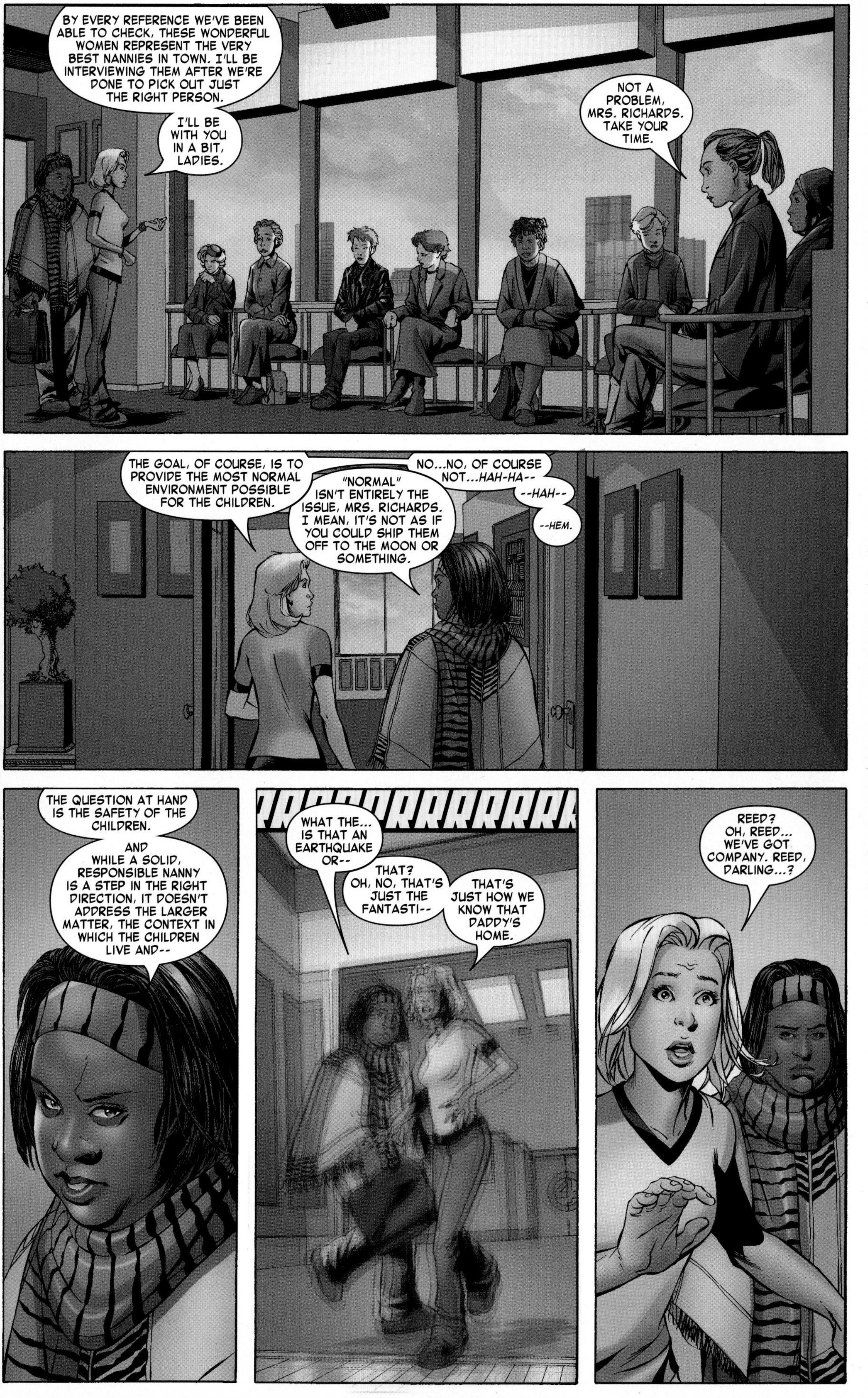
BY EVERY REFERENCE WE'VE BEEN ABLE TO CHECK, THESE WONDERFUL WOMEN REPRESENT THE VERY BEST NANNIES IN TOWN. I'LL BE INTERVIEWING THEM AFTER WE'RE DONE TO PICK OUT JUST THE RIGHT PERSON.
I'LL BE WITH YOU IN A BIT, LADIES.
NOT A PROBLEM, MRS. RICHARDS. TAKE YOUR TIME.
THE GOAL, OF COURSE, IS TO PROVIDE THE MOST NORMAL ENVIRONMENT POSSIBLE FOR THE CHILDREN.
"NORMAL" ISN'T ENTIRELY THE ISSUE, MRS. RICHARDS. I MEAN, IT'S NOT AS IF YOU COULD SHIP THEM OFF TO THE MOON OR SOMETHING.
NO...NO, OF COURSE NOT...HAH-HA--
--HAH--
--HEM.
THE QUESTION AT HAND IS THE SAFETY OF THE CHILDREN.
AND WHILE A SOLID, RESPONSIBLE NANNY IS A STEP IN THE RIGHT DIRECTION, IT DOESN'T ADDRESS THE LARGER MATTER, THE CONTEXT IN WHICH THE CHILDREN LIVE AND--
RRRRRRRRRRRR
WHAT THE... IS THAT AN EARTHQUAKE OR--
THAT? OH, NO, THAT'S JUST THE FANTASTI--
THAT'S JUST HOW WE KNOW THAT DADDY'S HOME.
REED? OH, REED... WE'VE GOT COMPANY. REED, DARLING...?

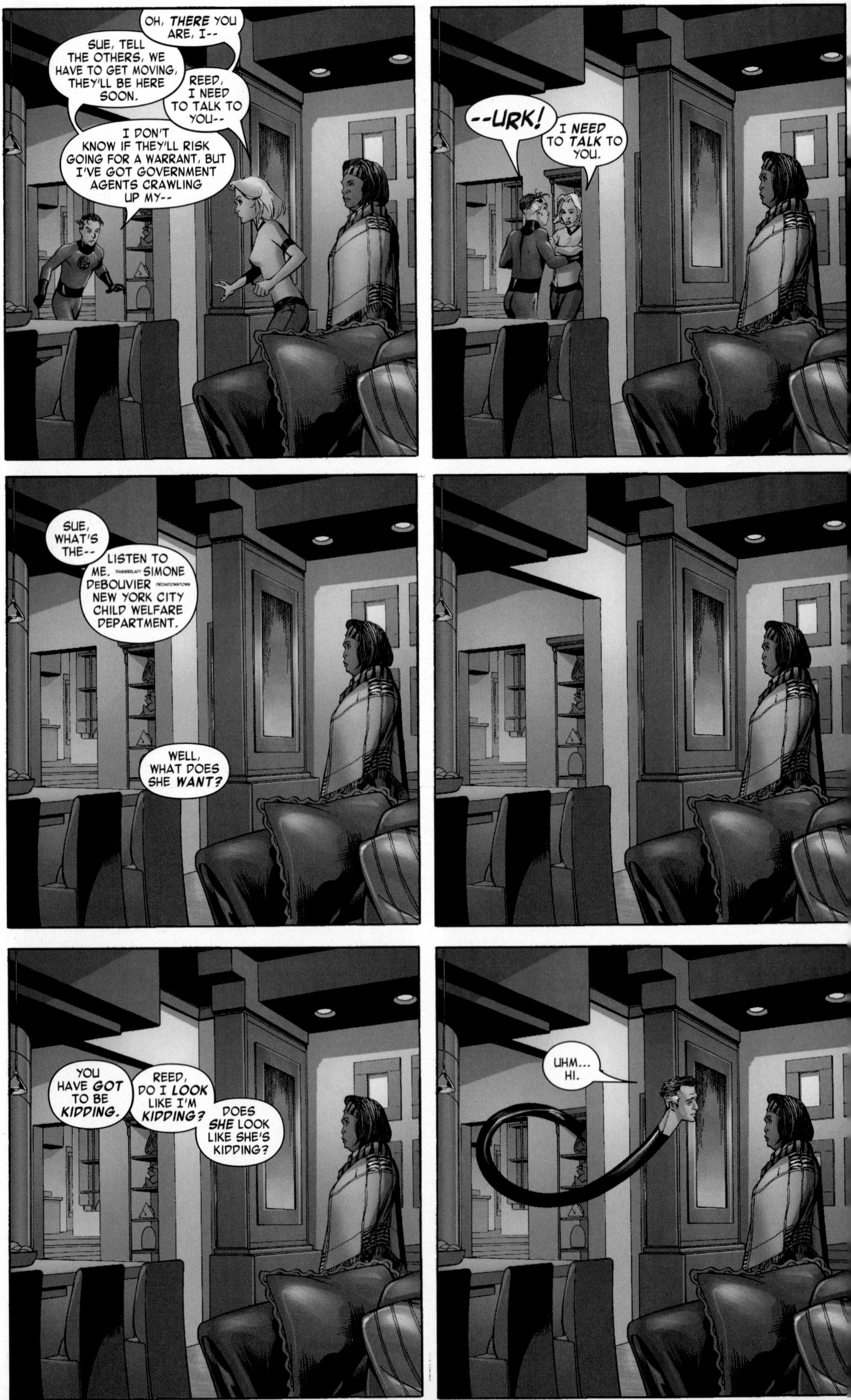
SUE, TELL THE OTHERS, WE HAVE TO GET MOVING, THEY'LL BE HERE SOON.
OH, THERE YOU ARE, I--
REED, I NEED TO TALK TO YOU--
I DON'T KNOW IF THEY'LL RISK GOING FOR A WARRANT, BUT I'VE GOT GOVERNMENT AGENTS CRAWLING UP MY--
--URK!
I NEED TO TALK TO YOU.
SUE, WHAT'S THE--
LISTEN TO ME. SIMONE DEBOUVIER NEW YORK CITY CHILD WELFARE DEPARTMENT.
WELL, WHAT DOES SHE WANT?
YOU HAVE GOT TO BE KIDDING.
REED, DO I LOOK LIKE I'M KIDDING?
DOES SHE LOOK LIKE SHE'S KIDDING?
UHM... HI.

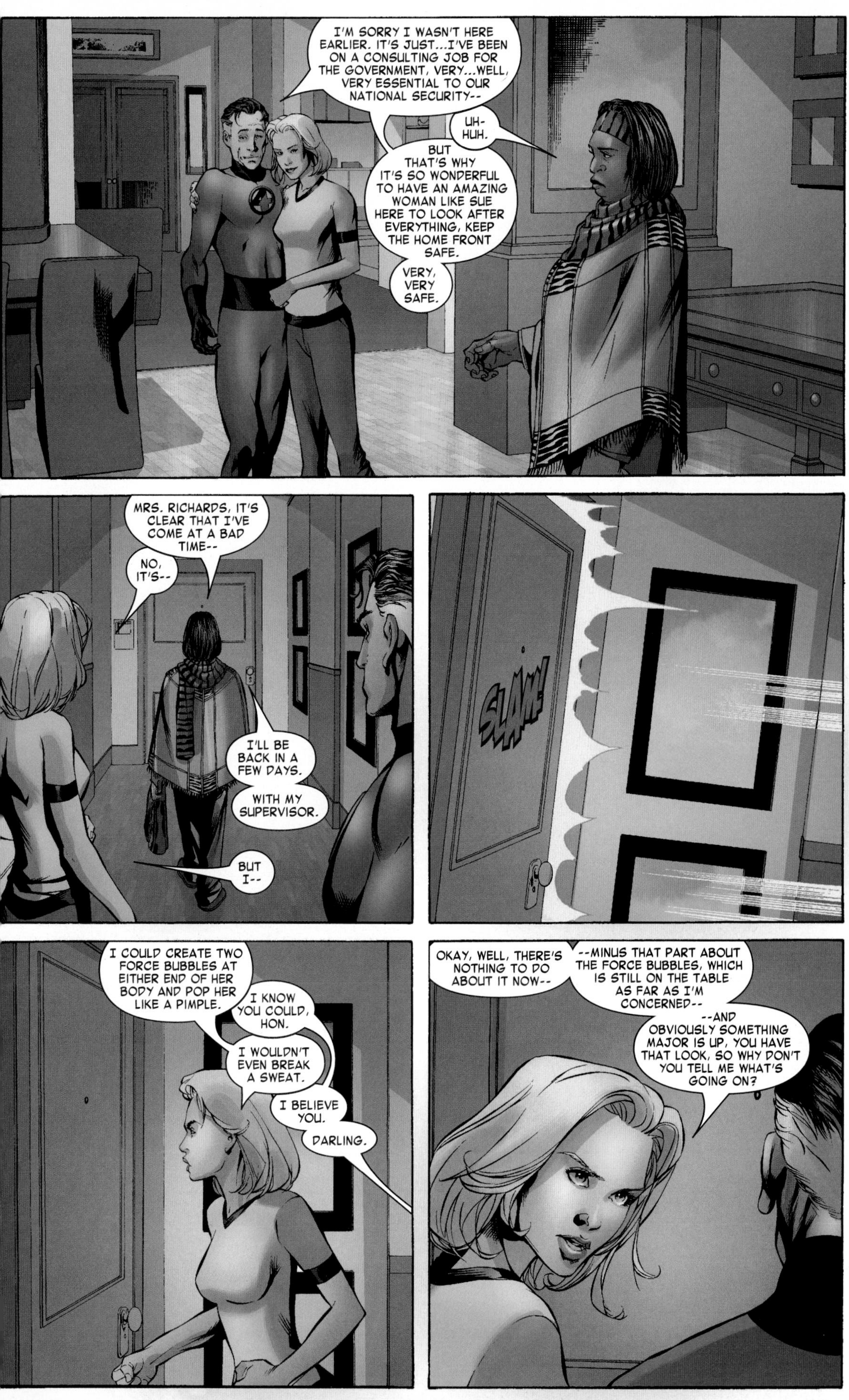

I'M SORRY I WASN'T HERE EARLIER. IT'S JUST...I'VE BEEN ON A CONSULTING JOB FOR THE GOVERNMENT, VERY...WELL, VERY ESSENTIAL TO OUR NATIONAL SECURITY--
UH-HUH.
BUT THAT'S WHY IT'S SO WONDERFUL TO HAVE AN AMAZING WOMAN LIKE SUE HERE TO LOOK AFTER EVERYTHING, KEEP THE HOME FRONT SAFE.
VERY, VERY SAFE.
MRS. RICHARDS, IT'S CLEAR THAT I'VE COME AT A BAD TIME--
NO, IT'S--
I'LL BE BACK IN A FEW DAYS.
WITH MY SUPERVISOR.
BUT I--
SLAM!
I COULD CREATE TWO FORCE BUBBLES AT EITHER END OF HER BODY AND POP HER LIKE A PIMPLE.
I KNOW YOU COULD, HON.
I WOULDN'T EVEN BREAK A SWEAT.
I BELIEVE YOU.
DARLING.
OKAY, WELL, THERE'S NOTHING TO DO ABOUT IT NOW--
--MINUS THAT PART ABOUT THE FORCE BUBBLES, WHICH IS STILL ON THE TABLE AS FAR AS I'M CONCERNED--
--AND OBVIOUSLY SOMETHING MAJOR IS UP, YOU HAVE THAT LOOK, SO WHY DON'T YOU TELL ME WHAT'S GOING ON?

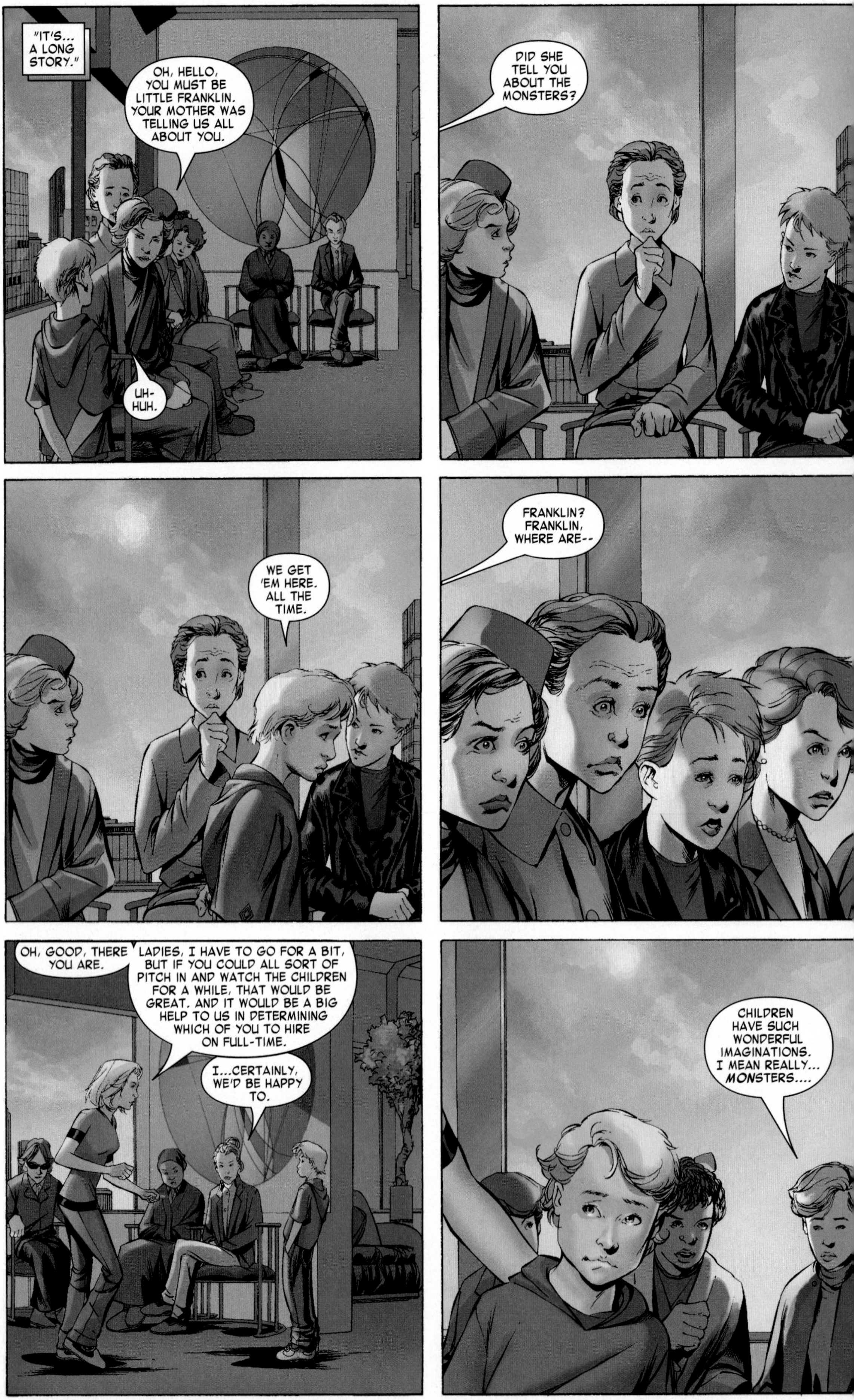
"IT'S... A LONG STORY."
OH, HELLO, YOU MUST BE LITTLE FRANKLIN. YOUR MOTHER WAS TELLING US ALL ABOUT YOU.
UH-HUH.
DID SHE TELL YOU ABOUT THE MONSTERS?
WE GET 'EM HERE. ALL THE TIME.
FRANKLIN? FRANKLIN, WHERE ARE--
OH, GOOD, THERE YOU ARE.
LADIES, I HAVE TO GO FOR A BIT, BUT IF YOU COULD ALL SORT OF PITCH IN AND WATCH THE CHILDREN FOR A WHILE, THAT WOULD BE GREAT. AND IT WOULD BE A BIG HELP TO US IN DETERMINING WHICH OF YOU TO HIRE ON FULL-TIME.
I...CERTAINLY, WE'D BE HAPPY TO.
CHILDREN HAVE SUCH WONDERFUL IMAGINATIONS. I MEAN REALLY... MONSTERS....

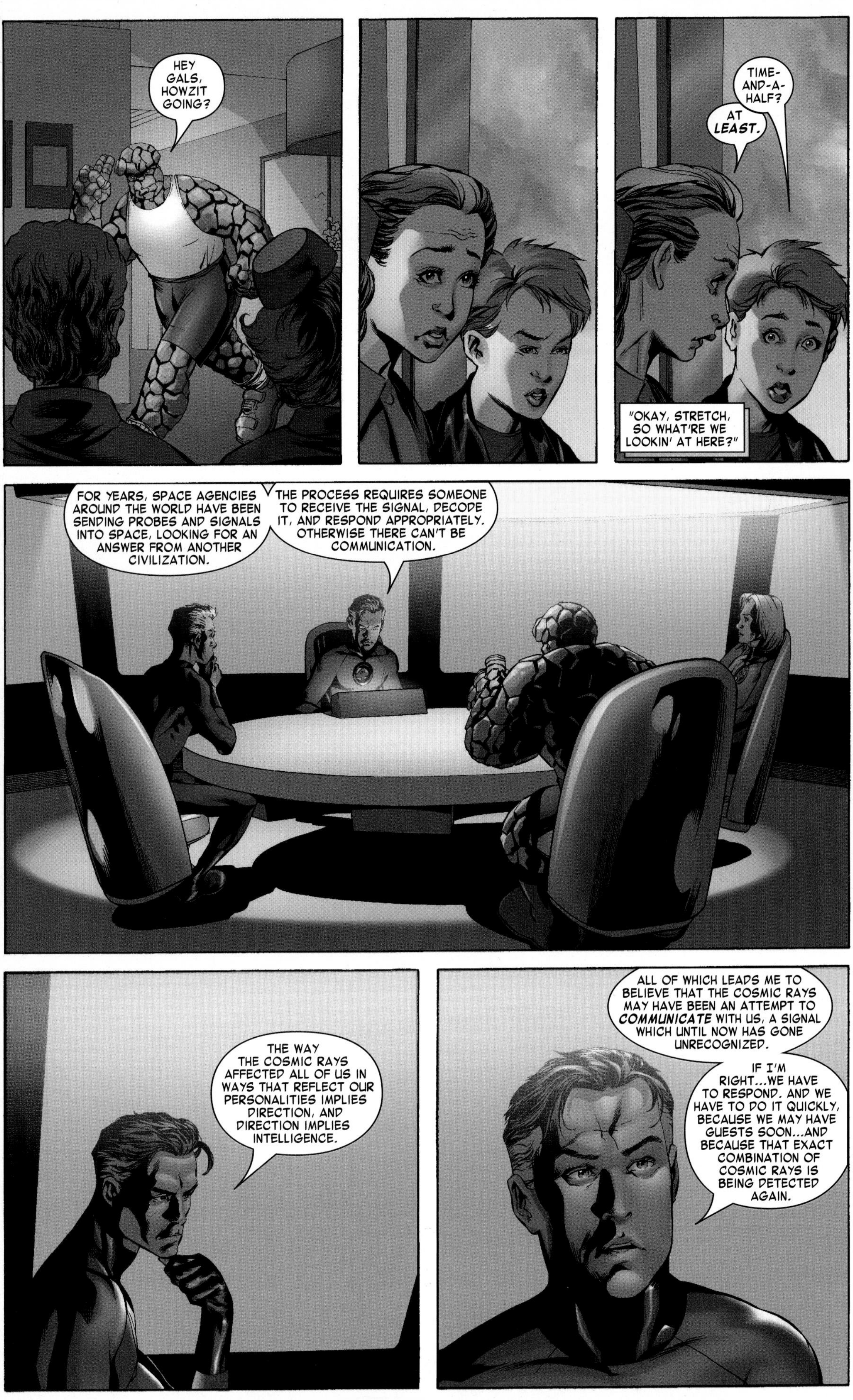
HEY GALS, HOWZIT GOING?
TIME-AND-A-HALF?
AT LEAST.
"OKAY, STRETCH, SO WHAT'RE WE LOOKIN' AT HERE?"
FOR YEARS, SPACE AGENCIES AROUND THE WORLD HAVE BEEN SENDING PROBES AND SIGNALS INTO SPACE, LOOKING FOR AN ANSWER FROM ANOTHER CIVILIZATION.
THE PROCESS REQUIRES SOMEONE TO RECEIVE THE SIGNAL, DECODE IT, AND RESPOND APPROPRIATELY. OTHERWISE THERE CAN'T BE COMMUNICATION.
THE WAY THE COSMIC RAYS AFFECTED ALL OF US IN WAYS THAT REFLECT OUR PERSONALITIES IMPLIES DIRECTION, AND DIRECTION IMPLIES INTELLIGENCE.
ALL OF WHICH LEADS ME TO BELIEVE THAT THE COSMIC RAYS MAY HAVE BEEN AN ATTEMPT TO COMMUNICATE WITH US, A SIGNAL WHICH UNTIL NOW HAS GONE UNRECOGNIZED.
IF I'M RIGHT...WE HAVE TO RESPOND. AND WE HAVE TO DO IT QUICKLY, BECAUSE WE MAY HAVE GUESTS SOON...AND BECAUSE THAT EXACT COMBINATION OF COSMIC RAYS IS BEING DETECTED AGAIN.

SO HOW DO WE ANSWER?

BY GOING BACK UP THERE, SHOWING THAT WE RECOGNIZE THE COMBINATION OF COSMIC RAYS...AND THAT ALL FOUR OF US ARE THERE TO SHOW WE RECOGNIZE THAT THERE WAS INTELLIGENCE IN HOW WE WERE AFFECTED.

AND THEN...?

I.... I DON'T KNOW, BEN. I DON'T KNOW WHAT'LL HAPPEN. MAYBE NOTHING. MAYBE EVERYTHING. I BELIEVE THAT THIS REPRESENTS A SIGNAL, BUT I DON'T HAVE ENOUGH DATA TO KNOW WHAT IT MEANS.

REED AND I TALKED ABOUT IT BEFORE WE CALLED YOU IN, AND OBVIOUSLY THERE ARE RISKS INVOLVED IN GOING BACK UP THERE.

WE KNOW HOW THE COSMIC RAYS AFFECTED US BEFORE. THIS TIME, THEY MAY HAVE NO EFFECT...OR THEY COULD HAVE EVEN MORE PROFOUND EFFECTS THAN THEY HAD BEFORE.

THEY COULD EVEN BE DEADLY. WE JUST DON'T KNOW.

SUE AND I ARE ON BOARD FOR THIS, BUT WE CAN'T SPEAK FOR YOU BECAUSE OF THE DANGER INVOLVED.

IF YOU BOTH AGREE, WE'LL GO. IF YOU DON'T, NOBODY GOES, BECAUSE I THINK IT HAS TO BE ALL FOUR OF US.

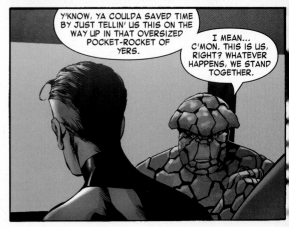

Y'KNOW, YA COULDA SAVED TIME BY JUST TELLIN' US THIS ON THE WAY UP IN THAT OVERSIZED POCKET-ROCKET OF YERS.

I MEAN... C'MON. THIS IS US, RIGHT? WHATEVER HAPPENS, WE STAND TOGETHER.

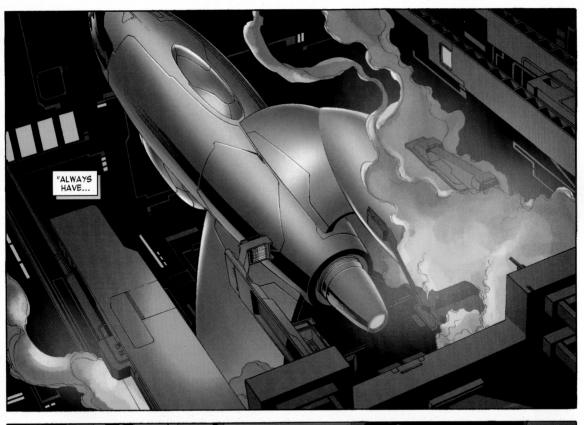

"ALWAYS HAVE...

"...ALWAYS WILL."

REED? WE'RE PICKING UP SOMETHING ON THE BUILDING MONITORS.

PATCH IT THROUGH.

DR. RICHARDS... MY NAME IS GENERAL CLEMENT BRAGG...YOU ARE ORDERED TO SURRENDER YOURSELF TO US AT ONCE. DO YOU HEAR ME?

I HEAR YOU, GENERAL, AND I'D LOVE TO COMPLY... BUT I'M AFRAID WE'VE ALREADY STARTED.

STARTED WHAT?

THE COUNTDOWN.

I SUGGEST YOU MOVE AWAY FROM THE BUILDING, FOR YOUR OWN SAFETY.

RUMBLERUMBLERUMBLE

AND DO IT QUICKLY.

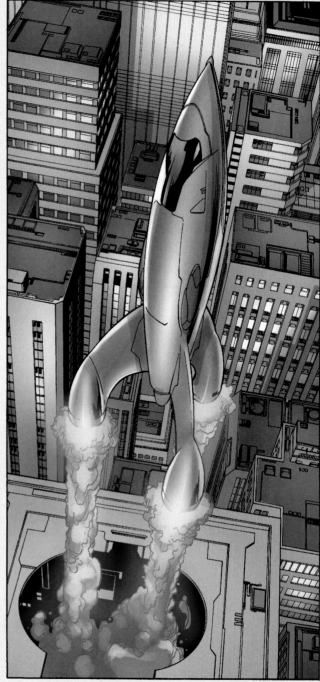

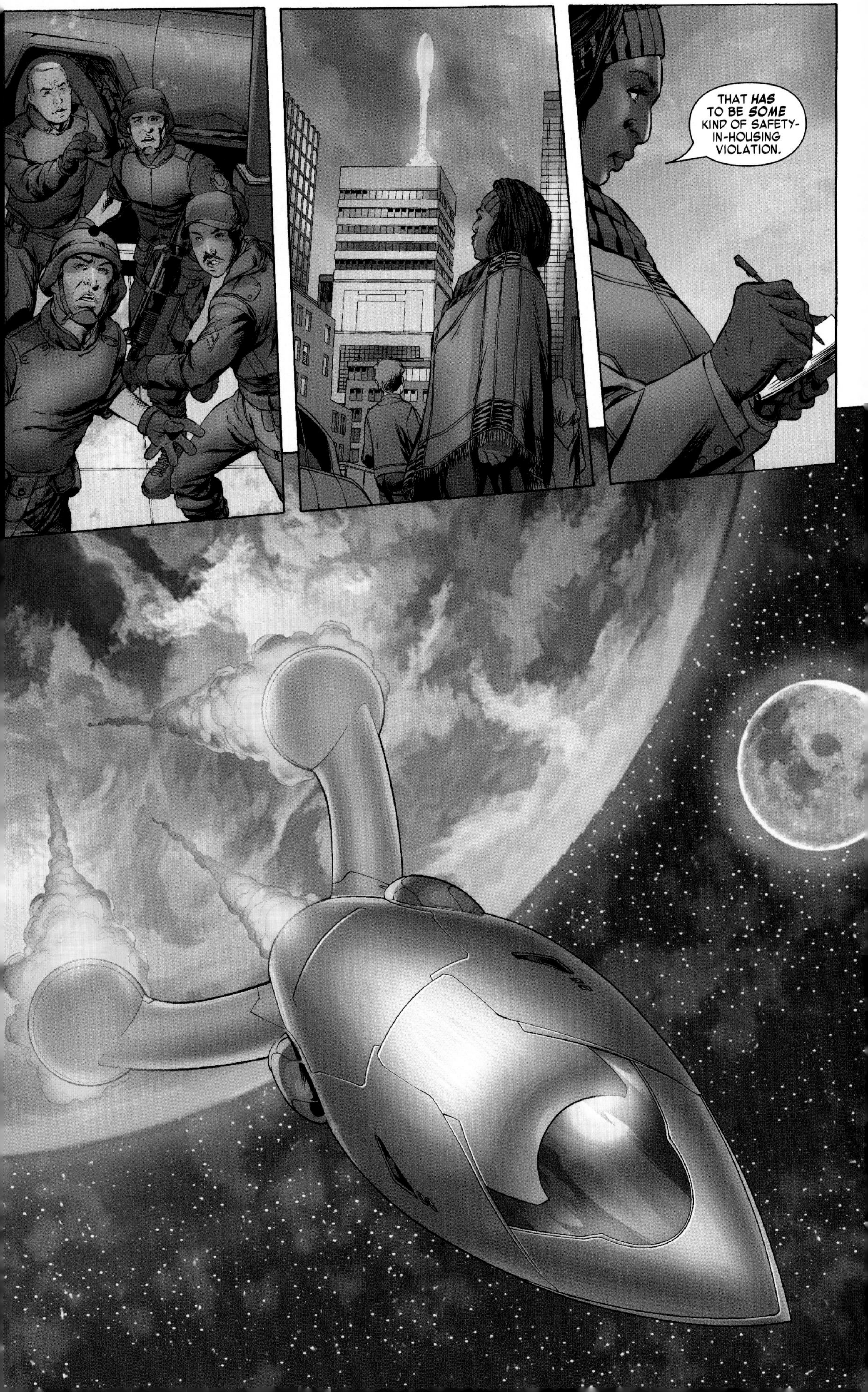
THAT HAS TO BE SOME KIND OF SAFETY-IN-HOUSING VIOLATION.

YA KNOW, ON THE WAY UP, RIGHT AFTER I LOST MY LUNCH--

THE FIRST OR THE SECOND TIME?

--THE SECOND TIME--

--I, THOUGHT, MAYBE THIS IS FATE.

FIRST I FIND OUT THAT I'VE GOT MORE MONEY THAN...WELL, WHOEVER'S GOT MORE MONEY THAN COMMON SENSE, EXCEPT I'VE *GOT* COMMON SENSE...

AND NOW THIS HAPPENS, AND I WAS THINKING... MAYBE GOING UP NOW, WITH THE SAME EXACT CIRCUMSTANCES THAT MADE US LIKE THIS THE FIRST TIME--

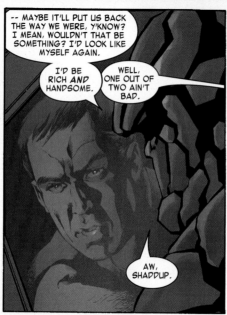

-- MAYBE IT'LL PUT US BACK THE WAY WE WERE, Y'KNOW? I MEAN, WOULDN'T THAT BE SOMETHING? I'D LOOK LIKE MYSELF AGAIN.

I'D BE RICH *AND* HANDSOME.

WELL, ONE OUT OF TWO AIN'T BAD.

AW, SHADDUP.

INSTRUMENTS ARE PICKING UP INCREASED COSMIC RAY ACTIVITY...ADJUSTING COURSE TO PUT US ON INTERCEPT.

CONTACT IN... ONE MINUTE.

REED...?

I JUST...IF ANYTHING HAPPENS--

I KNOW. I LOVE YOU TOO.

YEAH, AND I GOT MATCHSTICK HERE TA KISS ME IF I NEED IT, SO THANKS FOR ASKIN'.

WEIRD...NEVER OCCURRED TO ME UNTIL RIGHT NOW...WITH MITTS LIKE THIS, I CAN'T CROSS MY FINGERS.

HERE IT COMES!

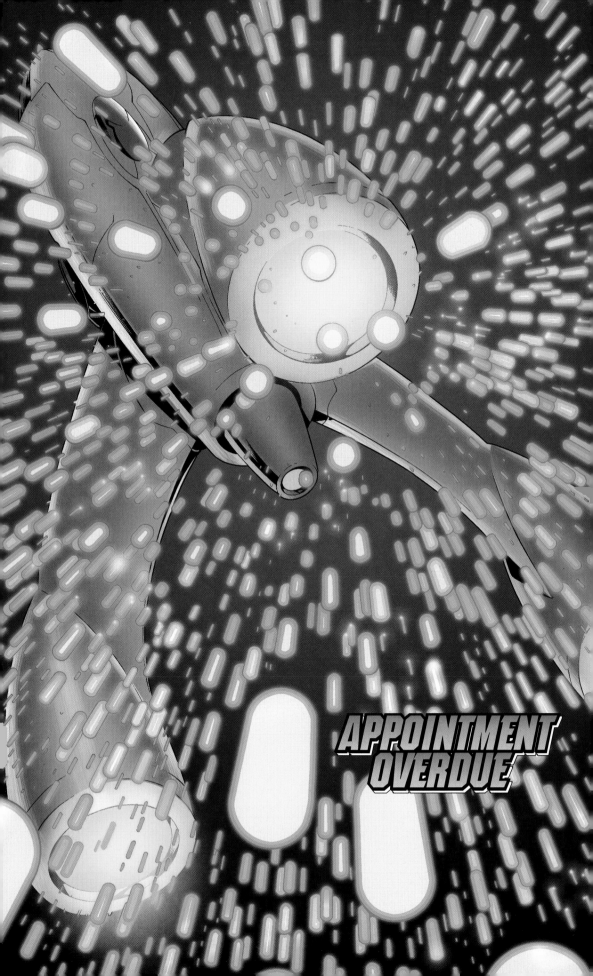

APPOINTMENT
OVERDUE

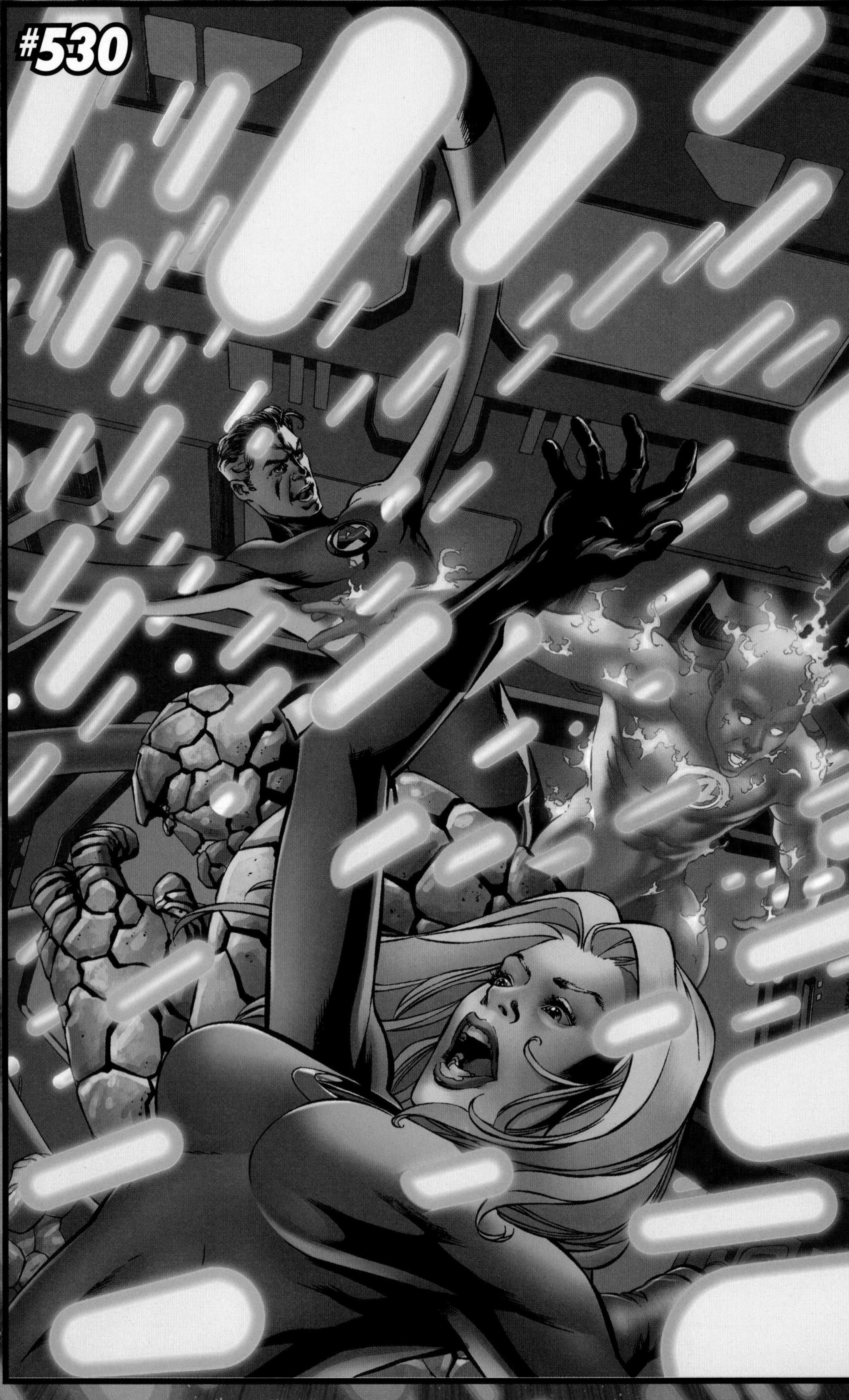
#530

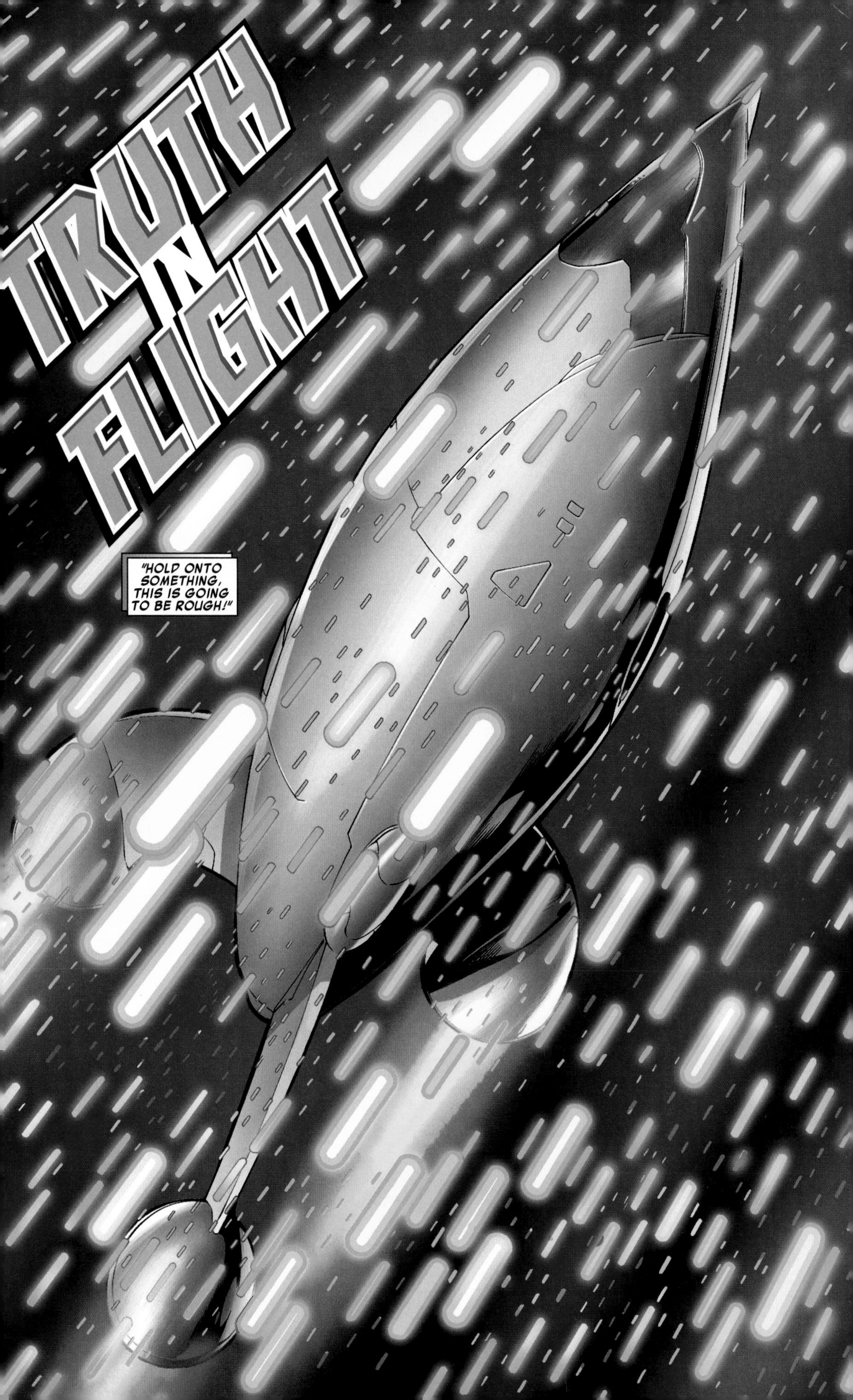
TRUTH IN FLIGHT
"HOLD ONTO SOMETHING, THIS IS GOING TO BE ROUGH!"

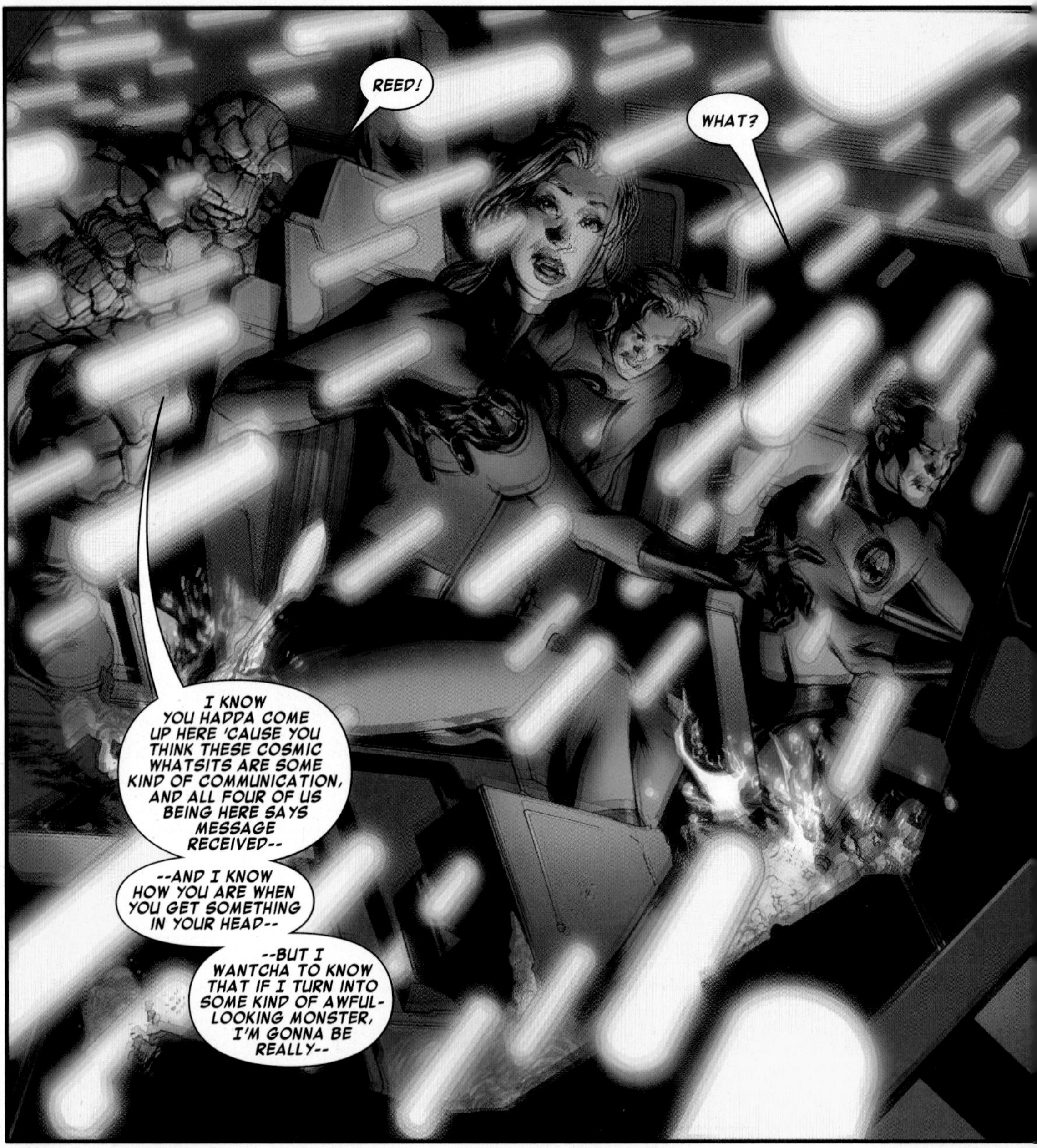
REED!
WHAT?
I KNOW YOU HADDA COME UP HERE 'CAUSE YOU THINK THESE COSMIC WHATSITS ARE SOME KIND OF COMMUNICATION, AND ALL FOUR OF US BEING HERE SAYS MESSAGE RECEIVED--
--AND I KNOW HOW YOU ARE WHEN YOU GET SOMETHING IN YOUR HEAD--
--BUT I WANTCHA TO KNOW THAT IF I TURN INTO SOME KIND OF AWFUL-LOOKING MONSTER, I'M GONNA BE REALLY--

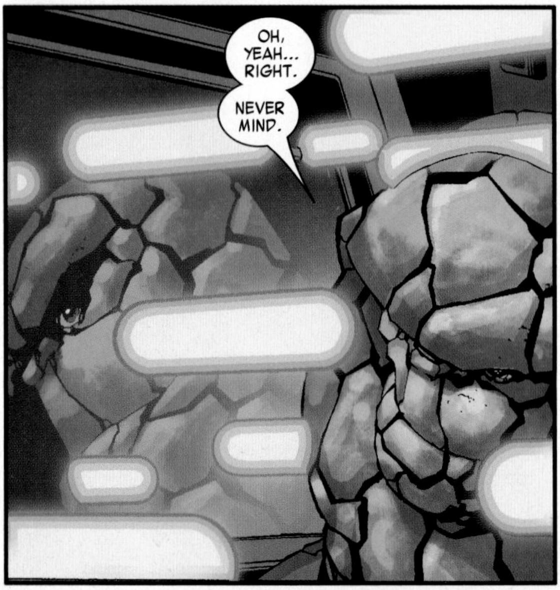
OH, YEAH... RIGHT.
NEVER MIND.

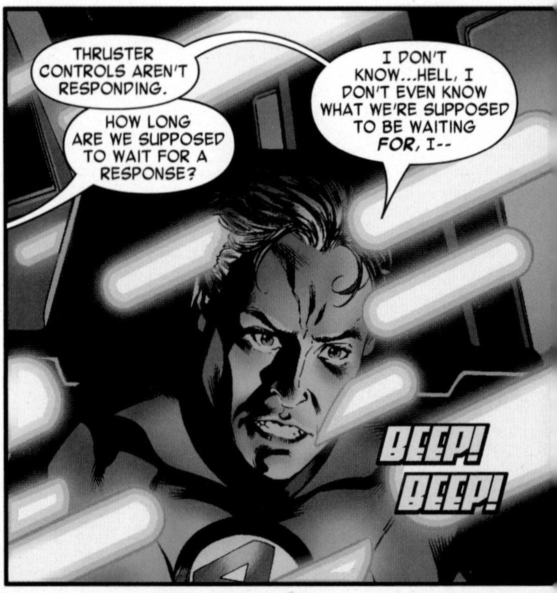
THRUSTER CONTROLS AREN'T RESPONDING.
HOW LONG ARE WE SUPPOSED TO WAIT FOR A RESPONSE?
I DON'T KNOW...HELL, I DON'T EVEN KNOW WHAT WE'RE SUPPOSED TO BE WAITING FOR, I--
BEEP! BEEP!

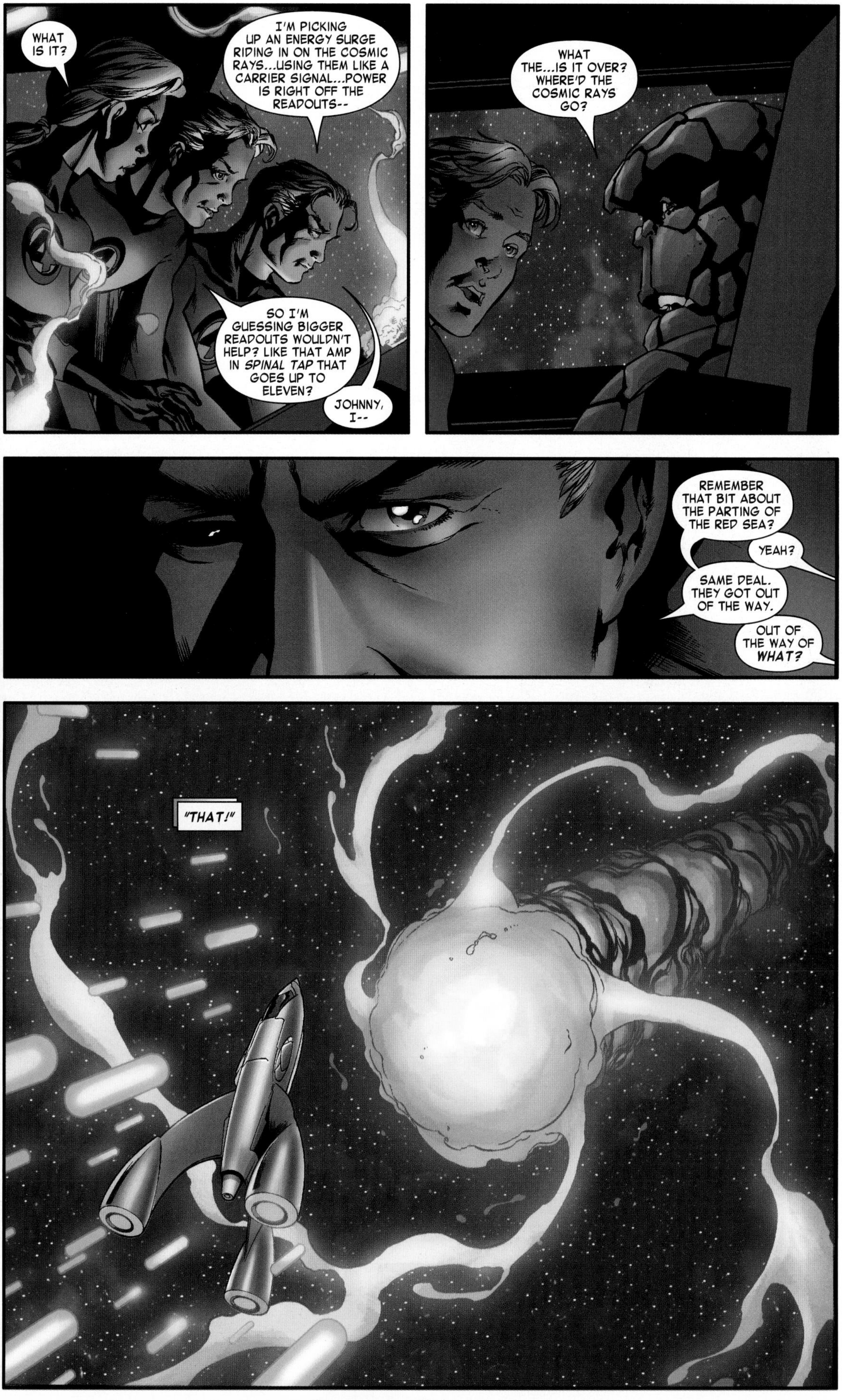
WHAT IS IT?
I'M PICKING UP AN ENERGY SURGE RIDING IN ON THE COSMIC RAYS...USING THEM LIKE A CARRIER SIGNAL...POWER IS RIGHT OFF THE READOUTS--
SO I'M GUESSING BIGGER READOUTS WOULDN'T HELP? LIKE THAT AMP IN *SPINAL TAP* THAT GOES UP TO ELEVEN?
JOHNNY, I--
WHAT THE...IS IT OVER? WHERE'D THE COSMIC RAYS GO?
REMEMBER THAT BIT ABOUT THE PARTING OF THE RED SEA?
YEAH?
SAME DEAL. THEY GOT OUT OF THE WAY.
OUT OF THE WAY OF ***WHAT?***
"THAT!"

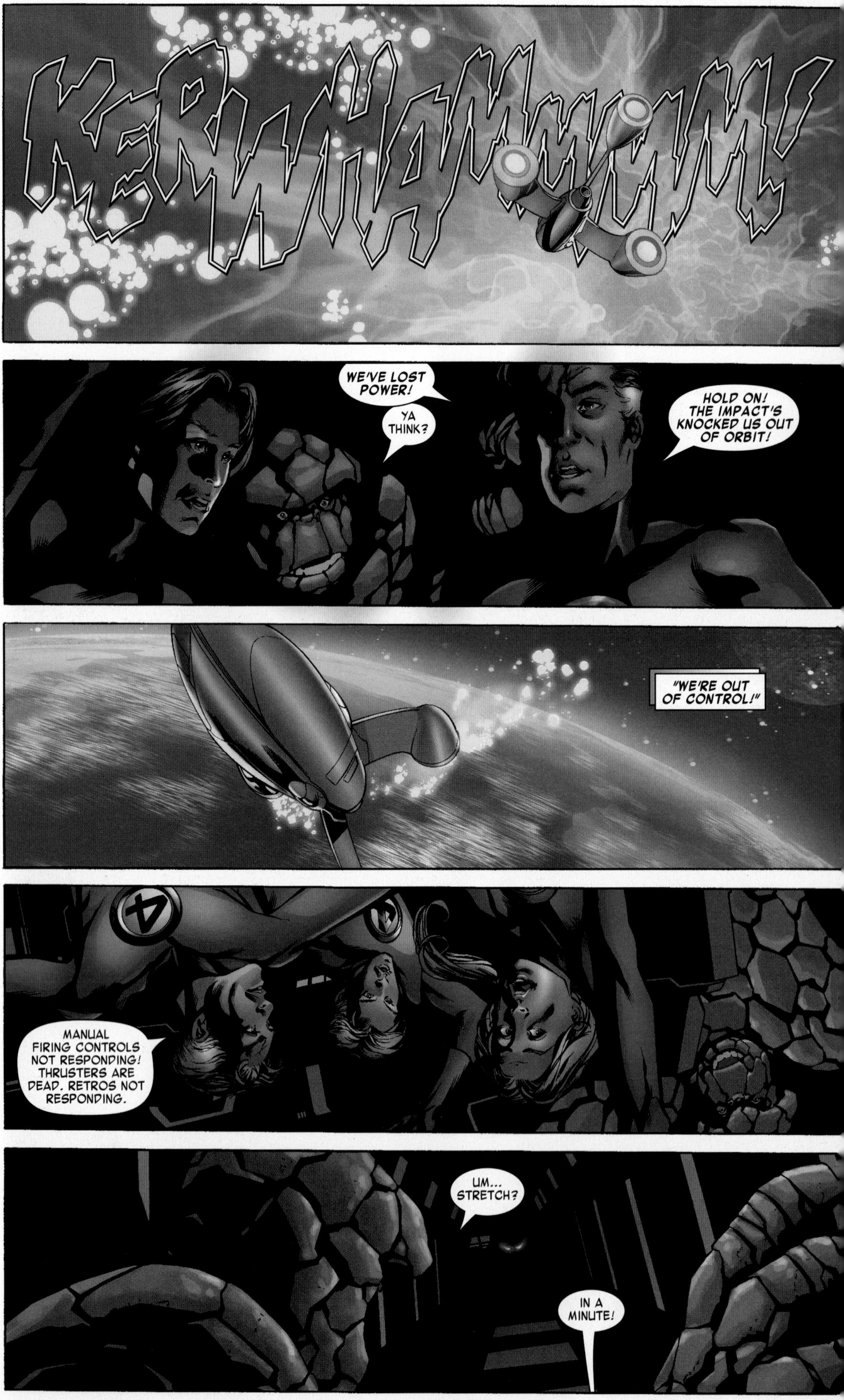
KERWHAMMMM!
WE'VE LOST POWER!
YA THINK?
HOLD ON! THE IMPACT'S KNOCKED US OUT OF ORBIT!
"WE'RE OUT OF CONTROL!"
MANUAL FIRING CONTROLS NOT RESPONDING! THRUSTERS ARE DEAD. RETROS NOT RESPONDING.
UM... STRETCH?
IN A MINUTE!

WE'VE GOT ONE CHANCE!

SUE, THROW A FORCE FIELD AROUND THE SHIP! THAT'LL KEEP US FROM BURNING UP ON RE-ENTRY.

WILL DO--

"--BUT EVEN THAT WON'T BE ABLE TO ABSORB THE IMPACT IF WE HIT THE GROUND AT FULL SPEED."

"IT WON'T HAVE TO."

JOHNNY, WE'RE DEEP ENOUGH IN THE ATMOSPHERE NOW FOR YOU TO FUNCTION OUTSIDE THE SHIP.

GET OUT THE AIRLOCK AND STAY BETWEEN THE SHIP'S HULL AND SUE'S FORCE FIELD, AND BE READY TO MOVE.

RIGHT.

YOU OKAY?

YOU KNOW WE GOT COMPANY, RIGHT?

NOT THE TIME FOR JOKES, BEN.

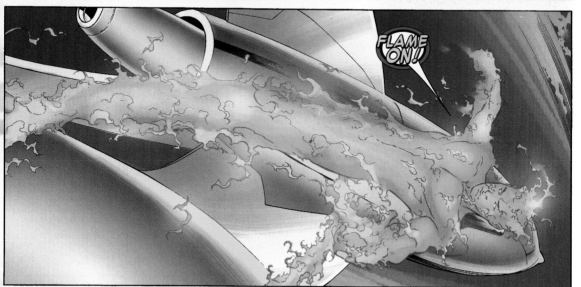

FLAME ON!

HE'S LIKE THAT ALLA TIME. HOTHEAD. NEVER LISTENS.

SO.

PARCHEESI?

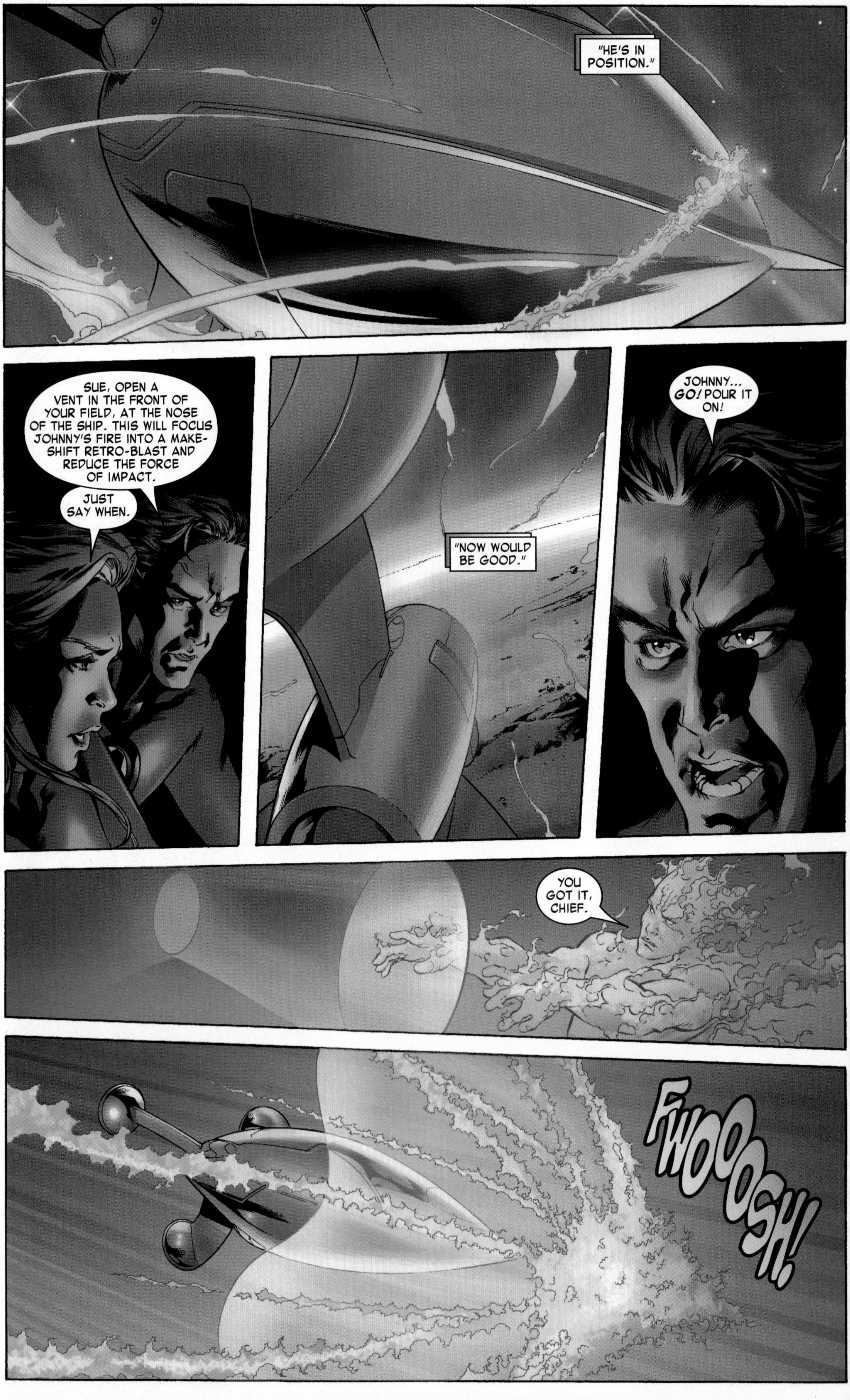
"HE'S IN POSITION."
SUE, OPEN A VENT IN THE FRONT OF YOUR FIELD, AT THE NOSE OF THE SHIP. THIS WILL FOCUS JOHNNY'S FIRE INTO A MAKE-SHIFT RETRO-BLAST AND REDUCE THE FORCE OF IMPACT.
JUST SAY WHEN.
"NOW WOULD BE GOOD."
JOHNNY... GO! POUR IT ON!
YOU GOT IT, CHIEF.
FWOOOOSH!

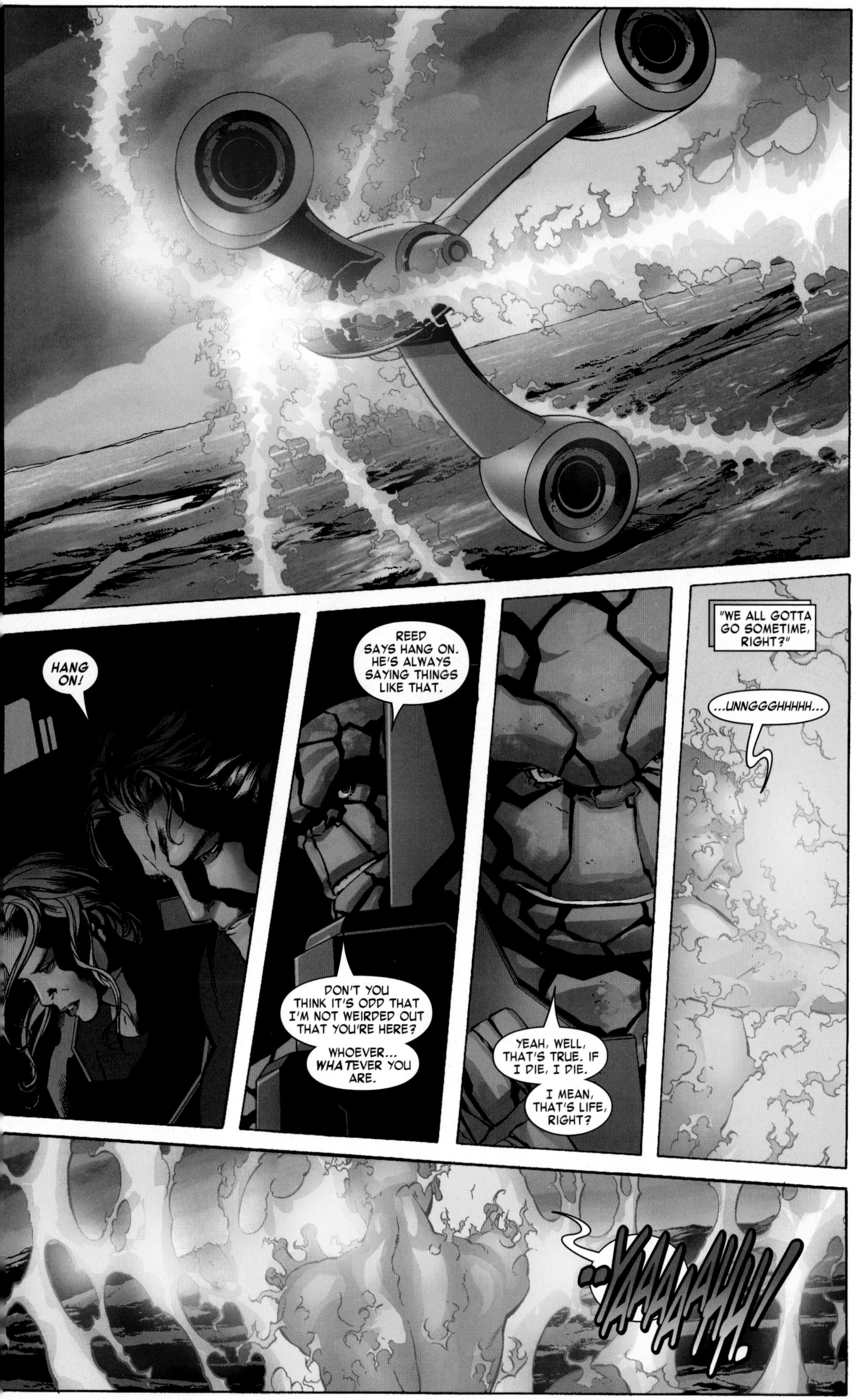
HANG ON!
REED SAYS HANG ON. HE'S ALWAYS SAYING THINGS LIKE THAT.
DON'T YOU THINK IT'S ODD THAT I'M NOT WEIRDED OUT THAT YOU'RE HERE?
WHOEVER... WHATEVER YOU ARE.
YEAH, WELL, THAT'S TRUE. IF I DIE, I DIE.
I MEAN, THAT'S LIFE, RIGHT?
"WE ALL GOTTA GO SOMETIME, RIGHT?"
...UNNGGGHHHHH...
..YAAAAAHH!

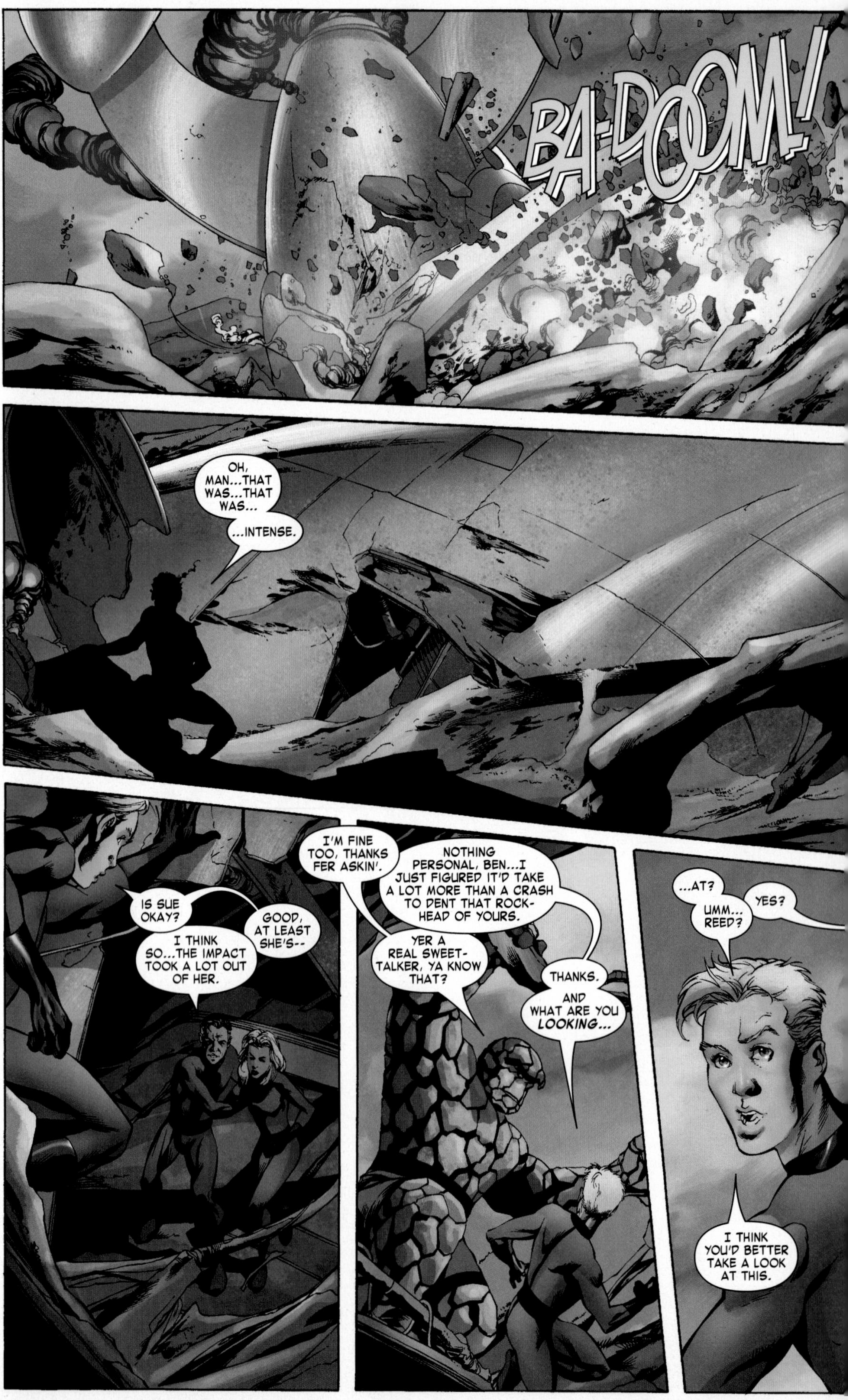
BA-DOOM!
OH, MAN...THAT WAS...THAT WAS...
...INTENSE.
IS SUE OKAY?
GOOD, AT LEAST SHE'S--
I THINK SO...THE IMPACT TOOK A LOT OUT OF HER.
I'M FINE TOO, THANKS FER ASKIN'.
NOTHING PERSONAL, BEN...I JUST FIGURED IT'D TAKE A LOT MORE THAN A CRASH TO DENT THAT ROCK-HEAD OF YOURS.
YER A REAL SWEET-TALKER, YA KNOW THAT?
THANKS.
AND WHAT ARE YOU *LOOKING*...
...AT?
UMM... REED?
YES?
I THINK YOU'D BETTER TAKE A LOOK AT THIS.

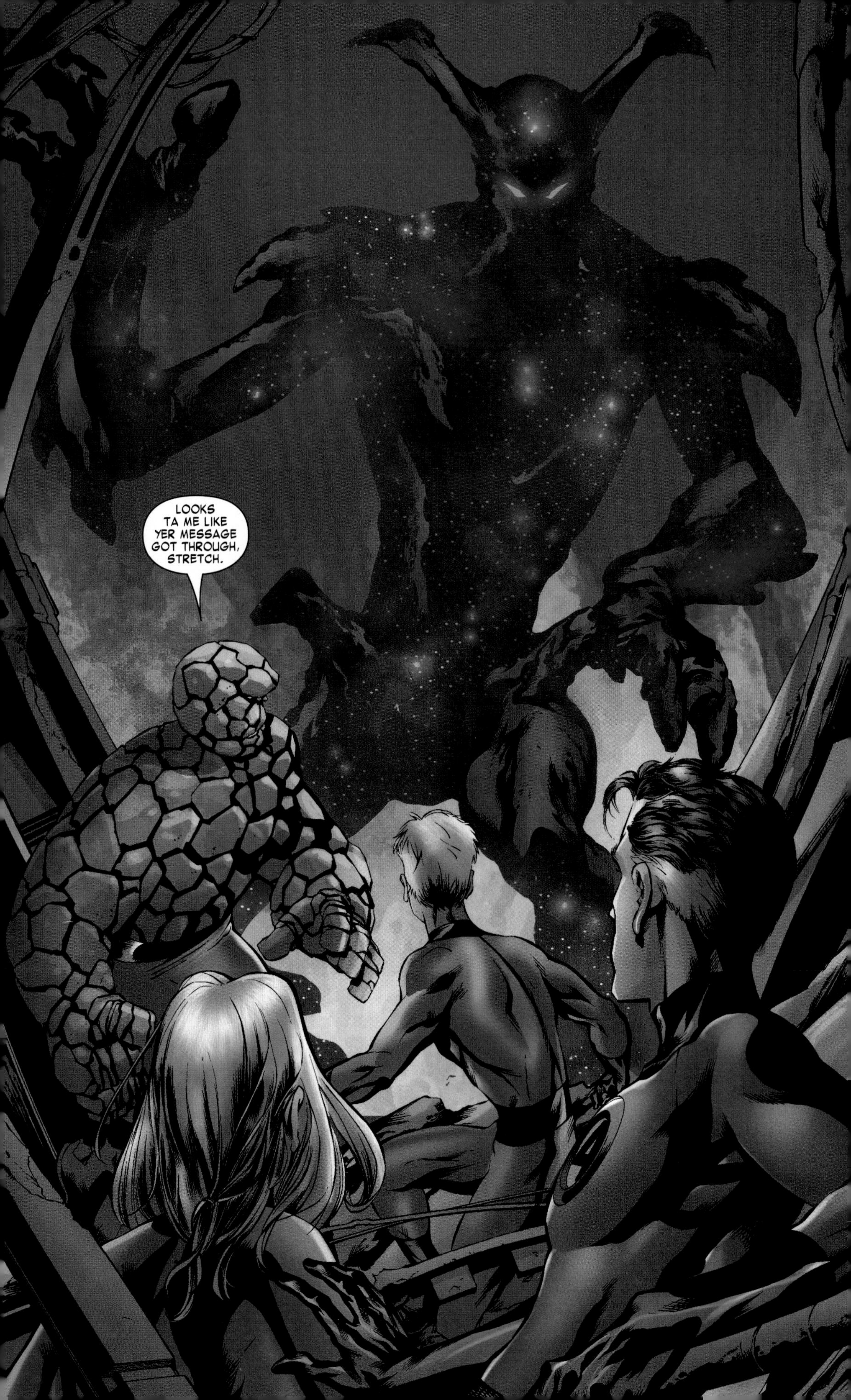
LOOKS TA ME LIKE YER MESSAGE GOT THROUGH, STRETCH.

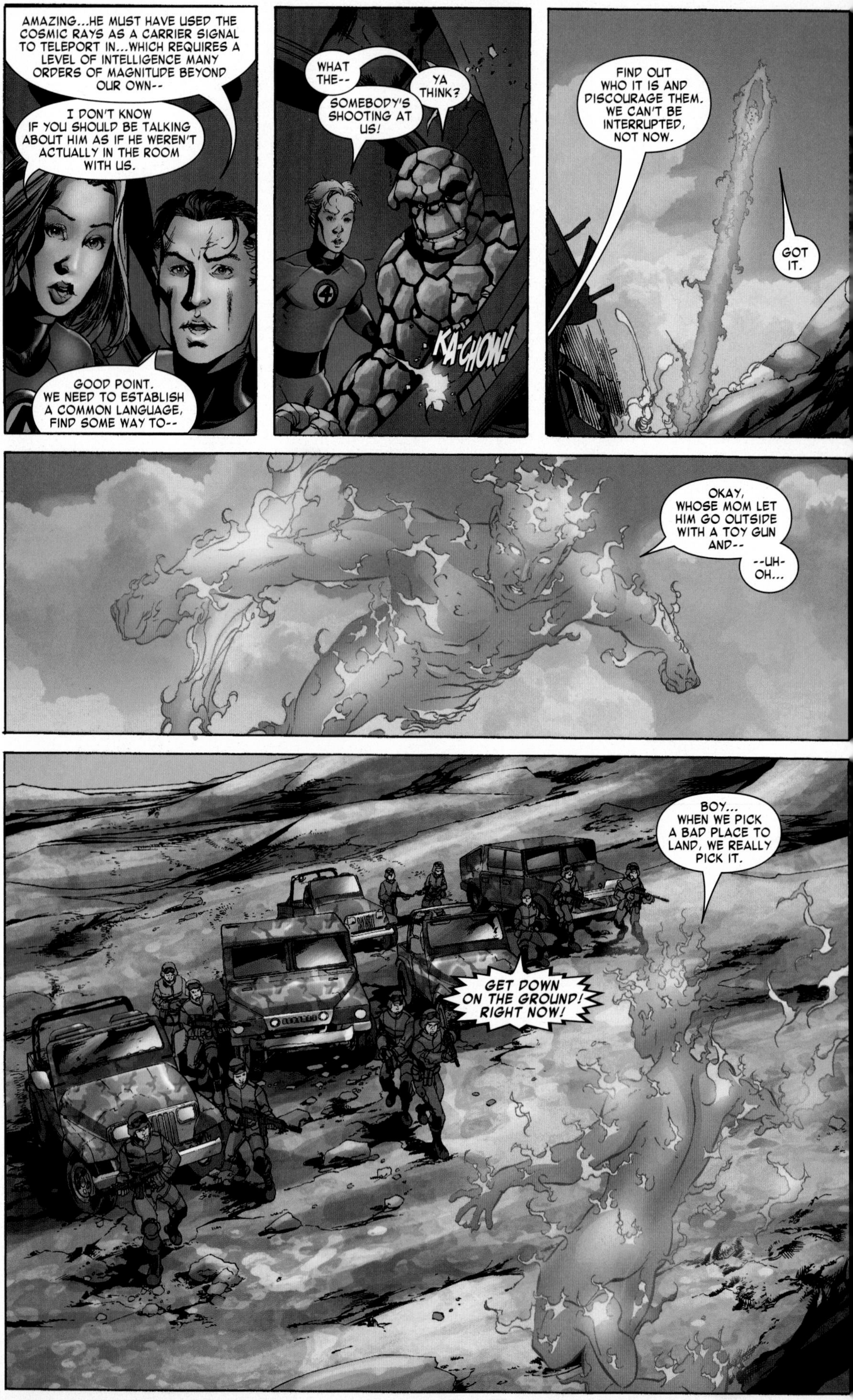
AMAZING...HE MUST HAVE USED THE COSMIC RAYS AS A CARRIER SIGNAL TO TELEPORT IN...WHICH REQUIRES A LEVEL OF INTELLIGENCE MANY ORDERS OF MAGNITUDE BEYOND OUR OWN--
I DON'T KNOW IF YOU SHOULD BE TALKING ABOUT HIM AS IF HE WEREN'T ACTUALLY IN THE ROOM WITH US.
GOOD POINT. WE NEED TO ESTABLISH A COMMON LANGUAGE, FIND SOME WAY TO--
WHAT THE--
SOMEBODY'S SHOOTING AT US!
YA THINK?
KA-CHOW!
FIND OUT WHO IT IS AND DISCOURAGE THEM. WE CAN'T BE INTERRUPTED, NOT NOW.
GOT IT.
OKAY, WHOSE MOM LET HIM GO OUTSIDE WITH A TOY GUN AND--
--UH-OH...
BOY... WHEN WE PICK A BAD PLACE TO LAND, WE REALLY PICK IT.
GET DOWN ON THE GROUND! RIGHT NOW!

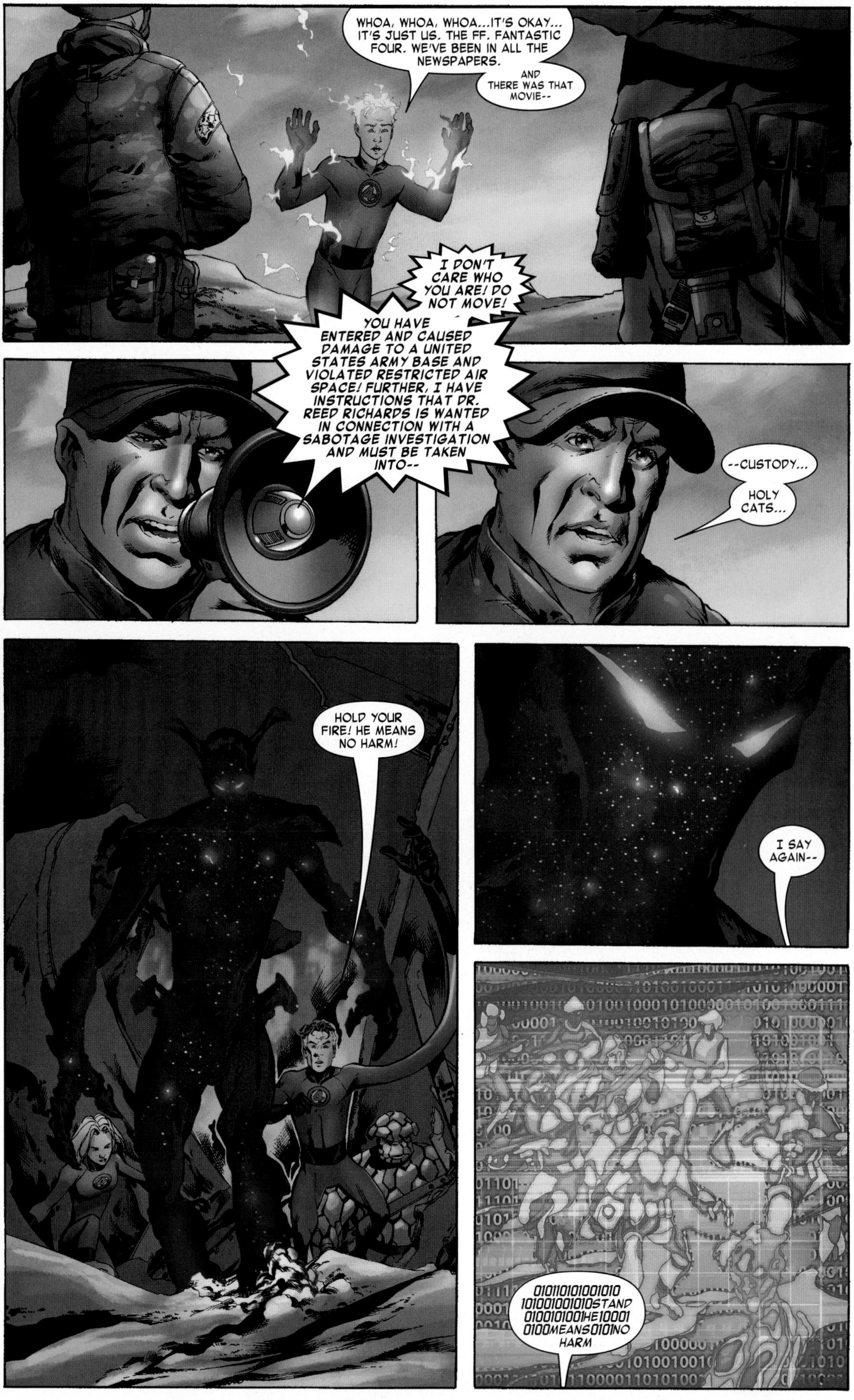
WHOA, WHOA, WHOA...IT'S OKAY... IT'S JUST US. THE FF. FANTASTIC FOUR. WE'VE BEEN IN ALL THE NEWSPAPERS.
AND THERE WAS THAT MOVIE--
I DON'T CARE WHO YOU ARE! DO NOT MOVE!
YOU HAVE ENTERED AND CAUSED DAMAGE TO A UNITED STATES ARMY BASE AND VIOLATED RESTRICTED AIR SPACE! FURTHER, I HAVE INSTRUCTIONS THAT DR. REED RICHARDS IS WANTED IN CONNECTION WITH A SABOTAGE INVESTIGATION AND MUST BE TAKEN INTO--
--CUSTODY...
HOLY CATS...
HOLD YOUR FIRE! HE MEANS NO HARM!
I SAY AGAIN--
0101101010010101010010010105TAND010010100IHE100010100MEANS0101NO HARM

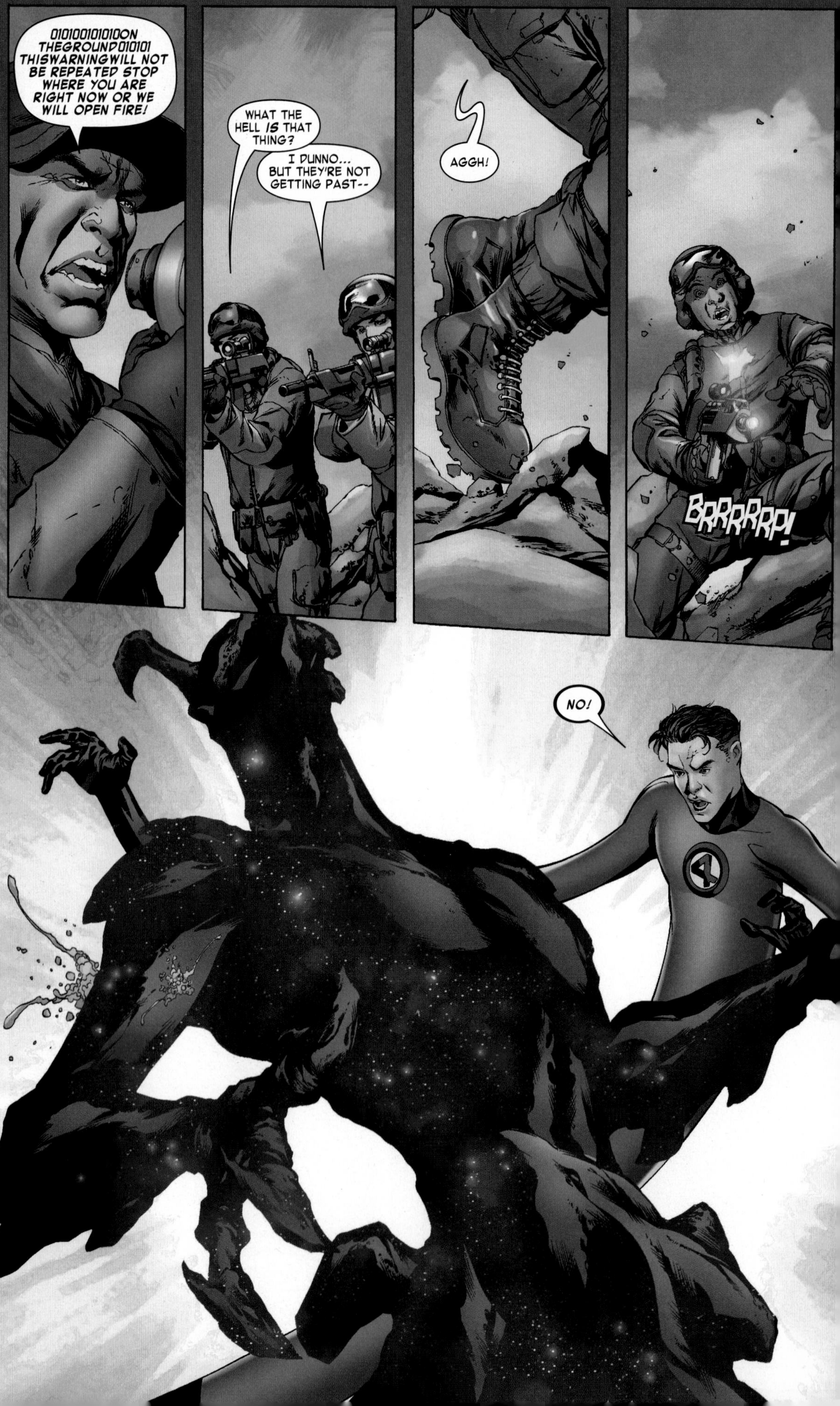
0101001010100N THEGROUND010101 THISWARNINGWILL NOT BE REPEATED STOP WHERE YOU ARE RIGHT NOW OR WE WILL OPEN FIRE!
WHAT THE HELL *IS* THAT THING?
I DUNNO... BUT THEY'RE NOT GETTING PAST--
AGGH!
BRRRRRP!
NO!

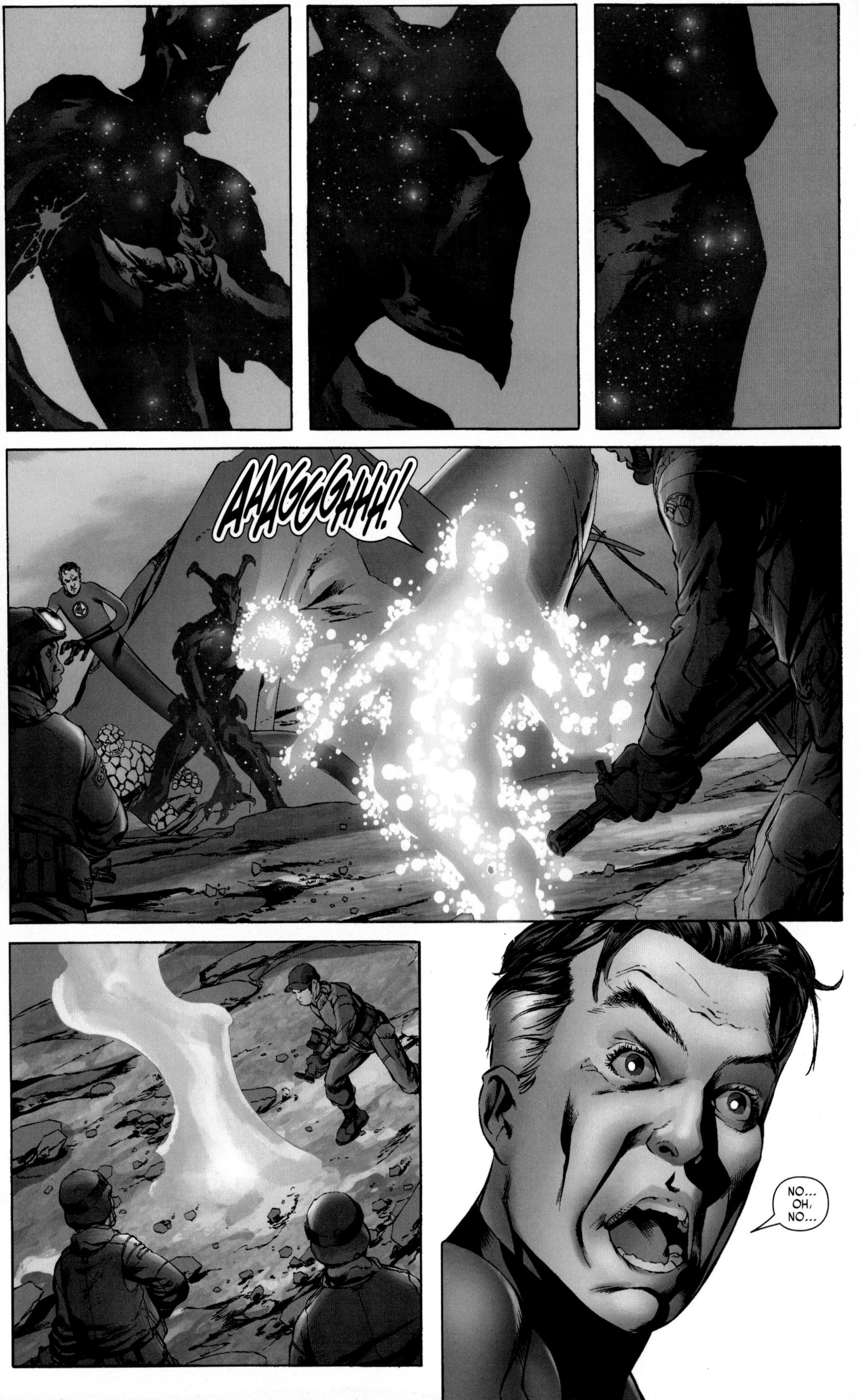
AAAGGGHHH!
NO... OH, NO...

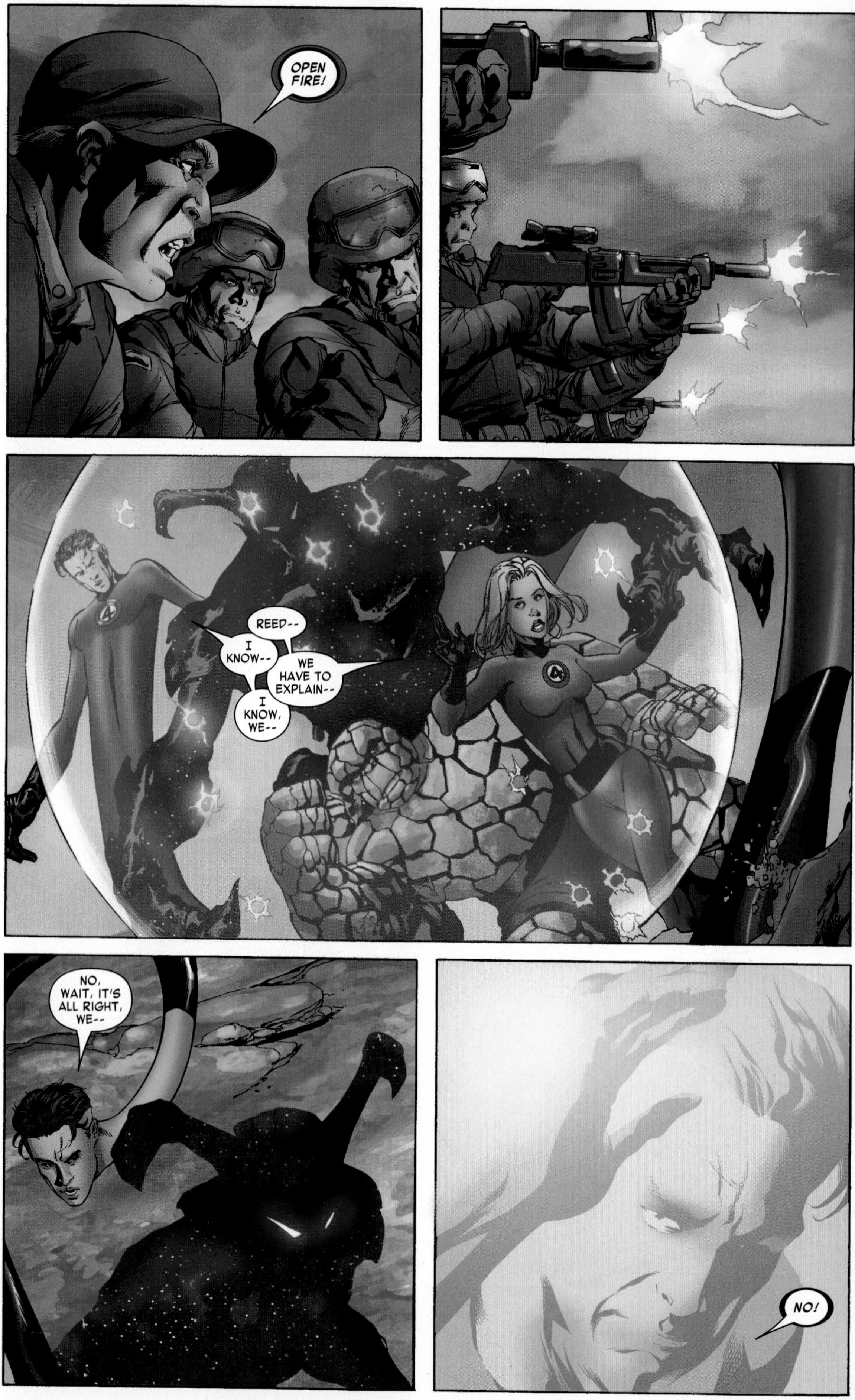
OPEN FIRE!
REED--
I KNOW--
WE HAVE TO EXPLAIN--
I KNOW, WE--
NO, WAIT, IT'S ALL RIGHT, WE--
NO!

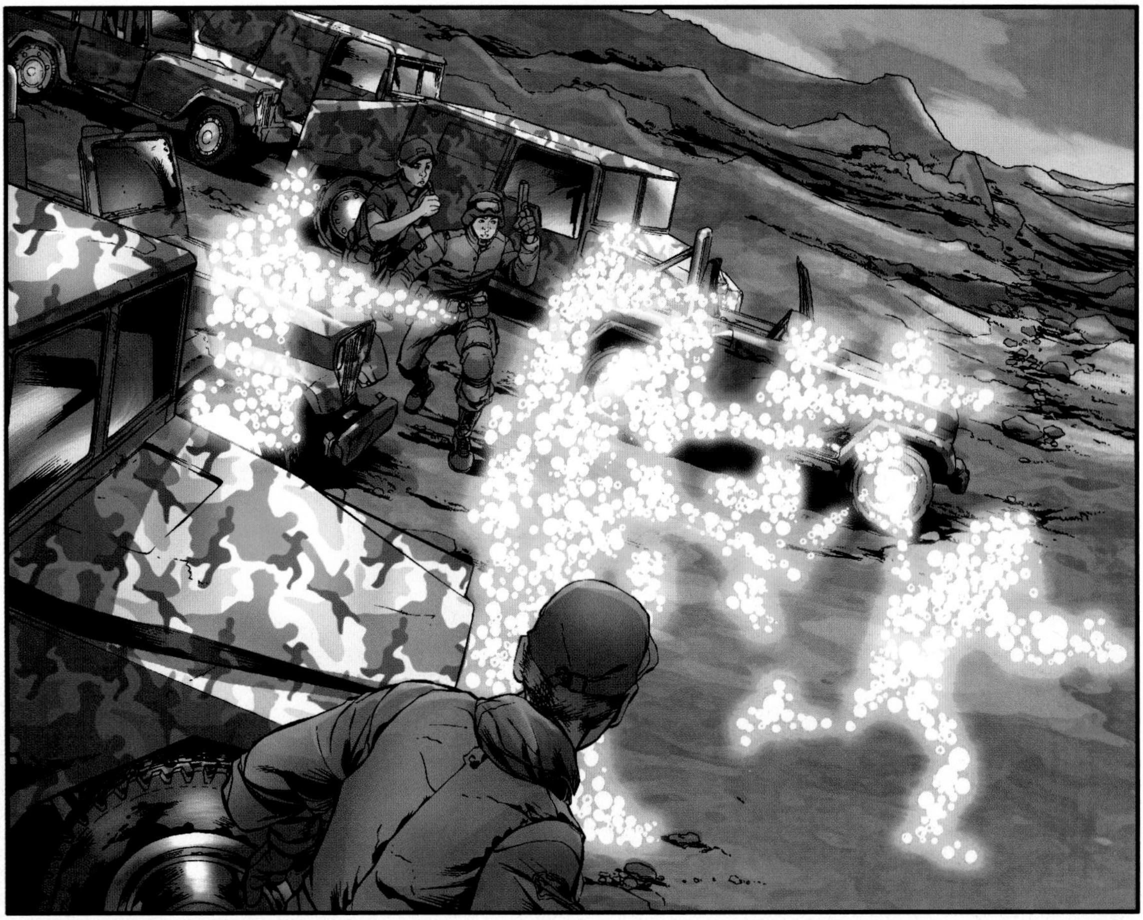
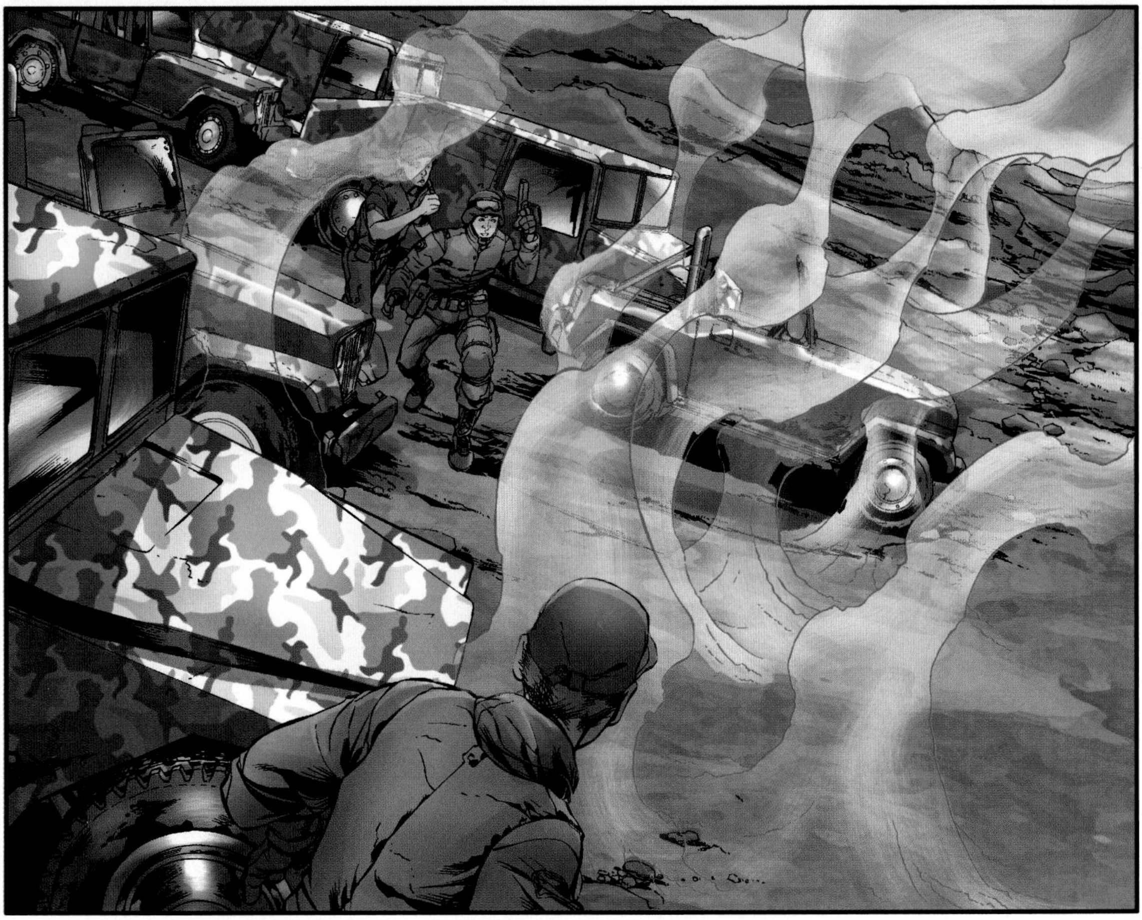

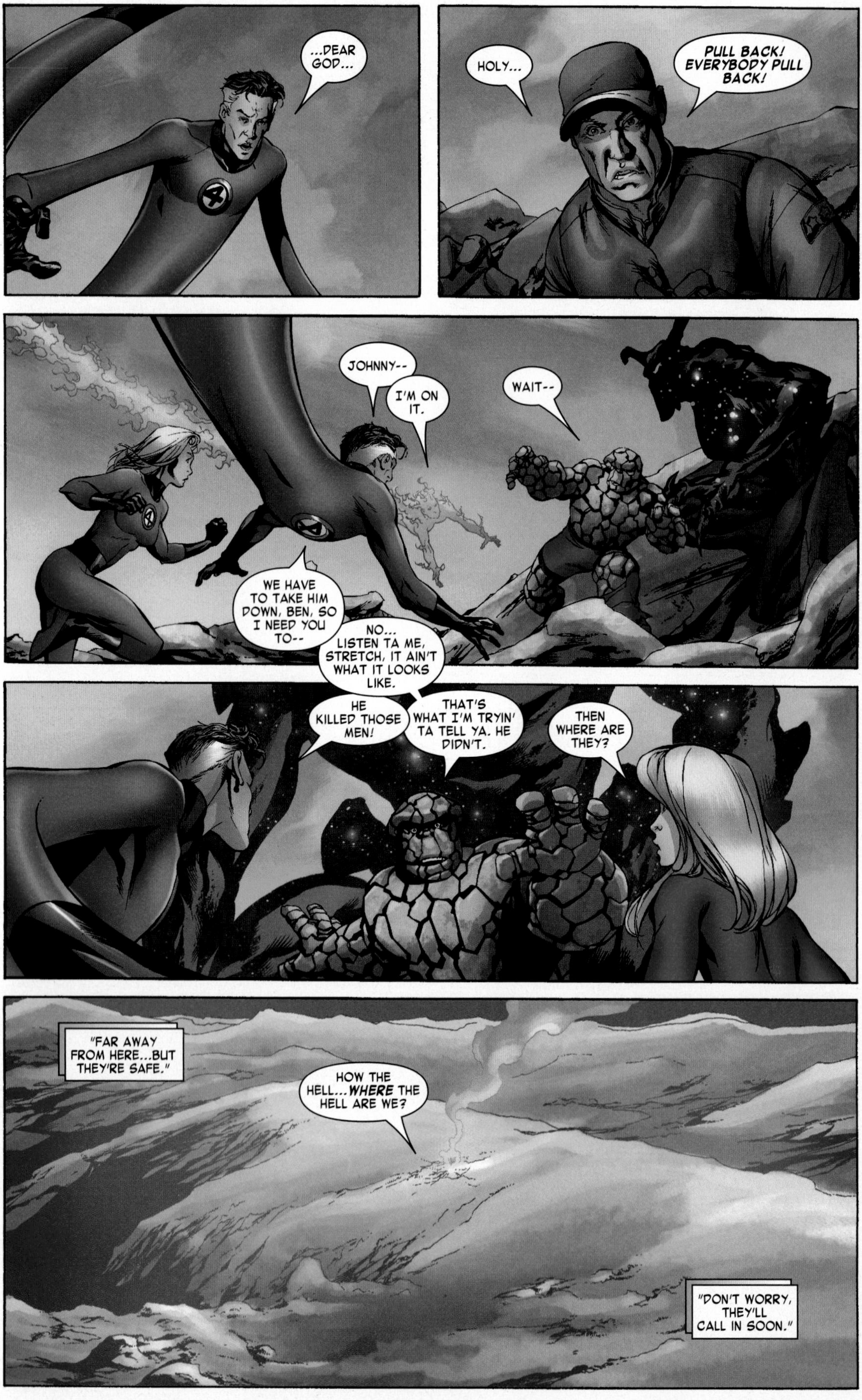
...DEAR GOD...
HOLY...
PULL BACK! EVERYBODY PULL BACK!
JOHNNY--
I'M ON IT.
WAIT--
WE HAVE TO TAKE HIM DOWN, BEN, SO I NEED YOU TO--
NO... LISTEN TA ME, STRETCH, IT AIN'T WHAT IT LOOKS LIKE.
HE KILLED THOSE MEN!
THAT'S WHAT I'M TRYIN' TA TELL YA. HE DIDN'T.
THEN WHERE ARE THEY?
"FAR AWAY FROM HERE...BUT THEY'RE SAFE."
HOW THE HELL...WHERE THE HELL ARE WE?
"DON'T WORRY, THEY'LL CALL IN SOON."

--YEAH, I DO. I JUST... I JUST KNOW, THAT'S ALL. YOU JUST GOTTA TRUST ME, OKAY?

IF THEY DON'T CALL IN, I'LL HELP YA CLOBBER THE GUY. BUT UNTIL THEN, JUST...GIVE HIM HALF A CHANCE.

HOW DO YOU KNOW?

BECAUSE HE'S TELLIN' ME SO. IN MY HEAD.

AND YOU *BELIEVE* HIM?

YEAH--

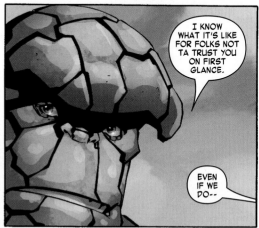

I KNOW WHAT IT'S LIKE FOR FOLKS NOT TA TRUST YOU ON FIRST GLANCE.

EVEN IF WE DO--

--THEY WON'T.

HE SAYS... HE SAYS HE UNDERSTANDS. SO THE BEST SOLUTION--

--IS TO BE SOMEWHERE ELSE. ME, I'M HAVIN' A DOROTHY MOMENT. THERE'S NO PLACE LIKE HOME. THERE'S--

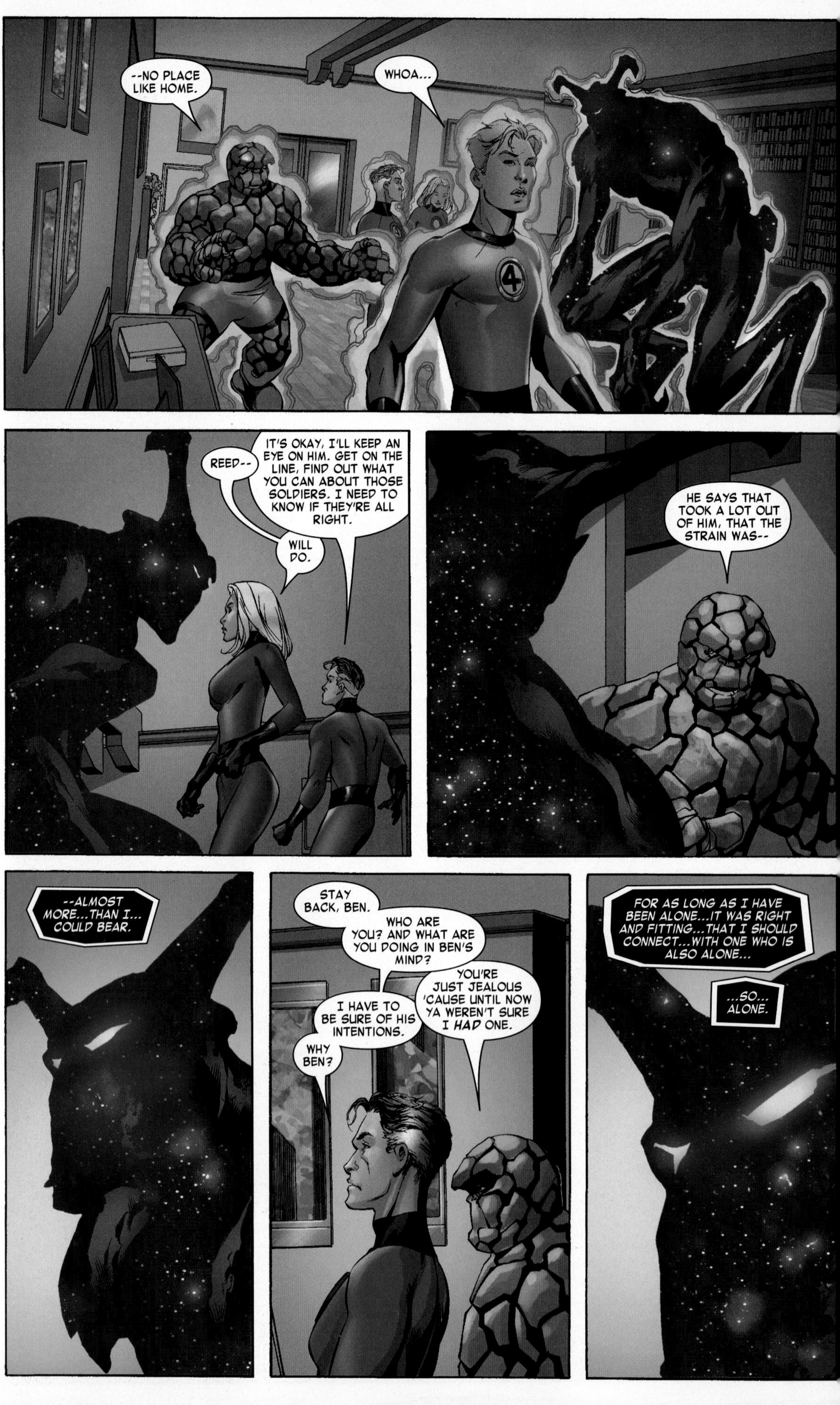
--NO PLACE LIKE HOME.
WHOA...
REED--
IT'S OKAY, I'LL KEEP AN EYE ON HIM. GET ON THE LINE, FIND OUT WHAT YOU CAN ABOUT THOSE SOLDIERS. I NEED TO KNOW IF THEY'RE ALL RIGHT.
WILL DO.
HE SAYS THAT TOOK A LOT OUT OF HIM, THAT THE STRAIN WAS--
--ALMOST MORE...THAN I... COULD BEAR.
STAY BACK, BEN.
WHO ARE YOU? AND WHAT ARE YOU DOING IN BEN'S MIND?
YOU'RE JUST JEALOUS 'CAUSE UNTIL NOW YA WEREN'T SURE I *HAD* ONE.
I HAVE TO BE SURE OF HIS INTENTIONS.
WHY BEN?
FOR AS LONG AS I HAVE BEEN ALONE...IT WAS RIGHT AND FITTING...THAT I SHOULD CONNECT...WITH ONE WHO IS ALSO ALONE...
...SO... ALONE.

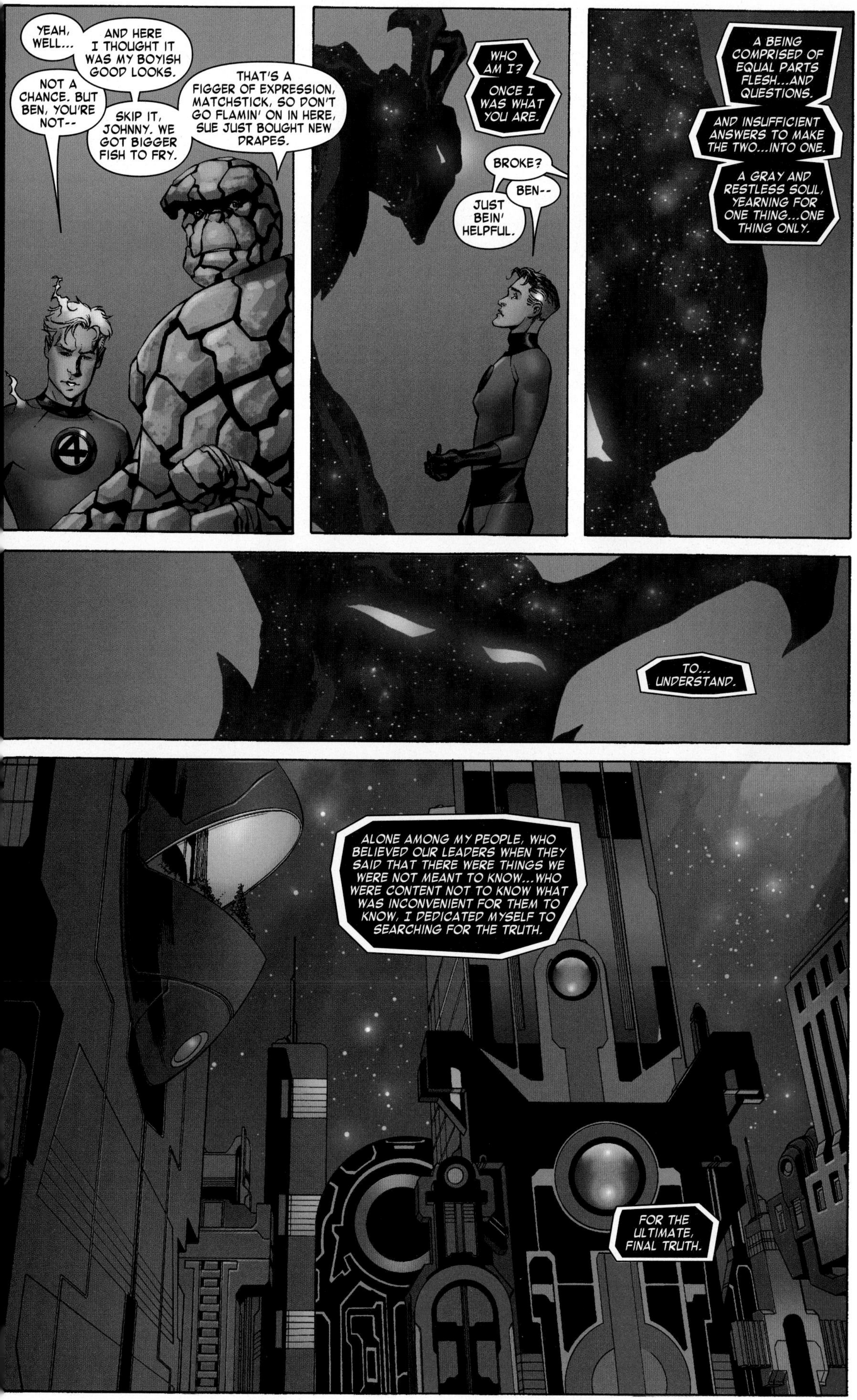
YEAH, WELL...
AND HERE I THOUGHT IT WAS MY BOYISH GOOD LOOKS.
NOT A CHANCE. BUT BEN, YOU'RE NOT--
SKIP IT, JOHNNY. WE GOT BIGGER FISH TO FRY.
THAT'S A FIGGER OF EXPRESSION, MATCHSTICK, SO DON'T GO FLAMIN' ON IN HERE, SUE JUST BOUGHT NEW DRAPES.
WHO AM I?
ONCE I WAS WHAT YOU ARE.
BROKE?
BEN--
JUST BEIN' HELPFUL.
A BEING COMPRISED OF EQUAL PARTS FLESH...AND QUESTIONS.
AND INSUFFICIENT ANSWERS TO MAKE THE TWO...INTO ONE.
A GRAY AND RESTLESS SOUL, YEARNING FOR ONE THING...ONE THING ONLY.
TO... UNDERSTAND.
ALONE AMONG MY PEOPLE, WHO BELIEVED OUR LEADERS WHEN THEY SAID THAT THERE WERE THINGS WE WERE NOT MEANT TO KNOW...WHO WERE CONTENT NOT TO KNOW WHAT WAS INCONVENIENT FOR THEM TO KNOW, I DEDICATED MYSELF TO SEARCHING FOR THE TRUTH.
FOR THE ULTIMATE, FINAL TRUTH.

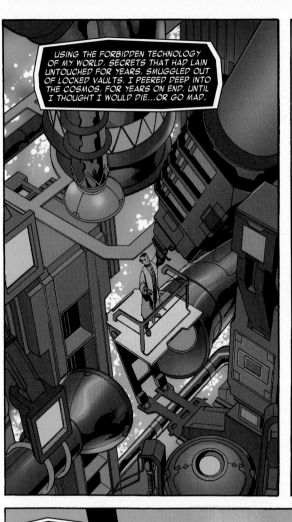

USING THE FORBIDDEN TECHNOLOGY OF MY WORLD, SECRETS THAT HAD LAIN UNTOUCHED FOR YEARS, SMUGGLED OUT OF LOCKED VAULTS, I PEERED DEEP INTO THE COSMOS, FOR YEARS ON END, UNTIL I THOUGHT I WOULD DIE...OR GO MAD.

AND I BEGAN TO UNDERSTAND...

...THAT THERE WERE GREATER TRUTHS...

...THAN OUR LEADERS ALLOWED US TO PERCEIVE. TRUTHS THAT CHALLENGED...

...WHAT WE BELIEVED.

MY BRAIN BURNED AS WITH A TERRIBLE FIRE...AND THOUGH I KNEW THE RISKS, I ALSO KNEW THAT I HAD TO TELL THE OTHERS...TELL MY PEOPLE WHAT I NOW UNDERSTOOD. SO THAT THEY WOULD UNDERSTAND.

AND THAT WAS MY MISTAKE.

BECAUSE I BELIEVED THAT ALL BEINGS, WHATEVER THEIR DIFFERENCES, WHATEVER THEIR BELIEFS, ARE DRAWN ALWAYS TO THE TRUTH...WILL RECOGNIZE THE TRUTH WHEN THEY HEAR IT...AND LOVE TRUTH MORE THAN THEIR FEARS AND PREJUDICES.

I WAS WRONG.

I FLED FOR MY LIFE... THEY PURSUED...I RAN TO MY HOME...TO LET THEM SEE THE TRUTH FOR THEMSELVES.

I THOUGHT I WOULD HAVE TIME... TIME ENOUGH TO SHOW THEM.

AND FOR A SECOND TIME... I WAS WRONG. THEY ATTACKED THE EQUIPMENT AT THE VERY MOMENT THAT I TOUCHED THE MIND OF THE UNIVERSE.

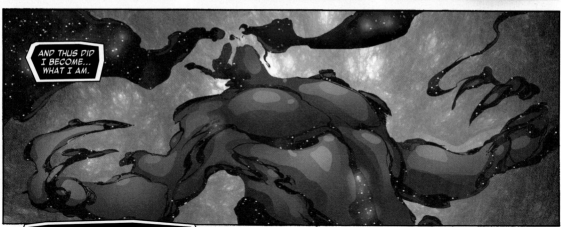

AND THUS DID I BECOME... WHAT I AM.

I HAD THE POWER TO FLEE...TO RIDE THE THOUGHTS OF THE UNIVERSE IN ITS WAVES AND ENERGIES...TO FIND OTHERS WHO WERE ALSO SEARCHING FOR THE ULTIMATE, FINAL TRUTH.

I CALIBRATED CERTAIN COSMIC RAYS AND USED THEM TO SEARCH FOR INTELLIGENCE...FINDING OTHERS, AS I FOUND YOU.

REED? I GOT THROUGH TO THE PENTAGON. THEY CONFIRM THE TROOPS ARE ALIVE, IF PRETTY COLD. BUT THEY STILL WANT TO KNOW--

IN THE PAST, I HAVE HAD TIME TO SPEAK, TO TEACH... TO ANSWER THE QUESTIONS THAT I KNOW YOU HOLD IN YOUR HEART.

BUT THOSE I KNEW FROM MY WORLD HAVE LEARNED TO TRACK ME MORE QUICKLY THAN BEFORE...ON A RELIGIOUS CRUSADE TO KEEP ME FROM TELLING OTHERS WHAT I KNOW.

UHM... REED? YOU'D BETTER TAKE A LOOK AT THIS.

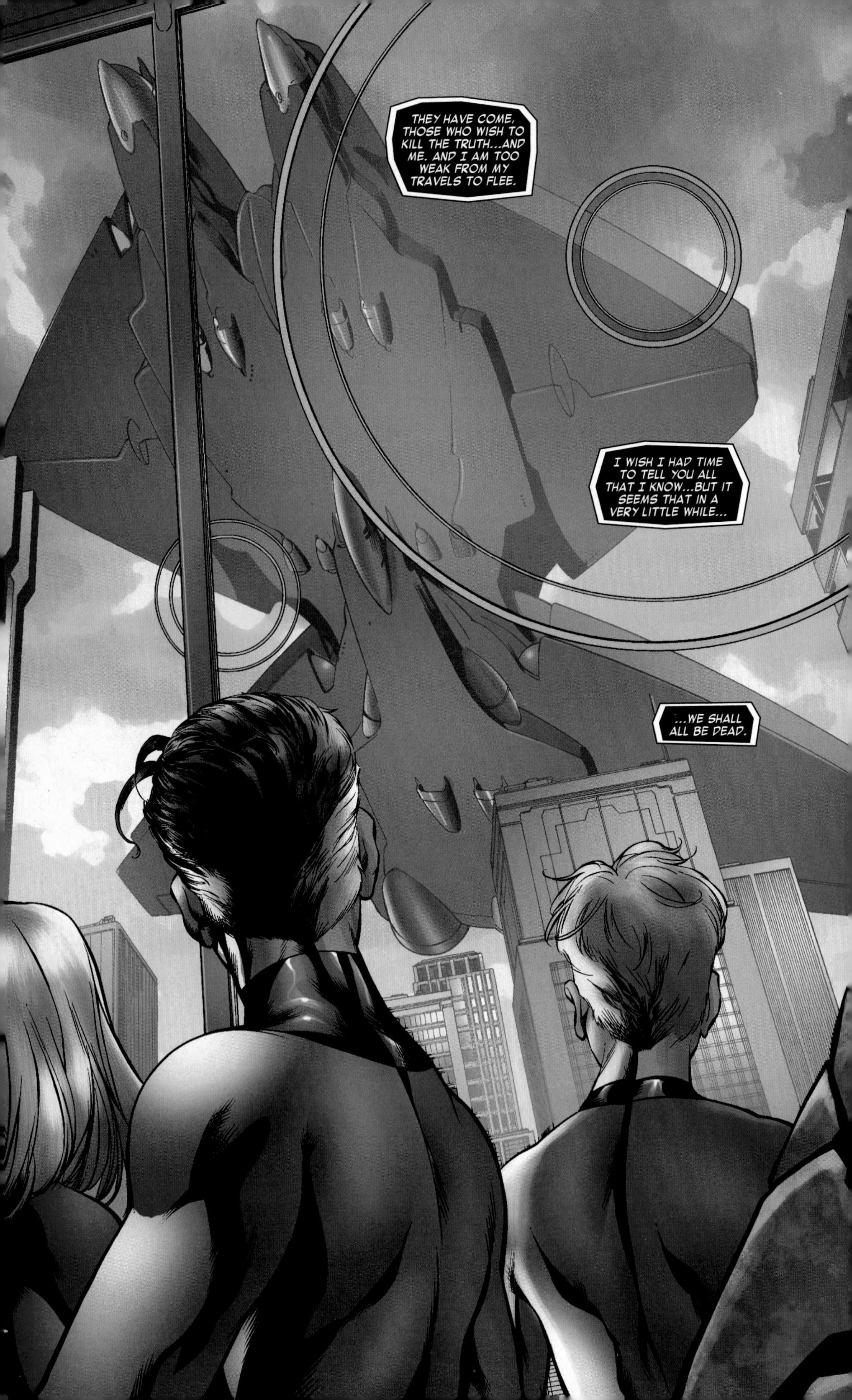
THEY HAVE COME, THOSE WHO WISH TO KILL THE TRUTH...AND ME. AND I AM TOO WEAK FROM MY TRAVELS TO FLEE.
I WISH I HAD TIME TO TELL YOU ALL THAT I KNOW...BUT IT SEEMS THAT IN A VERY LITTLE WHILE...
...WE SHALL ALL BE DEAD.

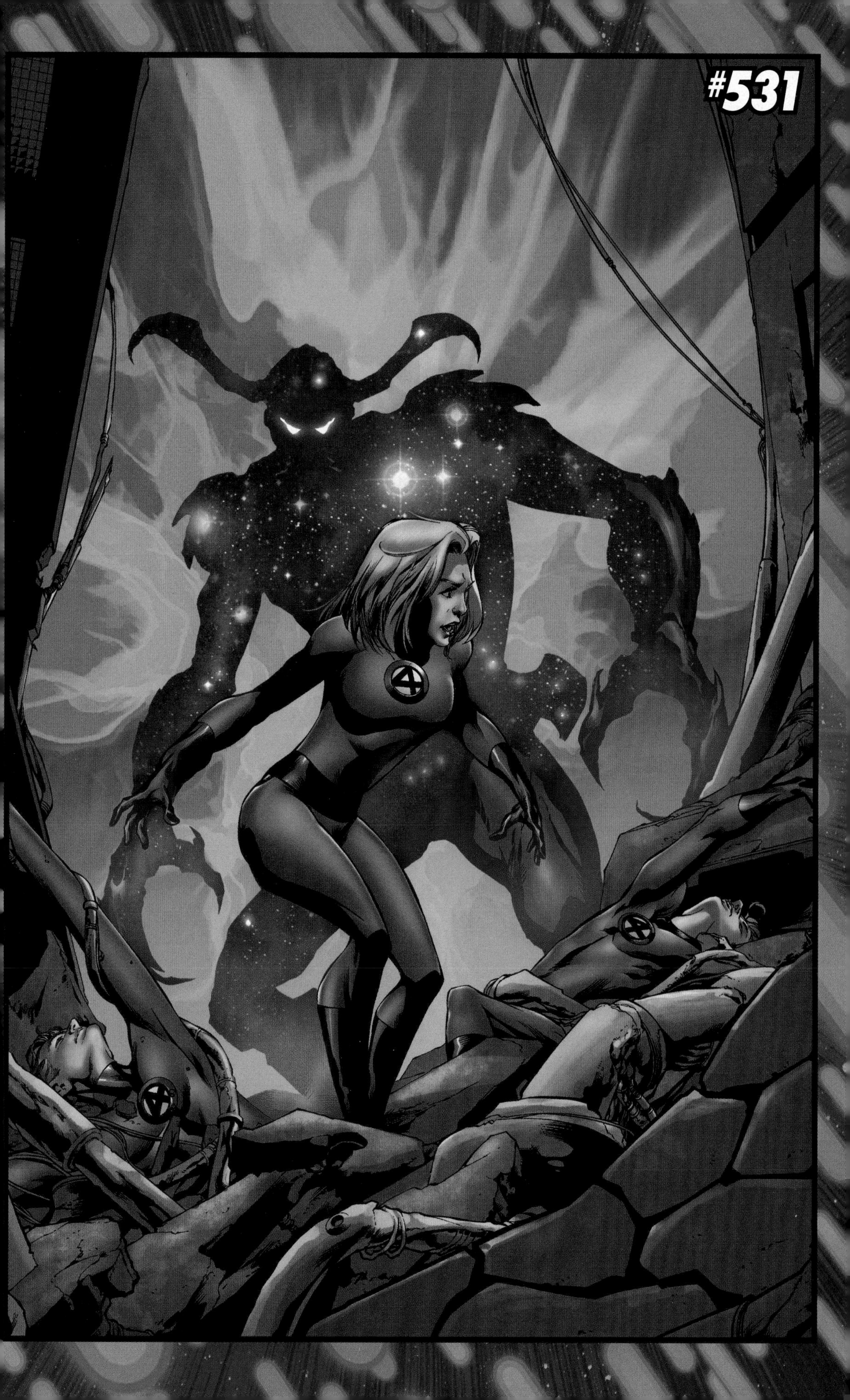
#531

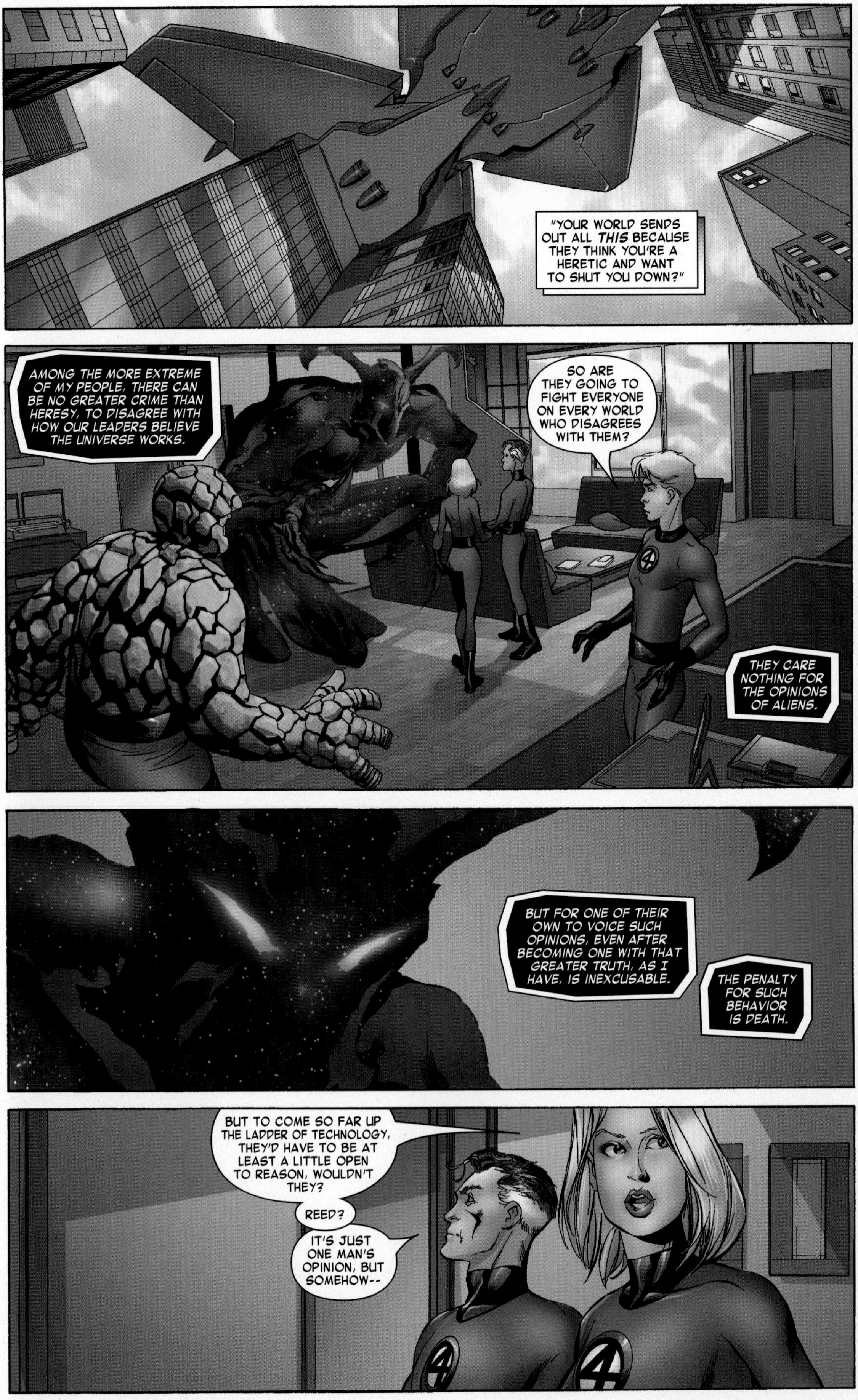
"YOUR WORLD SENDS OUT ALL THIS BECAUSE THEY THINK YOU'RE A HERETIC AND WANT TO SHUT YOU DOWN?"
AMONG THE MORE EXTREME OF MY PEOPLE, THERE CAN BE NO GREATER CRIME THAN HERESY, TO DISAGREE WITH HOW OUR LEADERS BELIEVE THE UNIVERSE WORKS.
SO ARE THEY GOING TO FIGHT EVERYONE ON EVERY WORLD WHO DISAGREES WITH THEM?
THEY CARE NOTHING FOR THE OPINIONS OF ALIENS.
BUT FOR ONE OF THEIR OWN TO VOICE SUCH OPINIONS, EVEN AFTER BECOMING ONE WITH THAT GREATER TRUTH, AS I HAVE, IS INEXCUSABLE.
THE PENALTY FOR SUCH BEHAVIOR IS DEATH.
BUT TO COME SO FAR UP THE LADDER OF TECHNOLOGY, THEY'D HAVE TO BE AT LEAST A LITTLE OPEN TO REASON, WOULDN'T THEY?
REED?
IT'S JUST ONE MAN'S OPINION, BUT SOMEHOW--

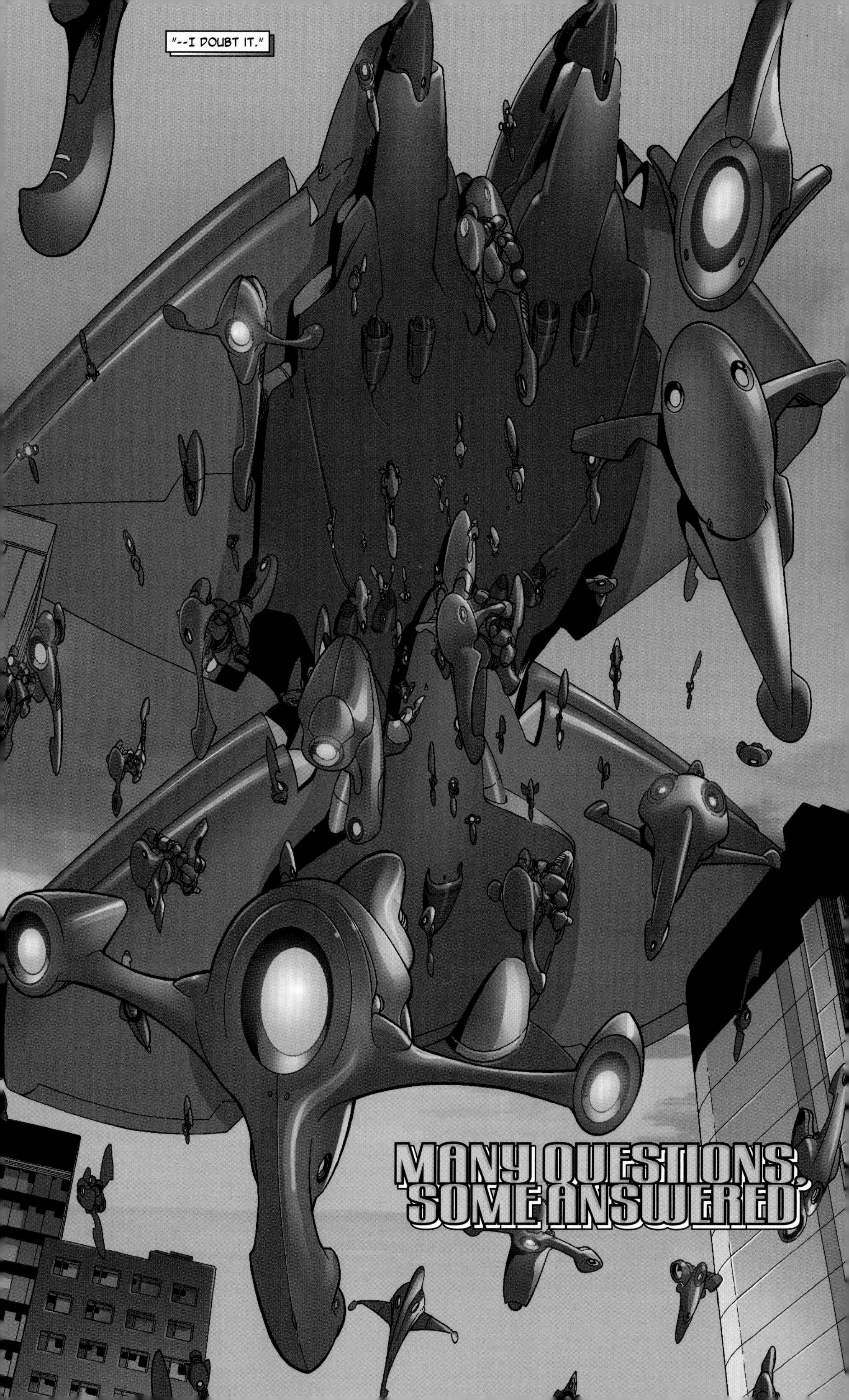
"--I DOUBT IT."
MANY QUESTIONS, SOME ANSWERED

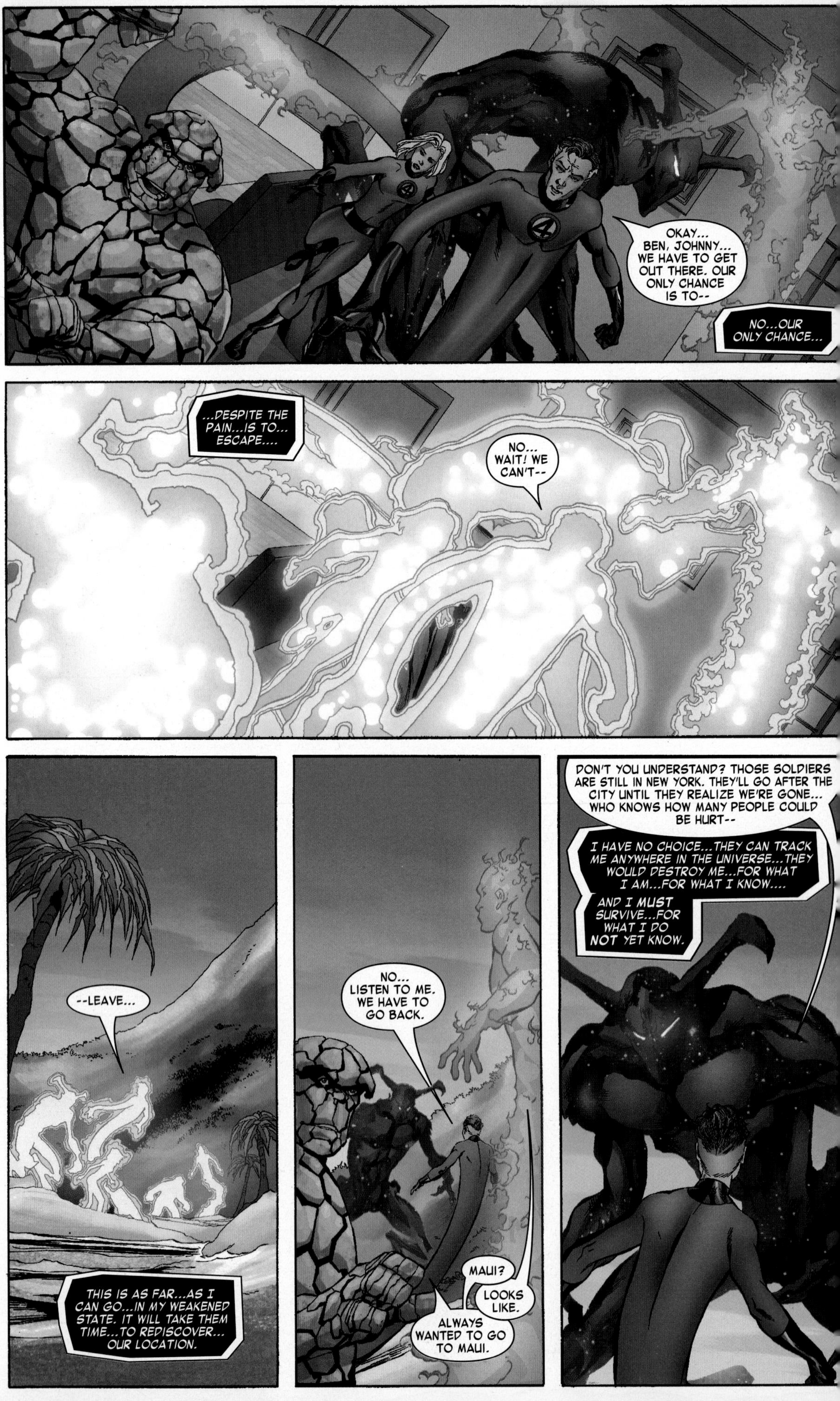
OKAY... BEN, JOHNNY... WE HAVE TO GET OUT THERE. OUR ONLY CHANCE IS TO--
NO...OUR ONLY CHANCE...
...DESPITE THE PAIN...IS TO... ESCAPE....
NO... WAIT! WE CAN'T--
--LEAVE...
THIS IS AS FAR...AS I CAN GO...IN MY WEAKENED STATE. IT WILL TAKE THEM TIME...TO REDISCOVER... OUR LOCATION.
NO... LISTEN TO ME. WE HAVE TO GO BACK.
MAUI?
LOOKS LIKE.
ALWAYS WANTED TO GO TO MAUI.
DON'T YOU UNDERSTAND? THOSE SOLDIERS ARE STILL IN NEW YORK. THEY'LL GO AFTER THE CITY UNTIL THEY REALIZE WE'RE GONE... WHO KNOWS HOW MANY PEOPLE COULD BE HURT--
I HAVE NO CHOICE...THEY CAN TRACK ME ANYWHERE IN THE UNIVERSE...THEY WOULD DESTROY ME...FOR WHAT I AM...FOR WHAT I KNOW....
AND I MUST SURVIVE...FOR WHAT I DO NOT YET KNOW.

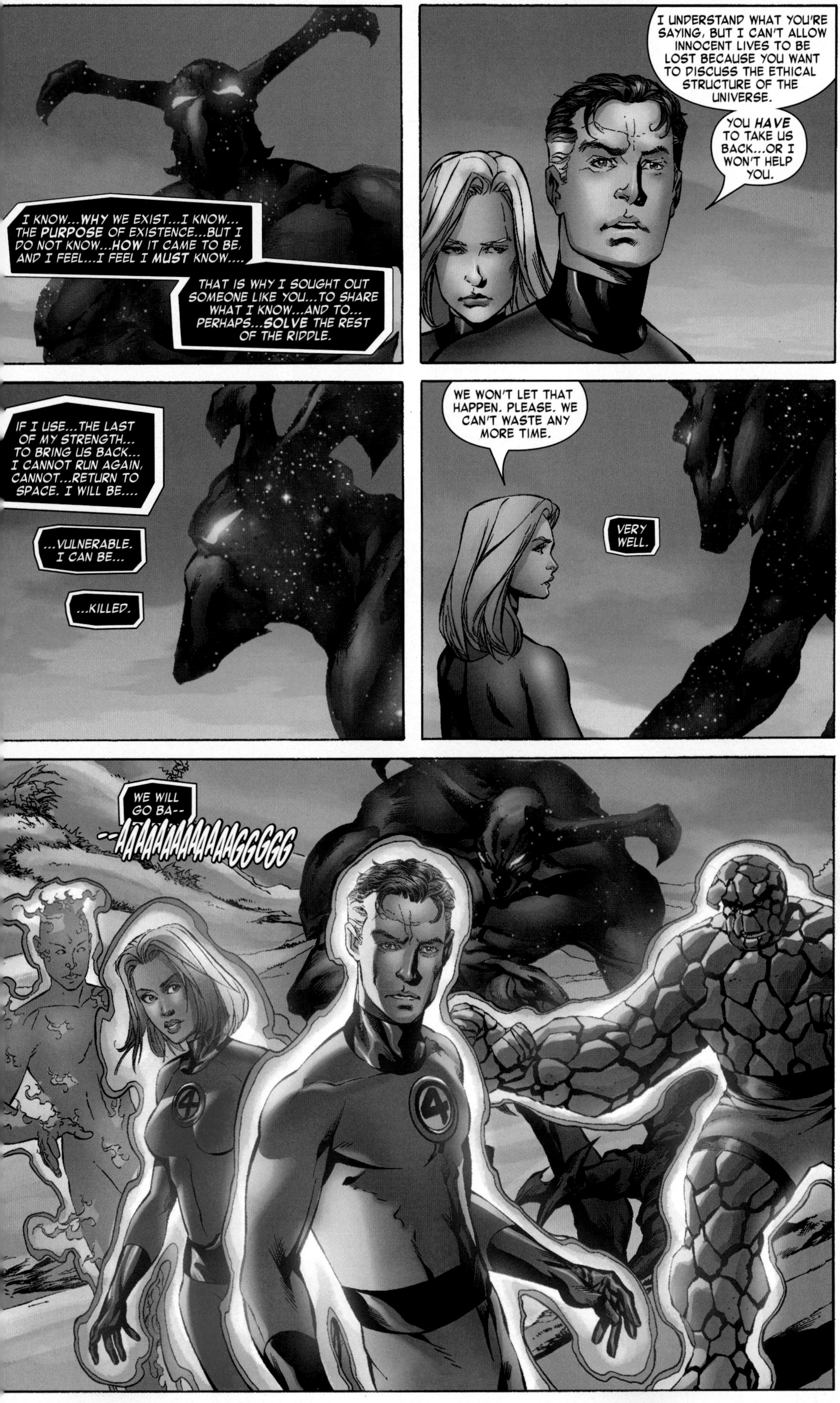
I KNOW...WHY WE EXIST...I KNOW... THE PURPOSE OF EXISTENCE...BUT I DO NOT KNOW...HOW IT CAME TO BE, AND I FEEL...I FEEL I MUST KNOW....
THAT IS WHY I SOUGHT OUT SOMEONE LIKE YOU...TO SHARE WHAT I KNOW...AND TO... PERHAPS...SOLVE THE REST OF THE RIDDLE.
I UNDERSTAND WHAT YOU'RE SAYING, BUT I CAN'T ALLOW INNOCENT LIVES TO BE LOST BECAUSE YOU WANT TO DISCUSS THE ETHICAL STRUCTURE OF THE UNIVERSE.
YOU HAVE TO TAKE US BACK...OR I WON'T HELP YOU.
IF I USE...THE LAST OF MY STRENGTH... TO BRING US BACK... I CANNOT RUN AGAIN, CANNOT...RETURN TO SPACE. I WILL BE....
...VULNERABLE. I CAN BE...
...KILLED.
WE WON'T LET THAT HAPPEN. PLEASE. WE CAN'T WASTE ANY MORE TIME.
VERY WELL.
WE WILL GO BA--
--AAAAAAAAAAAAGGGGG

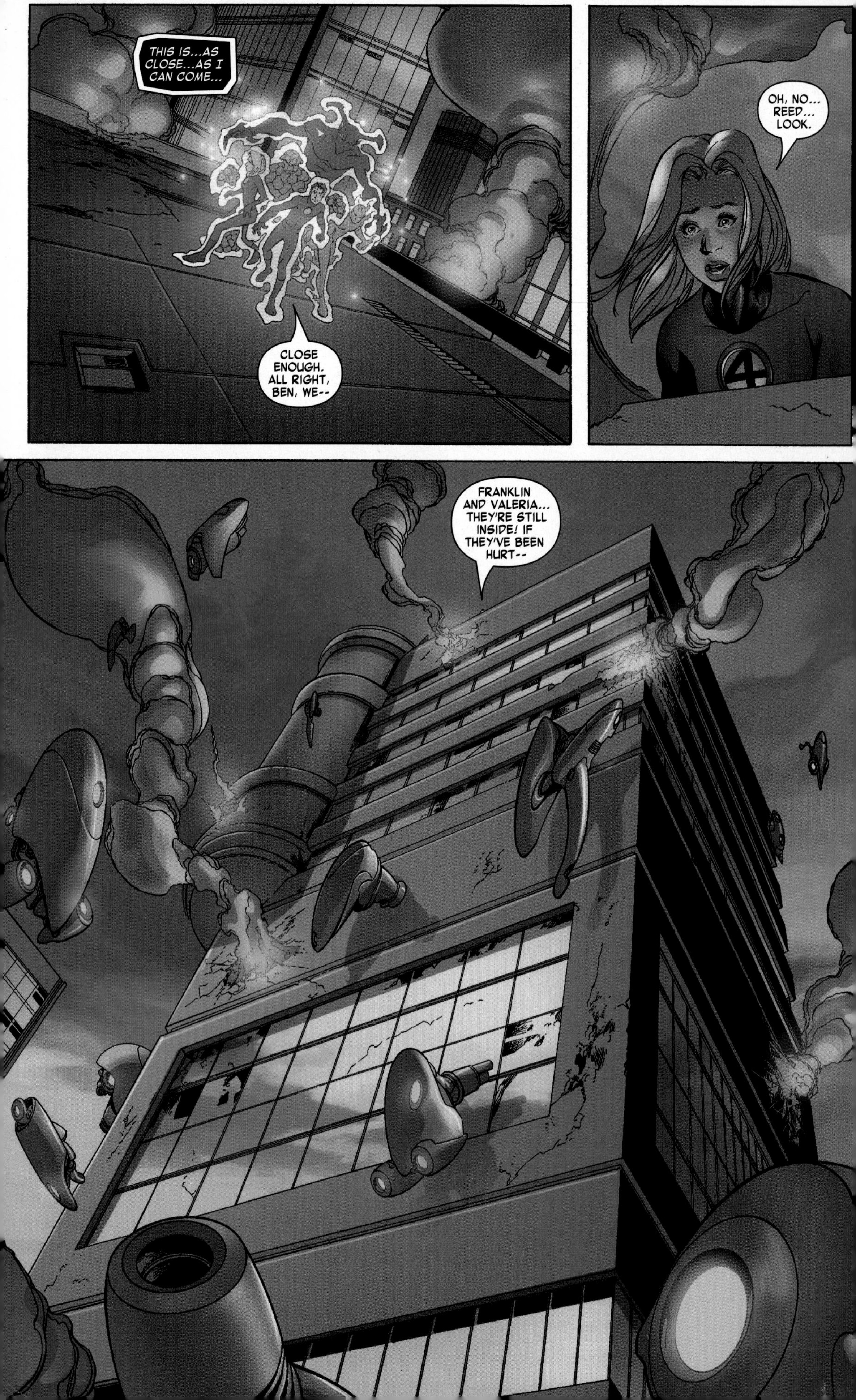
THIS IS...AS CLOSE...AS I CAN COME...
CLOSE ENOUGH. ALL RIGHT, BEN, WE--
OH, NO... REED... LOOK.
FRANKLIN AND VALERIA... THEY'RE STILL INSIDE! IF THEY'VE BEEN HURT--

SUE...GET THE ENTITY DOWNSTAIRS, INTO THE LAB....

BUT--

TRUST ME, I KNOW WHAT I'M DOING.

JOHNNY?

GET THE KIDS OUT OF THERE!

I'M ALREADY THERE!

FLAME ON!

YER GONNA THROW ME, AIN'TCHA?

YOU HAVE ANY OBJECTIONS?

NOT A ONE.

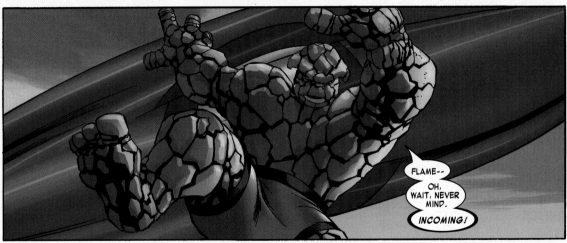

FLAME-- OH, WAIT, NEVER MIND.

INCOMING!

OKAY PAL, LEMME SEE YER LICENSE AND REGISTRATION FOR THIS CRATE!

YEAH, YEAH, TELL IT TO THE JUDGE.

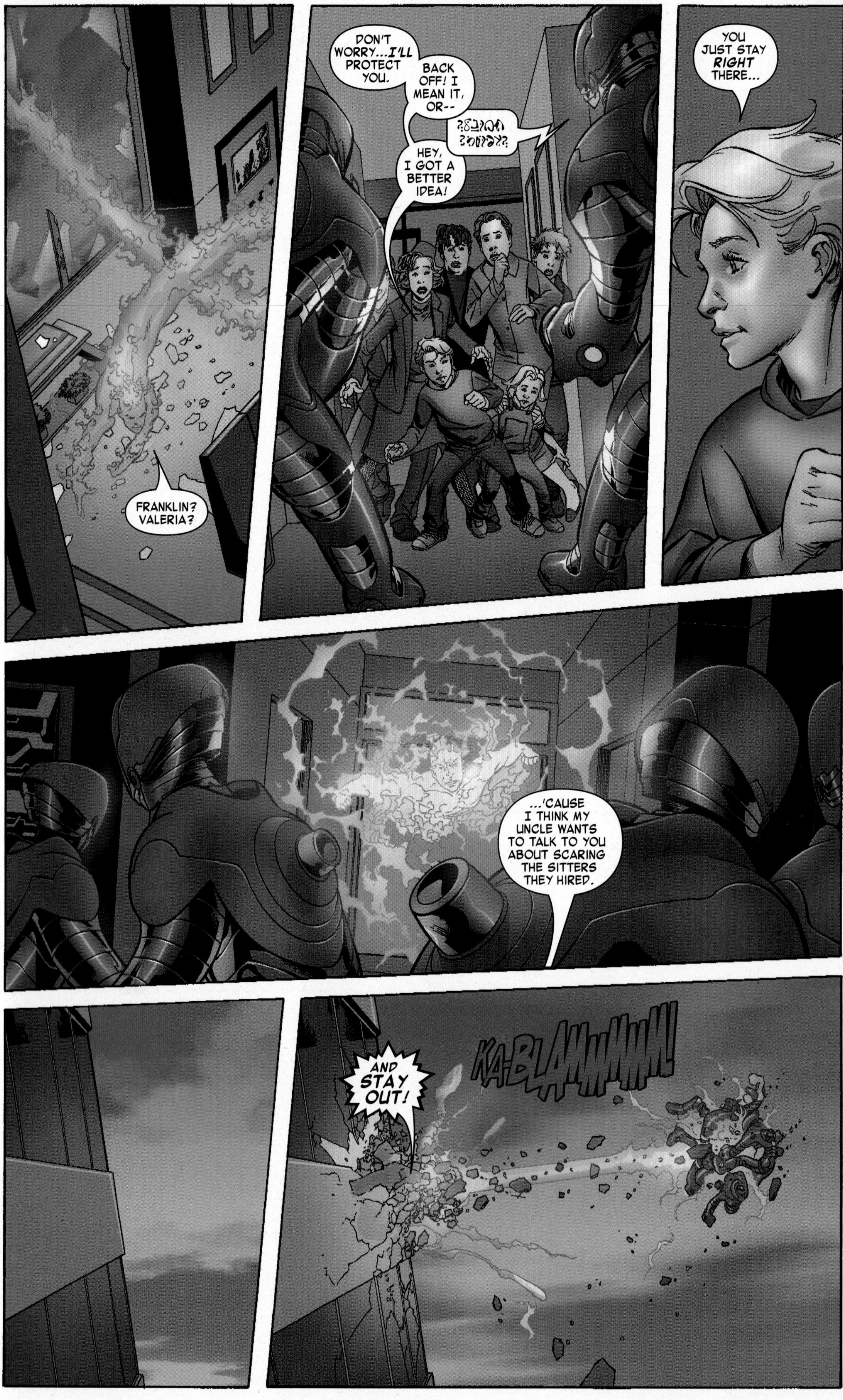
FRANKLIN? VALERIA?
DON'T WORRY...I'LL PROTECT YOU.
BACK OFF! I MEAN IT, OR--
HEY, I GOT A BETTER IDEA!
YOU JUST STAY RIGHT THERE...
...'CAUSE I THINK MY UNCLE WANTS TO TALK TO YOU ABOUT SCARING THE SITTERS THEY HIRED.
AND STAY OUT!
KA-BLAMMMMM!

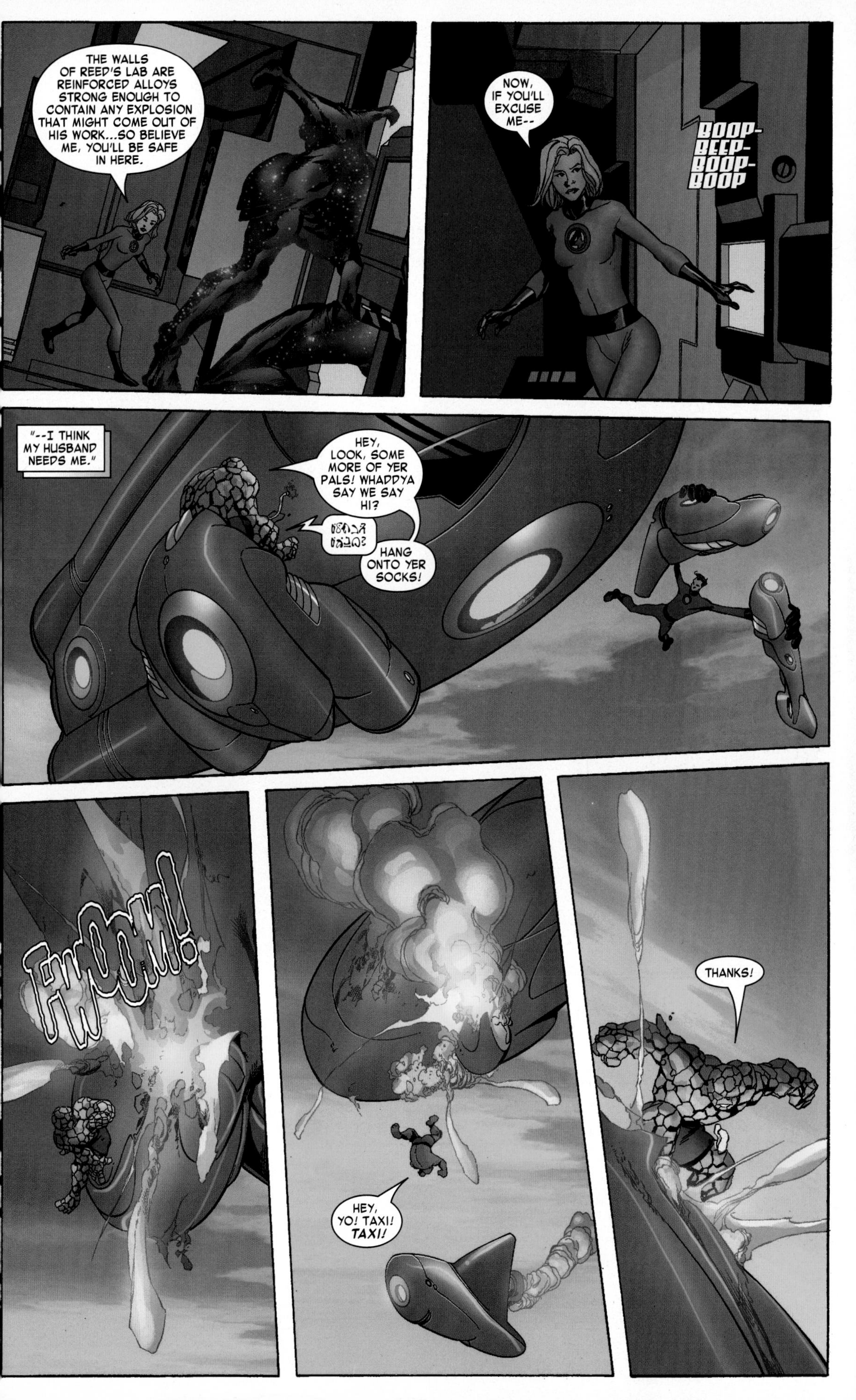
THE WALLS OF REED'S LAB ARE REINFORCED ALLOYS STRONG ENOUGH TO CONTAIN ANY EXPLOSION THAT MIGHT COME OUT OF HIS WORK...SO BELIEVE ME, YOU'LL BE SAFE IN HERE.
NOW, IF YOU'LL EXCUSE ME--
BOOP-BEEP-BOOP-BOOP
"--I THINK MY HUSBAND NEEDS ME."
HEY, LOOK, SOME MORE OF YER PALS! WHADDYA SAY WE SAY HI?
HANG ONTO YER SOCKS!
FWOOM!
HEY, YO! TAXI! TAXI!
THANKS!

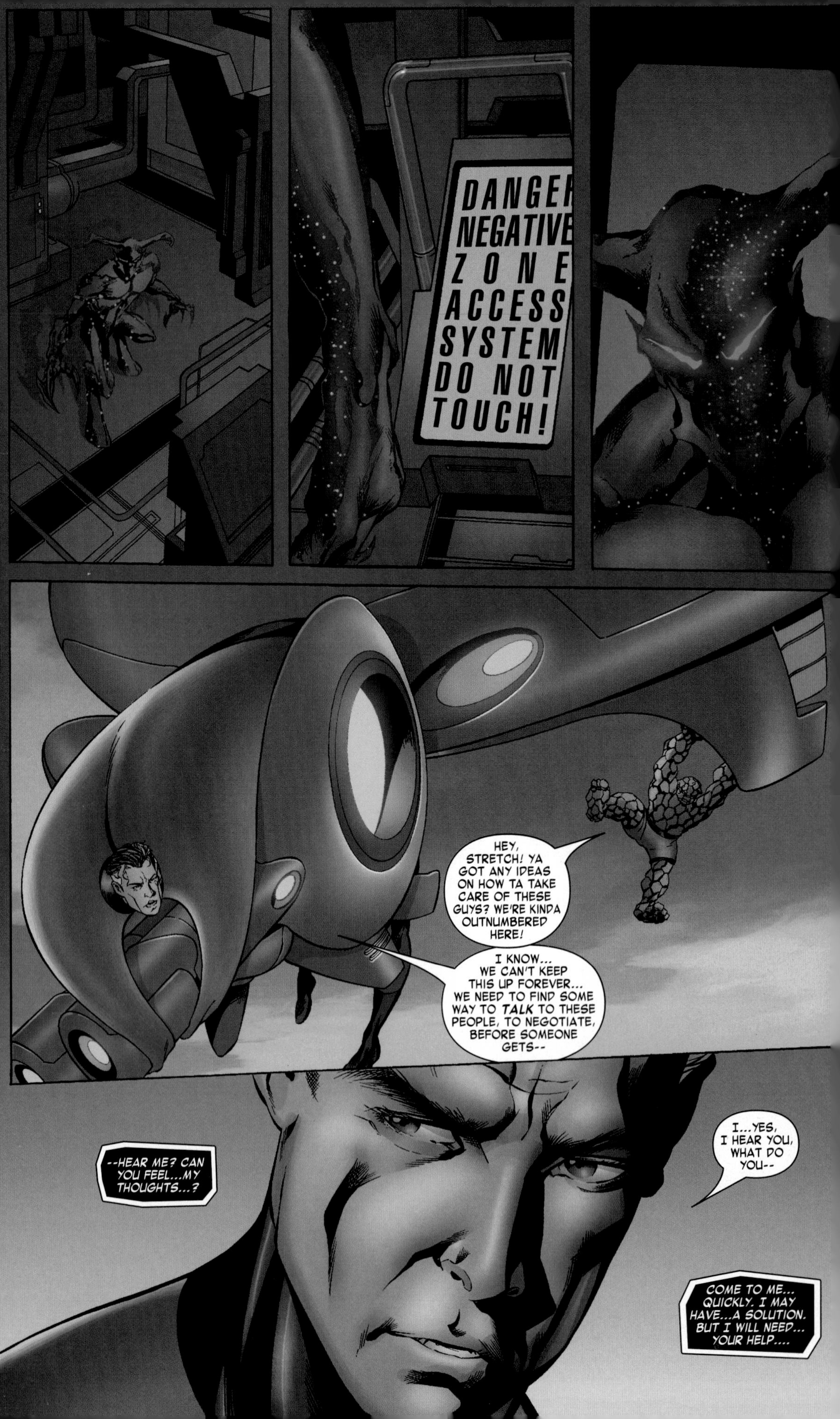
DANGER
NEGATIVE
ZONE
ACCESS
SYSTEM
DO NOT
TOUCH!
HEY, STRETCH! YA GOT ANY IDEAS ON HOW TA TAKE CARE OF THESE GUYS? WE'RE KINDA OUTNUMBERED HERE!
I KNOW... WE CAN'T KEEP THIS UP FOREVER... WE NEED TO FIND SOME WAY TO *TALK* TO THESE PEOPLE, TO NEGOTIATE, BEFORE SOMEONE GETS--
--HEAR ME? CAN YOU FEEL...MY THOUGHTS...?
I...YES, I HEAR YOU, WHAT DO YOU--
COME TO ME... QUICKLY. I MAY HAVE...A SOLUTION. BUT I WILL NEED... YOUR HELP....

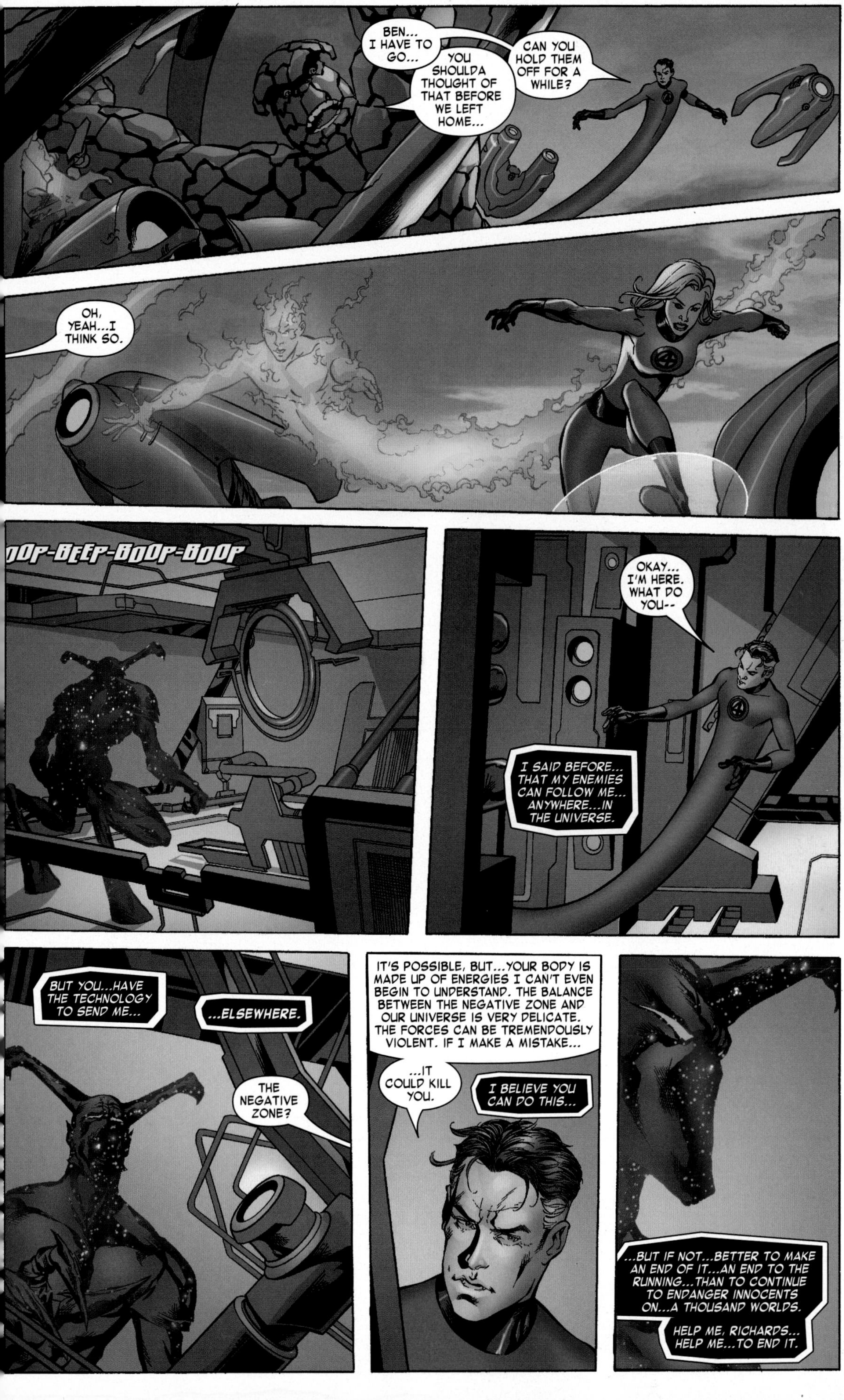
BEN... I HAVE TO GO...
YOU SHOULDA THOUGHT OF THAT BEFORE WE LEFT HOME...
CAN YOU HOLD THEM OFF FOR A WHILE?
OH, YEAH...I THINK SO.
OOP-BEEP-BOOP-BOOP
OKAY... I'M HERE. WHAT DO YOU--
I SAID BEFORE... THAT MY ENEMIES CAN FOLLOW ME... ANYWHERE...IN THE UNIVERSE.
BUT YOU...HAVE THE TECHNOLOGY TO SEND ME...
...ELSEWHERE.
THE NEGATIVE ZONE?
IT'S POSSIBLE, BUT...YOUR BODY IS MADE UP OF ENERGIES I CAN'T EVEN BEGIN TO UNDERSTAND. THE BALANCE BETWEEN THE NEGATIVE ZONE AND OUR UNIVERSE IS VERY DELICATE. THE FORCES CAN BE TREMENDOUSLY VIOLENT. IF I MAKE A MISTAKE...
...IT COULD KILL YOU.
I BELIEVE YOU CAN DO THIS...
...BUT IF NOT...BETTER TO MAKE AN END OF IT...AN END TO THE RUNNING...THAN TO CONTINUE TO ENDANGER INNOCENTS ON...A THOUSAND WORLDS.
HELP ME, RICHARDS... HELP ME...TO END IT.

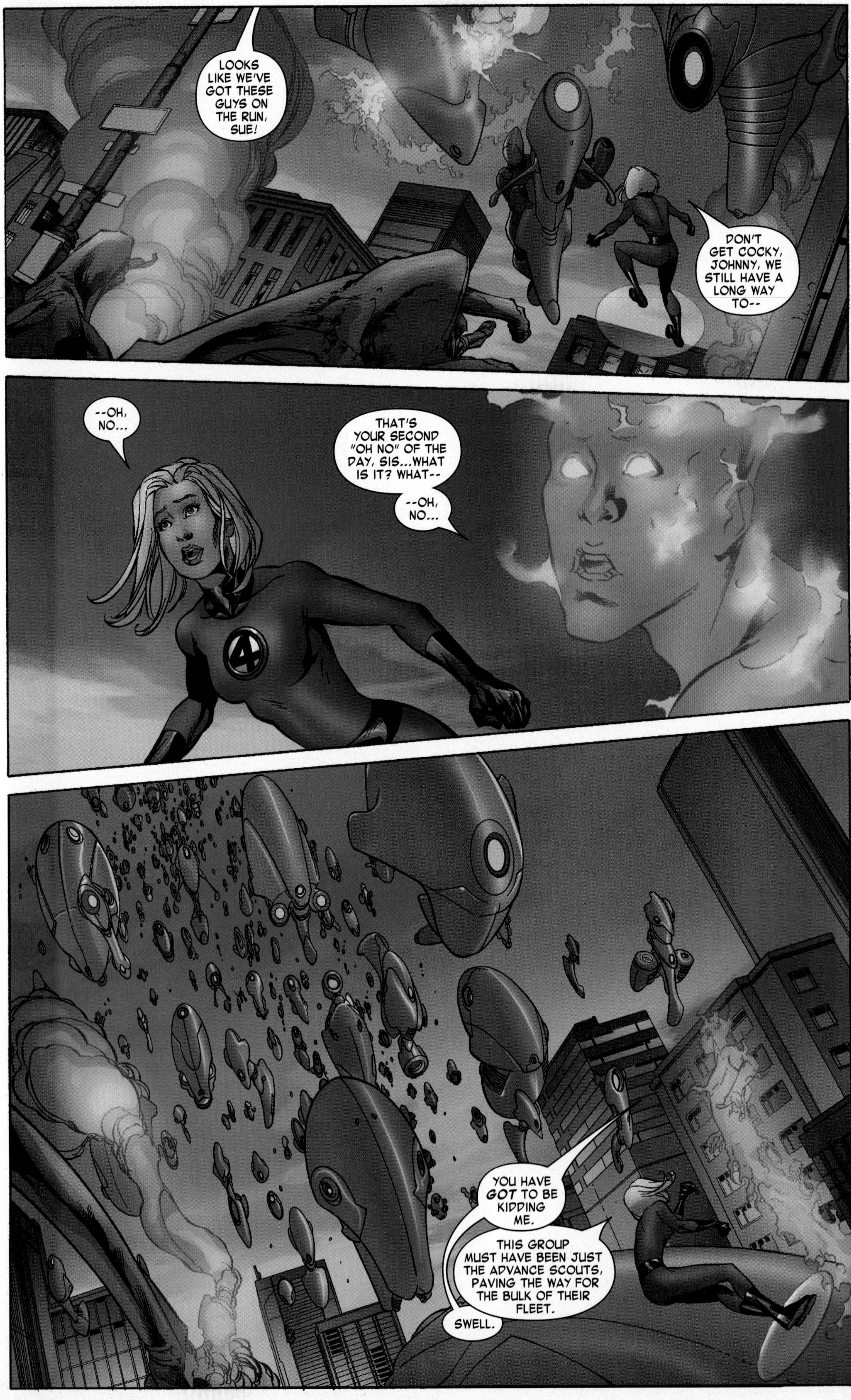
LOOKS LIKE WE'VE GOT THESE GUYS ON THE RUN, SUE!
DON'T GET COCKY, JOHNNY, WE STILL HAVE A LONG WAY TO--
--OH, NO...
THAT'S YOUR SECOND "OH NO" OF THE DAY, SIS...WHAT IS IT? WHAT--
--OH, NO...
YOU HAVE GOT TO BE KIDDING ME.
THIS GROUP MUST HAVE BEEN JUST THE ADVANCE SCOUTS, PAVING THE WAY FOR THE BULK OF THEIR FLEET.
SWELL.

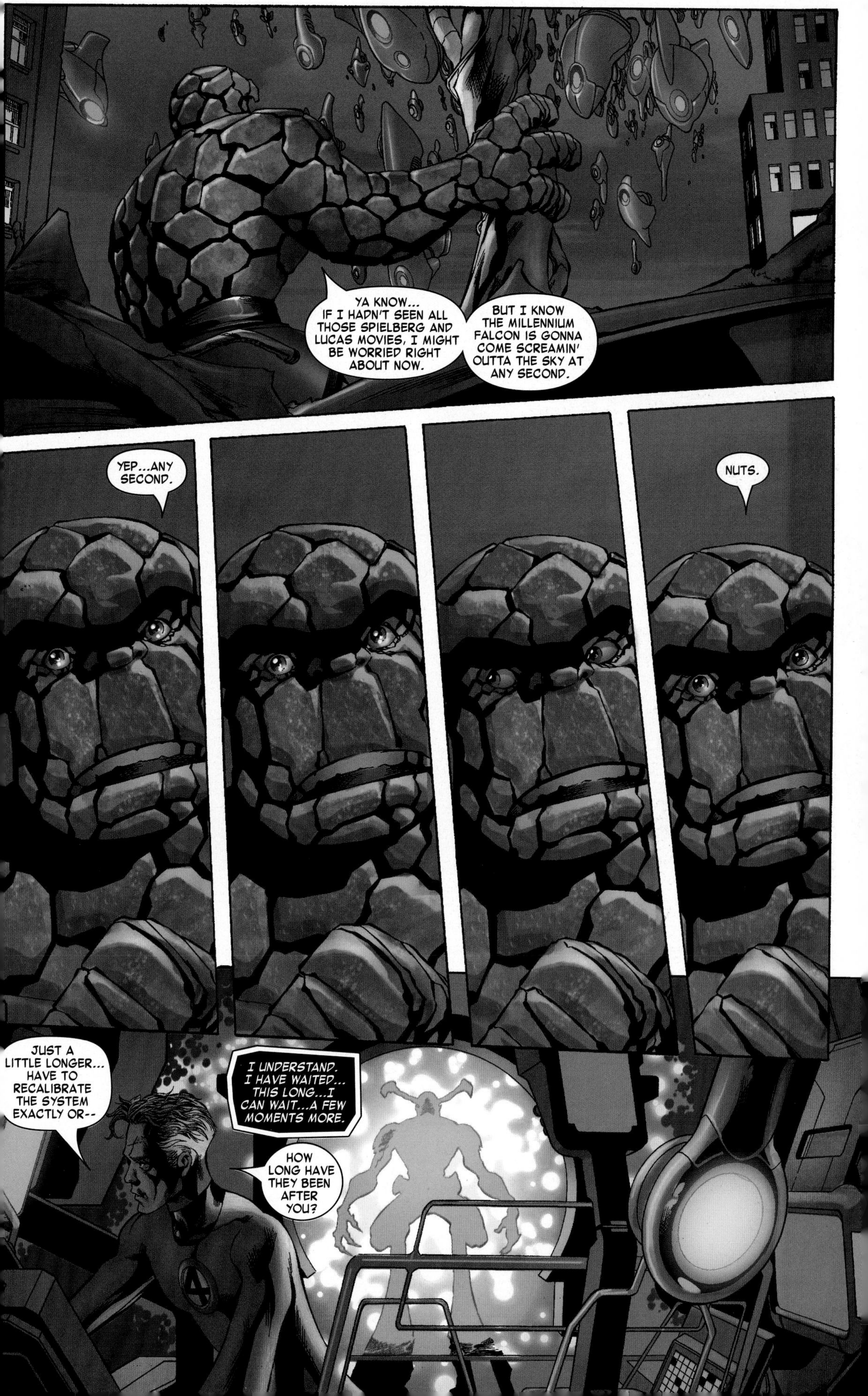
YA KNOW... IF I HADN'T SEEN ALL THOSE SPIELBERG AND LUCAS MOVIES, I MIGHT BE WORRIED RIGHT ABOUT NOW.
BUT I KNOW THE MILLENNIUM FALCON IS GONNA COME SCREAMIN' OUTTA THE SKY AT ANY SECOND.
YEP...ANY SECOND.
NUTS.
JUST A LITTLE LONGER... HAVE TO RECALIBRATE THE SYSTEM EXACTLY OR--
I UNDERSTAND. I HAVE WAITED... THIS LONG...I CAN WAIT...A FEW MOMENTS MORE.
HOW LONG HAVE THEY BEEN AFTER YOU?

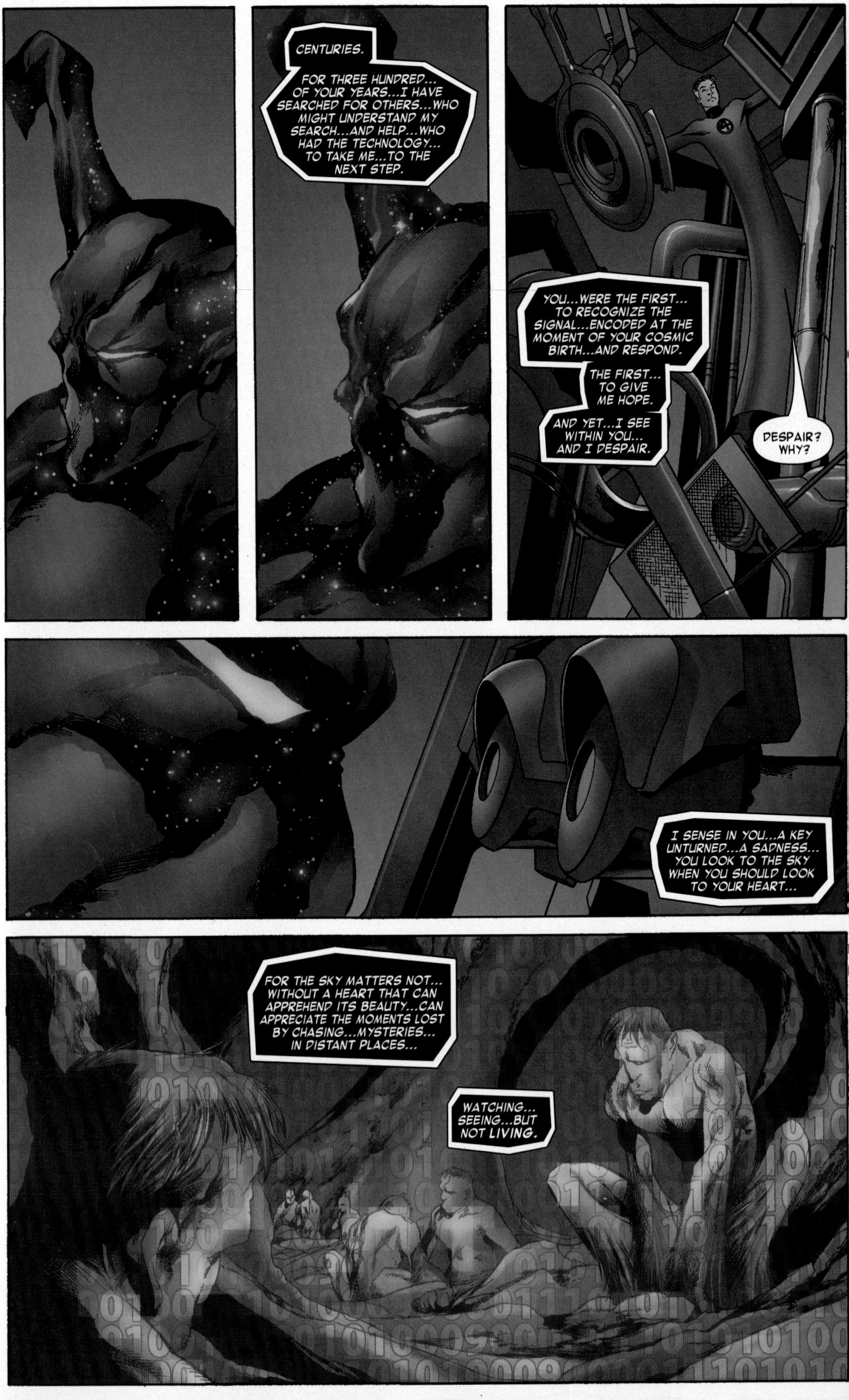
CENTURIES.
FOR THREE HUNDRED... OF YOUR YEARS...I HAVE SEARCHED FOR OTHERS...WHO MIGHT UNDERSTAND MY SEARCH...AND HELP...WHO HAD THE TECHNOLOGY... TO TAKE ME...TO THE NEXT STEP.
YOU...WERE THE FIRST... TO RECOGNIZE THE SIGNAL...ENCODED AT THE MOMENT OF YOUR COSMIC BIRTH...AND RESPOND.
THE FIRST... TO GIVE ME HOPE.
AND YET...I SEE WITHIN YOU... AND I DESPAIR.
DESPAIR? WHY?
I SENSE IN YOU...A KEY UNTURNED...A SADNESS... YOU LOOK TO THE SKY WHEN YOU SHOULD LOOK TO YOUR HEART...
FOR THE SKY MATTERS NOT... WITHOUT A HEART THAT CAN APPREHEND ITS BEAUTY...CAN APPRECIATE THE MOMENTS LOST BY CHASING...MYSTERIES... IN DISTANT PLACES...
WATCHING... SEEING...BUT NOT LIVING.

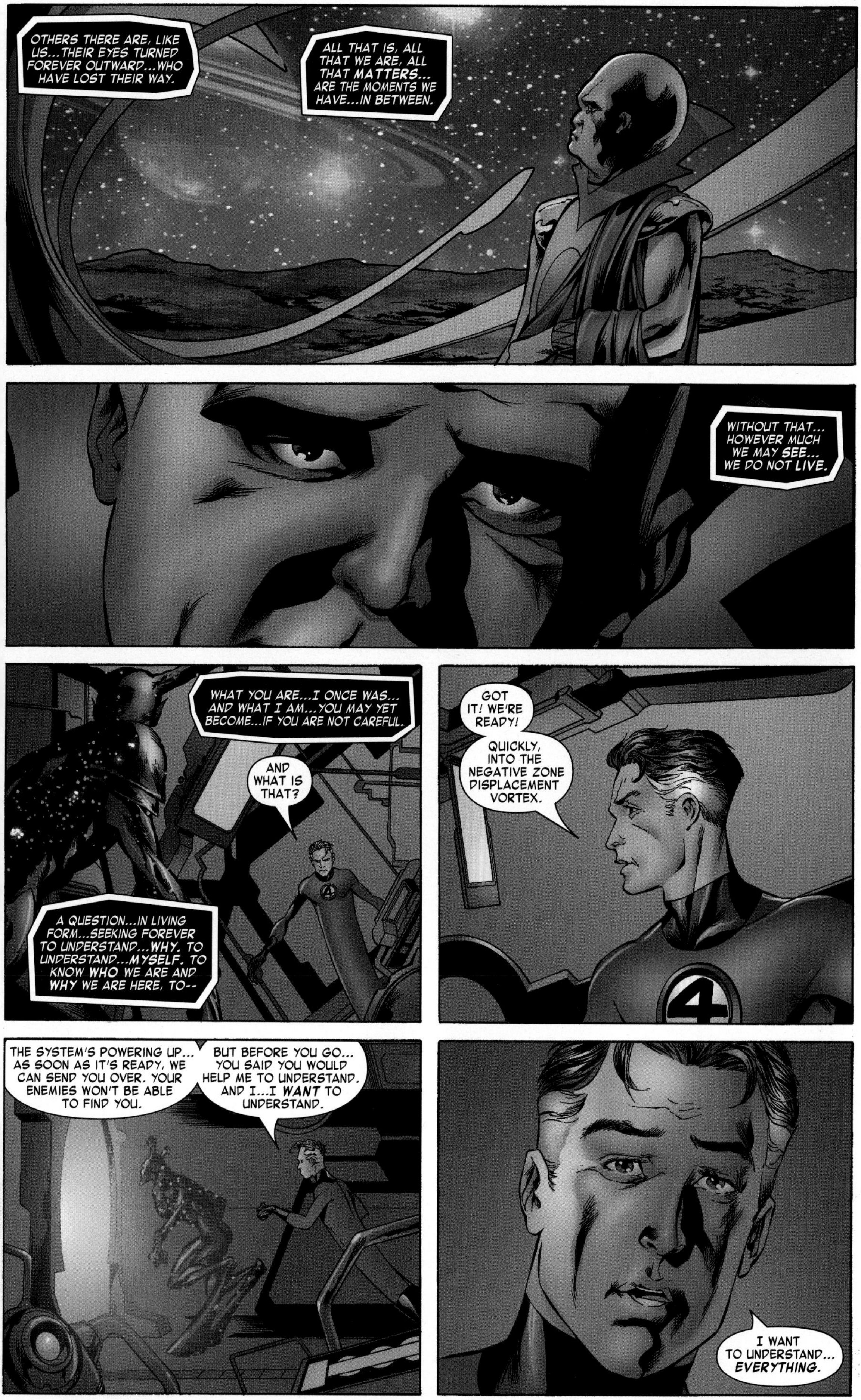
OTHERS THERE ARE, LIKE US...THEIR EYES TURNED FOREVER OUTWARD...WHO HAVE LOST THEIR WAY.
ALL THAT IS, ALL THAT WE ARE, ALL THAT MATTERS... ARE THE MOMENTS WE HAVE...IN BETWEEN.
WITHOUT THAT... HOWEVER MUCH WE MAY SEE... WE DO NOT LIVE.
WHAT YOU ARE...I ONCE WAS... AND WHAT I AM...YOU MAY YET BECOME...IF YOU ARE NOT CAREFUL.
AND WHAT IS THAT?
A QUESTION...IN LIVING FORM...SEEKING FOREVER TO UNDERSTAND...WHY. TO UNDERSTAND...MYSELF. TO KNOW WHO WE ARE AND WHY WE ARE HERE, TO--
GOT IT! WE'RE READY!
QUICKLY, INTO THE NEGATIVE ZONE DISPLACEMENT VORTEX.
THE SYSTEM'S POWERING UP... AS SOON AS IT'S READY, WE CAN SEND YOU OVER. YOUR ENEMIES WON'T BE ABLE TO FIND YOU.
BUT BEFORE YOU GO... YOU SAID YOU WOULD HELP ME TO UNDERSTAND. AND I...I WANT TO UNDERSTAND.
I WANT TO UNDERSTAND... EVERYTHING.

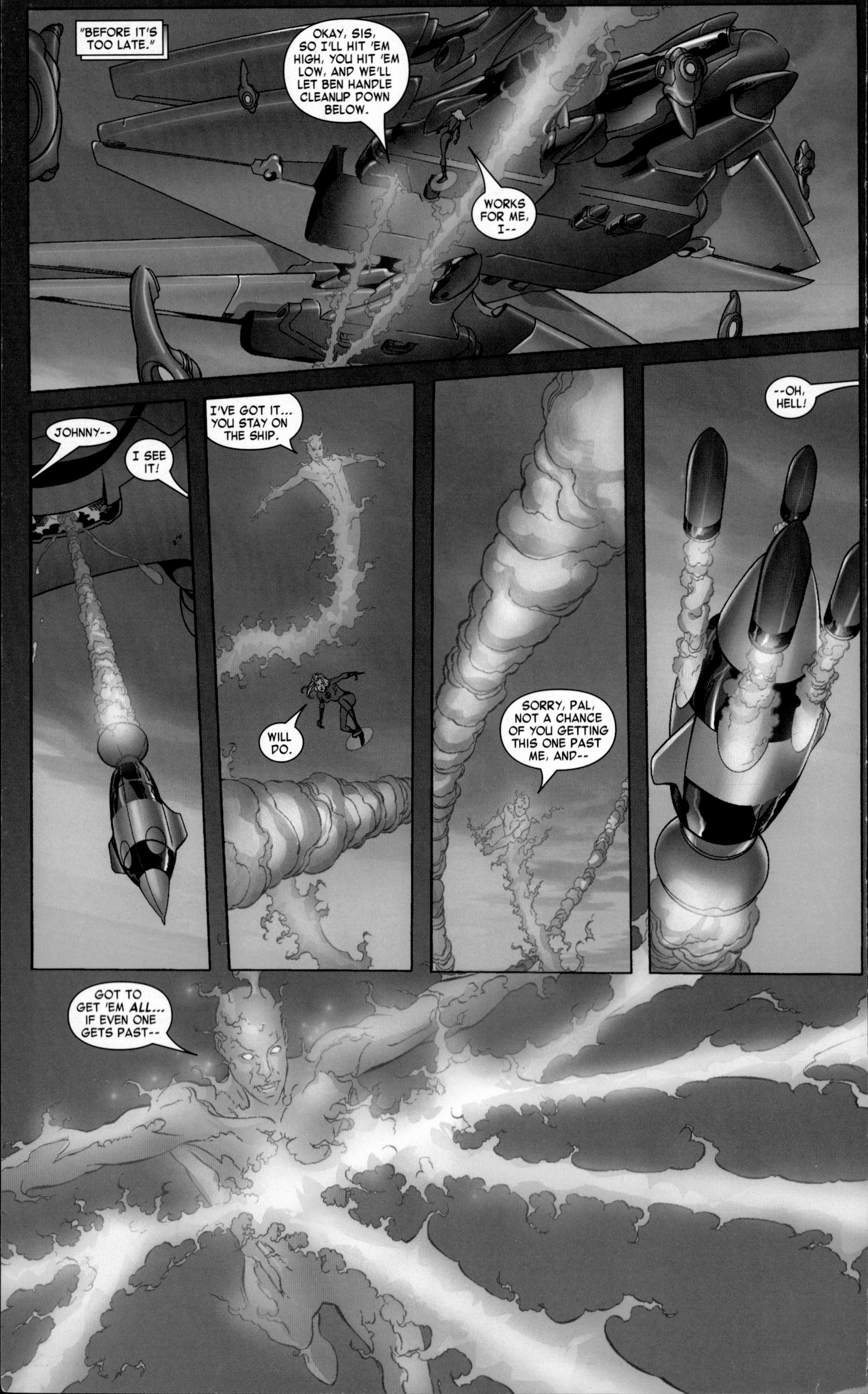
"BEFORE IT'S TOO LATE."
OKAY, SIS, SO I'LL HIT 'EM HIGH, YOU HIT 'EM LOW, AND WE'LL LET BEN HANDLE CLEANUP DOWN BELOW.
WORKS FOR ME, I--
JOHNNY--
I SEE IT!
I'VE GOT IT... YOU STAY ON THE SHIP.
WILL DO.
SORRY, PAL, NOT A CHANCE OF YOU GETTING THIS ONE PAST ME, AND--
--OH, HELL!
GOT TO GET 'EM ALL... IF EVEN ONE GETS PAST--

NO!

TAKE MY HAND...AND YOU WILL SEE...ALL THAT I KNOW...AND ALL...THAT I STILL SEEK.

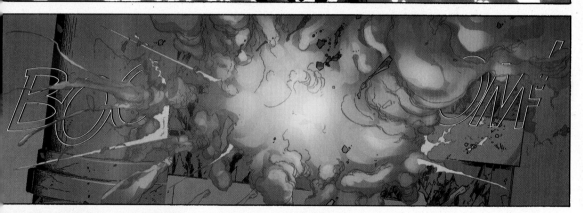

SYSTEM'S OUT OF CONTROL... OVERLOADING...HAVE TO STOP IT...HAVE TO STOP--

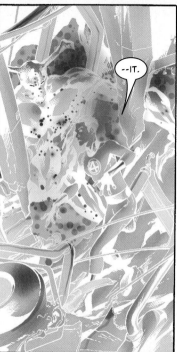

--IT.

AND IN THE INSTANT BEFORE THE DARKNESS TAKES ME, I THINK--

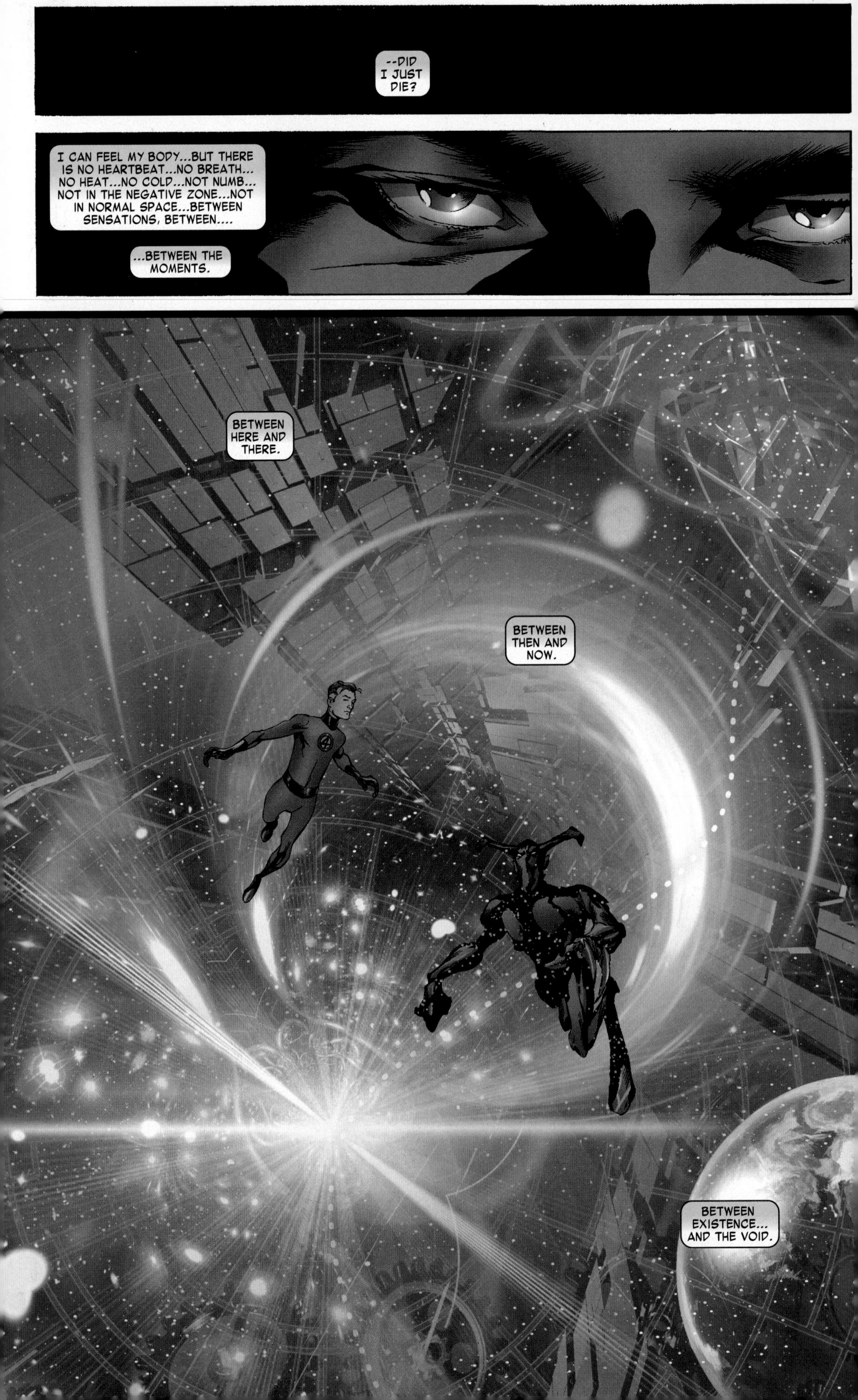
--DID I JUST DIE?
I CAN FEEL MY BODY...BUT THERE IS NO HEARTBEAT...NO BREATH... NO HEAT...NO COLD...NOT NUMB... NOT IN THE NEGATIVE ZONE...NOT IN NORMAL SPACE...BETWEEN SENSATIONS, BETWEEN....
...BETWEEN THE MOMENTS.
BETWEEN HERE AND THERE.
BETWEEN THEN AND NOW.
BETWEEN EXISTENCE... AND THE VOID.

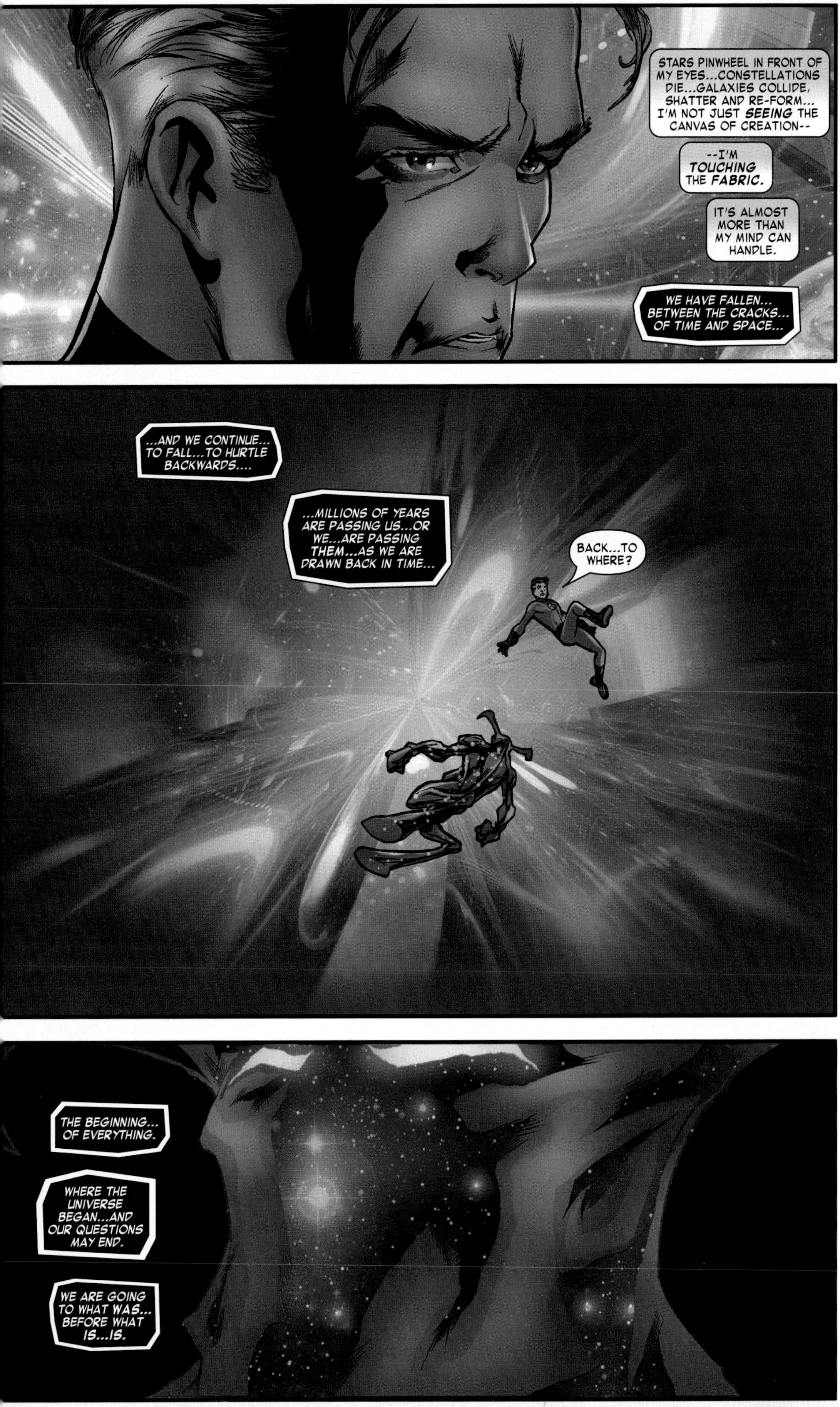
STARS PINWHEEL IN FRONT OF MY EYES...CONSTELLATIONS DIE...GALAXIES COLLIDE, SHATTER AND RE-FORM... I'M NOT JUST *SEEING* THE CANVAS OF CREATION--
--I'M *TOUCHING* THE *FABRIC.*
IT'S ALMOST MORE THAN MY MIND CAN HANDLE.
WE HAVE FALLEN... BETWEEN THE CRACKS... OF TIME AND SPACE...
...AND WE CONTINUE... TO FALL...TO HURTLE BACKWARDS....
...MILLIONS OF YEARS ARE PASSING US...OR WE...ARE PASSING *THEM*...AS WE ARE DRAWN BACK IN TIME...
BACK...TO WHERE?
THE BEGINNING... OF EVERYTHING.
WHERE THE UNIVERSE BEGAN...AND OUR QUESTIONS MAY END.
WE ARE GOING TO WHAT *WAS*... BEFORE WHAT *IS...IS*.

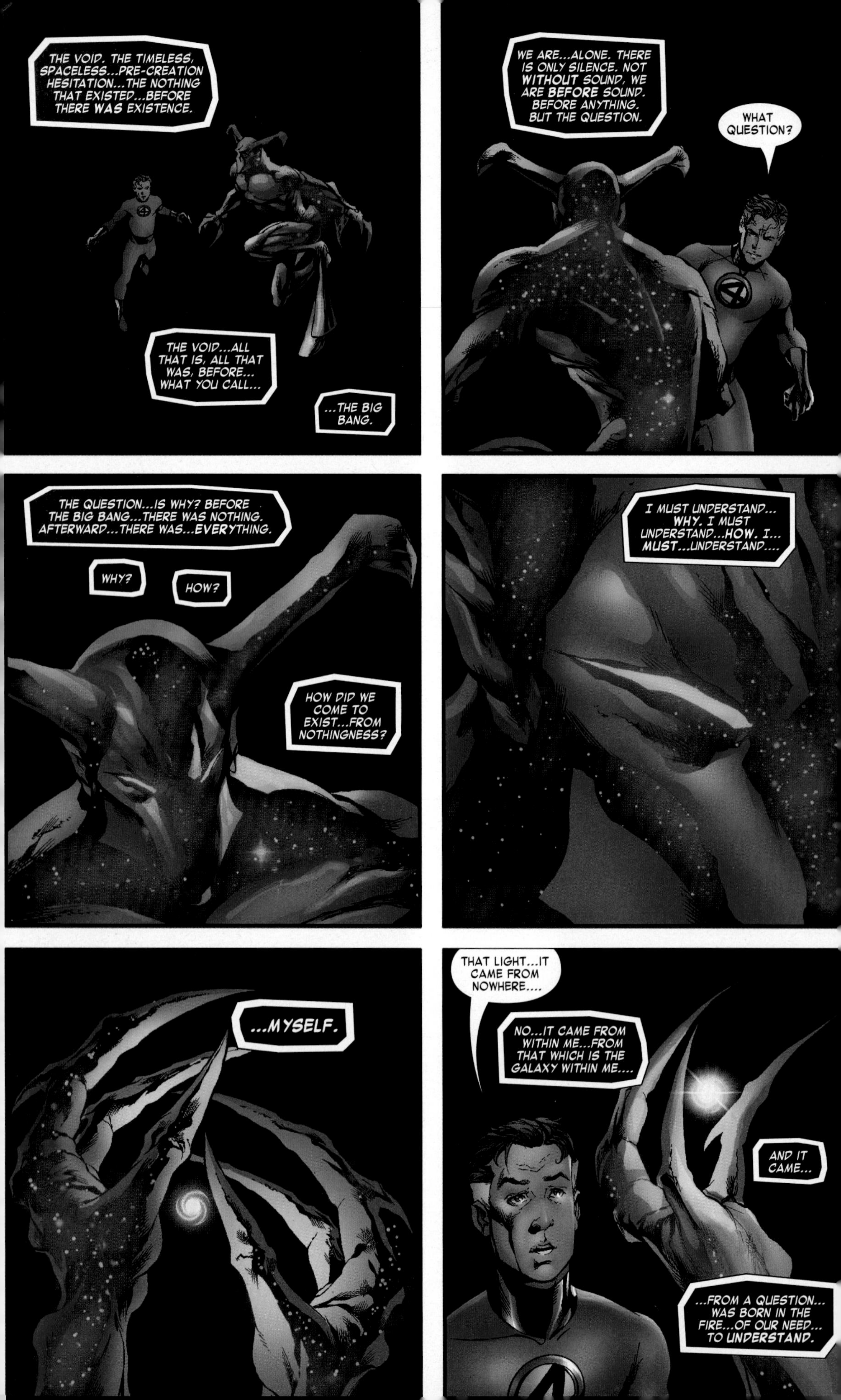
THE VOID. THE TIMELESS, SPACELESS...PRE-CREATION HESITATION...THE NOTHING THAT EXISTED...BEFORE THERE WAS EXISTENCE.
THE VOID...ALL THAT IS, ALL THAT WAS, BEFORE... WHAT YOU CALL...
...THE BIG BANG.
WE ARE...ALONE. THERE IS ONLY SILENCE. NOT WITHOUT SOUND, WE ARE BEFORE SOUND. BEFORE ANYTHING. BUT THE QUESTION.
WHAT QUESTION?
THE QUESTION...IS WHY? BEFORE THE BIG BANG...THERE WAS NOTHING. AFTERWARD...THERE WAS...EVERYTHING.
WHY?
HOW?
HOW DID WE COME TO EXIST...FROM NOTHINGNESS?
I MUST UNDERSTAND... WHY. I MUST UNDERSTAND...HOW. I... MUST...UNDERSTAND....
...MYSELF.
THAT LIGHT...IT CAME FROM NOWHERE....
NO...IT CAME FROM WITHIN ME...FROM THAT WHICH IS THE GALAXY WITHIN ME....
AND IT CAME...
...FROM A QUESTION... WAS BORN IN THE FIRE...OF OUR NEED... TO UNDERSTAND.

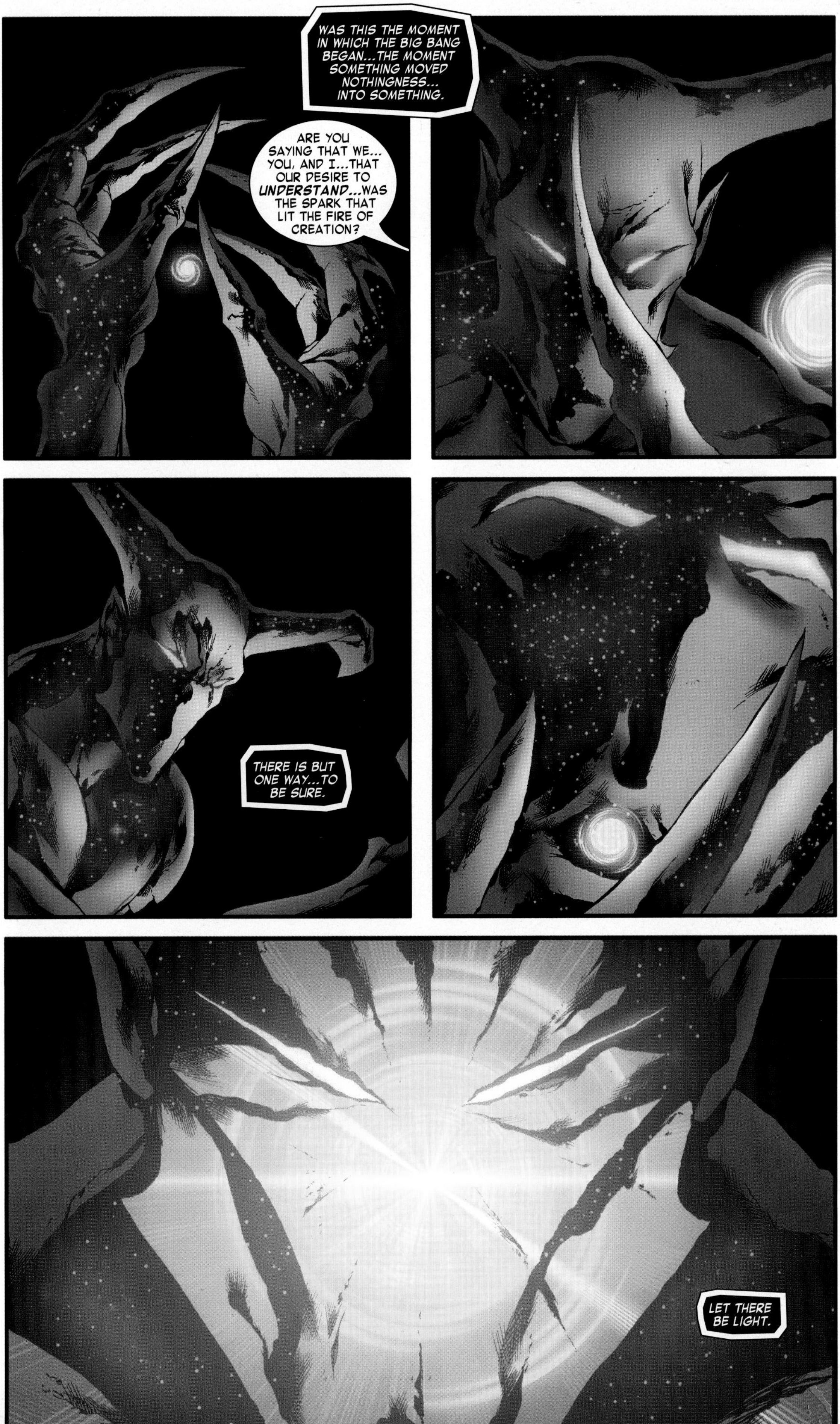
WAS THIS THE MOMENT IN WHICH THE BIG BANG BEGAN...THE MOMENT SOMETHING MOVED NOTHINGNESS... INTO SOMETHING.
ARE YOU SAYING THAT WE... YOU, AND I...THAT OUR DESIRE TO UNDERSTAND...WAS THE SPARK THAT LIT THE FIRE OF CREATION?
THERE IS BUT ONE WAY...TO BE SURE.
LET THERE BE LIGHT.

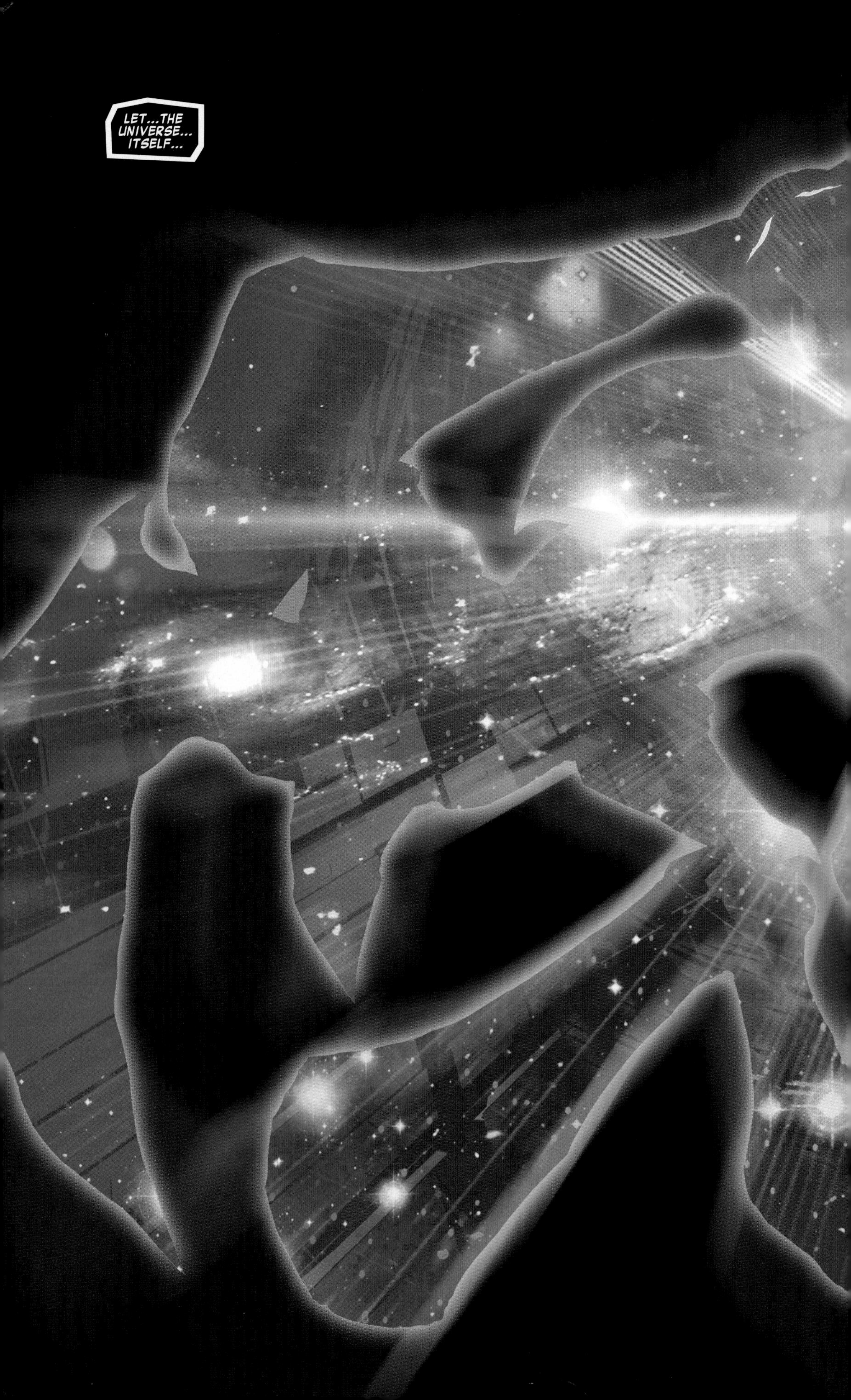
LET...THE UNIVERSE... ITSELF...

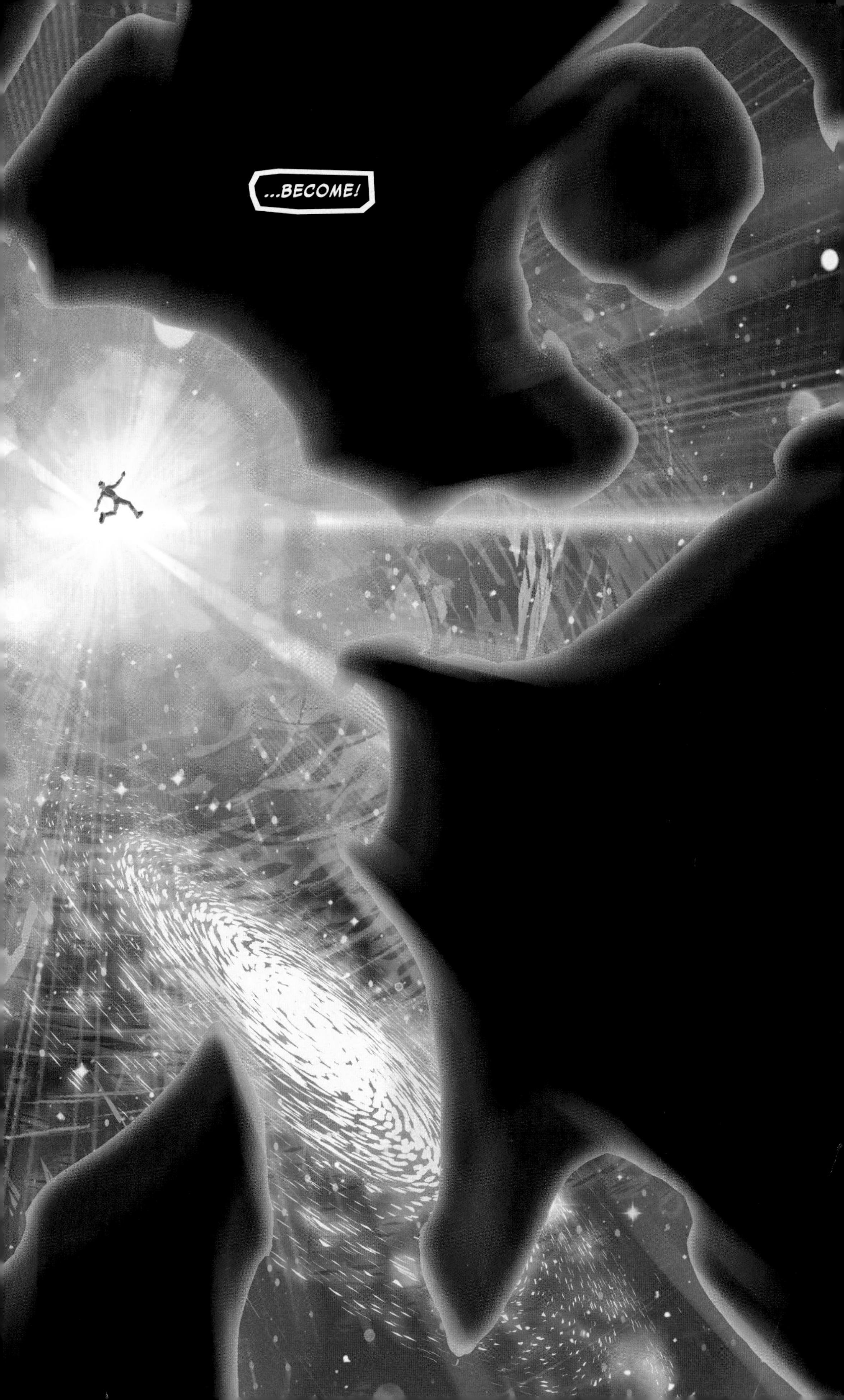
...BECOME!

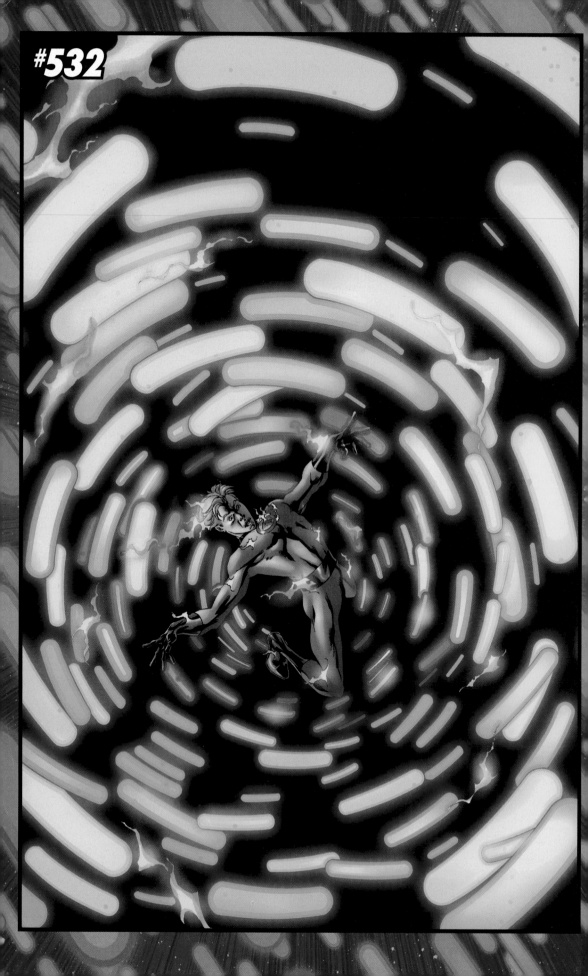

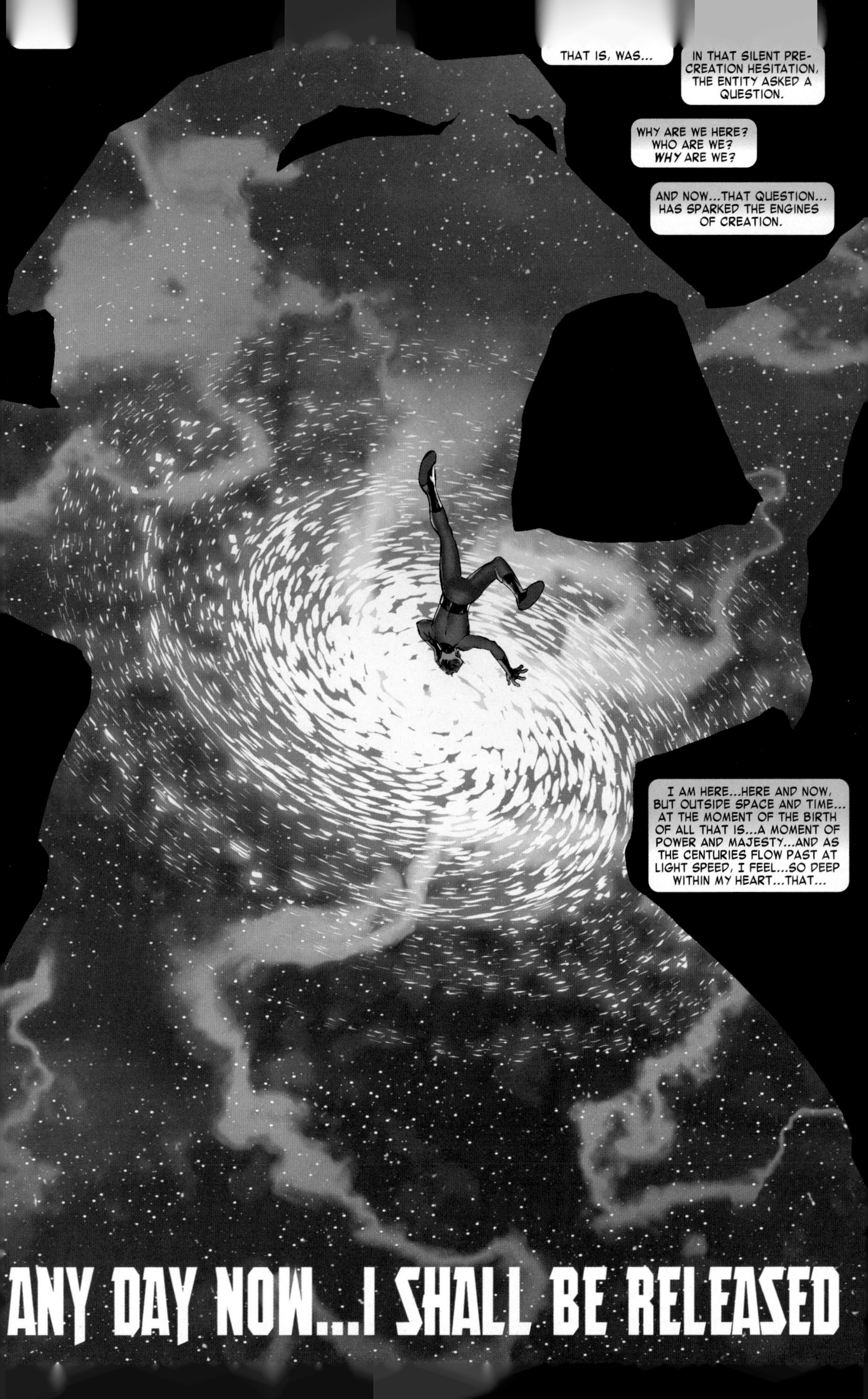
THAT IS, WAS...
IN THAT SILENT PRE-CREATION HESITATION, THE ENTITY ASKED A QUESTION.
WHY ARE WE HERE? WHO ARE WE? *WHY* ARE WE?
AND NOW...THAT QUESTION... HAS SPARKED THE ENGINES OF CREATION.
I AM HERE...HERE AND NOW, BUT OUTSIDE SPACE AND TIME... AT THE MOMENT OF THE BIRTH OF ALL THAT IS...A MOMENT OF POWER AND MAJESTY...AND AS THE CENTURIES FLOW PAST AT LIGHT SPEED, I FEEL...SO DEEP WITHIN MY HEART...THAT...
ANY DAY NOW...I SHALL BE RELEASED

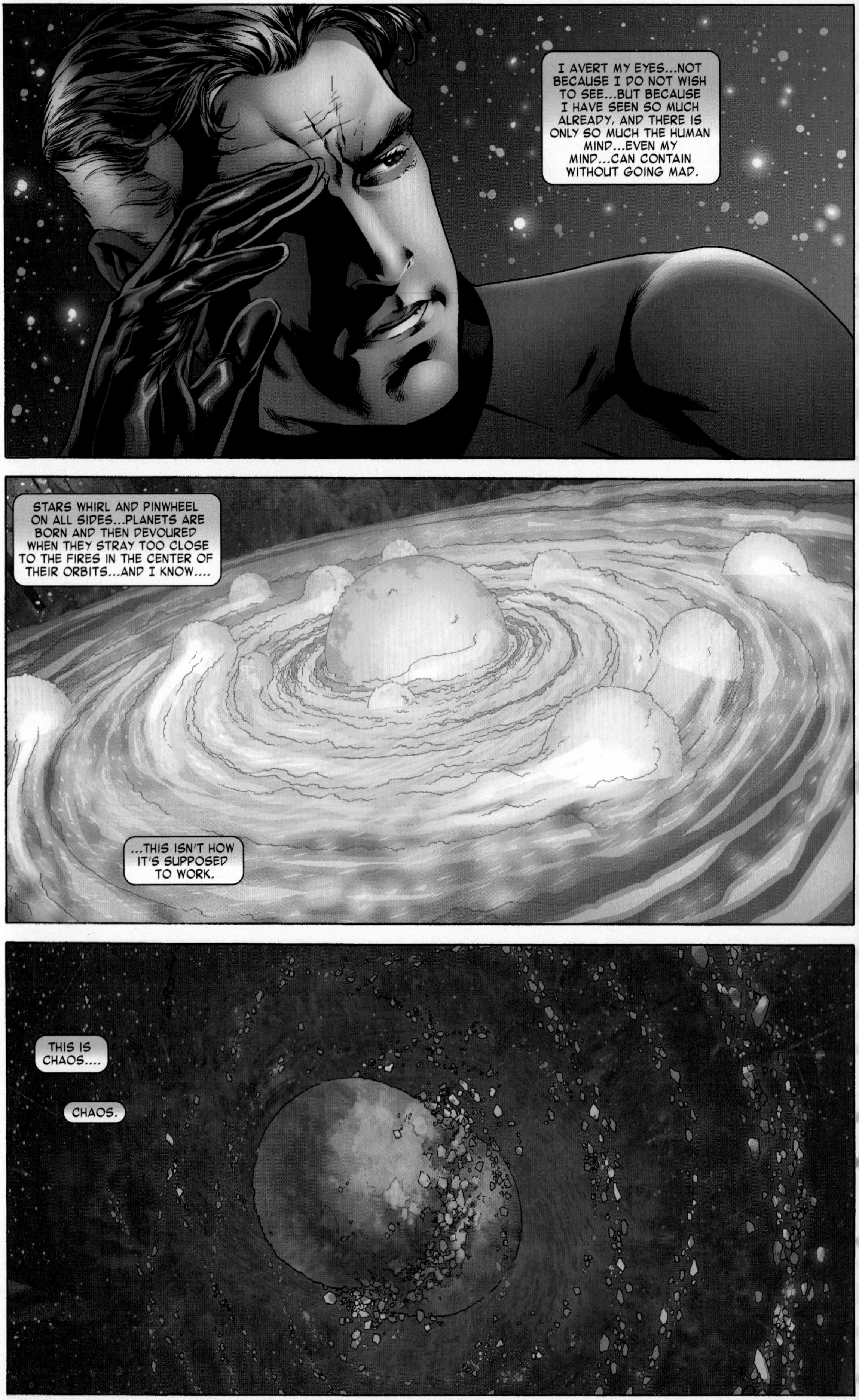
I AVERT MY EYES...NOT BECAUSE I DO NOT WISH TO SEE...BUT BECAUSE I HAVE SEEN SO MUCH ALREADY, AND THERE IS ONLY SO MUCH THE HUMAN MIND...EVEN MY MIND...CAN CONTAIN WITHOUT GOING MAD.
STARS WHIRL AND PINWHEEL ON ALL SIDES...PLANETS ARE BORN AND THEN DEVOURED WHEN THEY STRAY TOO CLOSE TO THE FIRES IN THE CENTER OF THEIR ORBITS...AND I KNOW....
...THIS ISN'T HOW IT'S SUPPOSED TO WORK.
THIS IS CHAOS....
CHAOS.

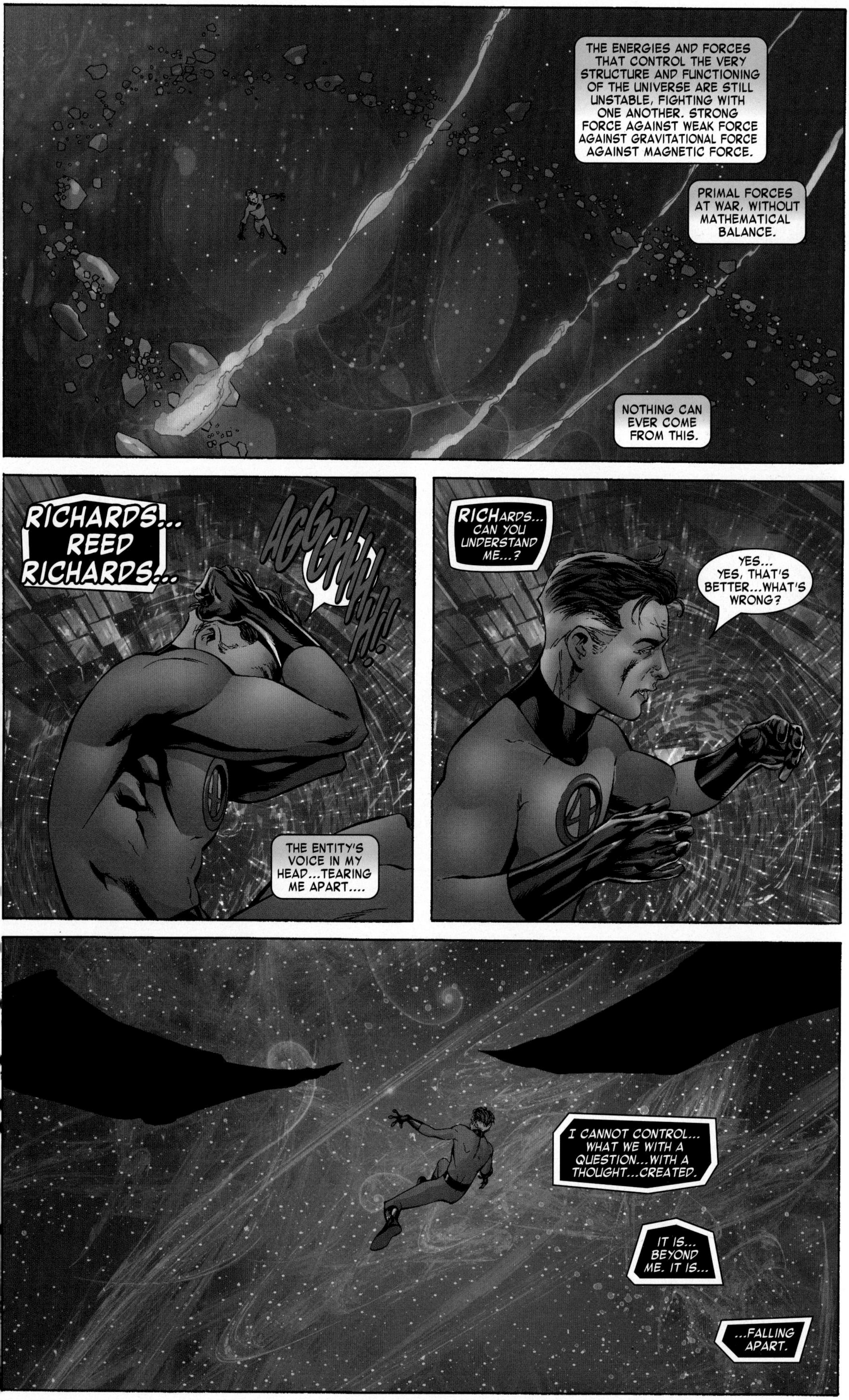

THE ENERGIES AND FORCES THAT CONTROL THE VERY STRUCTURE AND FUNCTIONING OF THE UNIVERSE ARE STILL UNSTABLE, FIGHTING WITH ONE ANOTHER. STRONG FORCE AGAINST WEAK FORCE AGAINST GRAVITATIONAL FORCE AGAINST MAGNETIC FORCE.
PRIMAL FORCES AT WAR, WITHOUT MATHEMATICAL BALANCE.
NOTHING CAN EVER COME FROM THIS.
RICHARDS... REED RICHARDS...
AGGGHHHH!!
THE ENTITY'S VOICE IN MY HEAD...TEARING ME APART....
RICHards... CAN YOU UNDERSTAND ME...?
YES... YES, THAT'S BETTER...WHAT'S WRONG?
I CANNOT CONTROL... WHAT WE WITH A QUESTION...WITH A THOUGHT...CREATED.
IT IS... BEYOND ME. IT IS...
...FALLING APART.

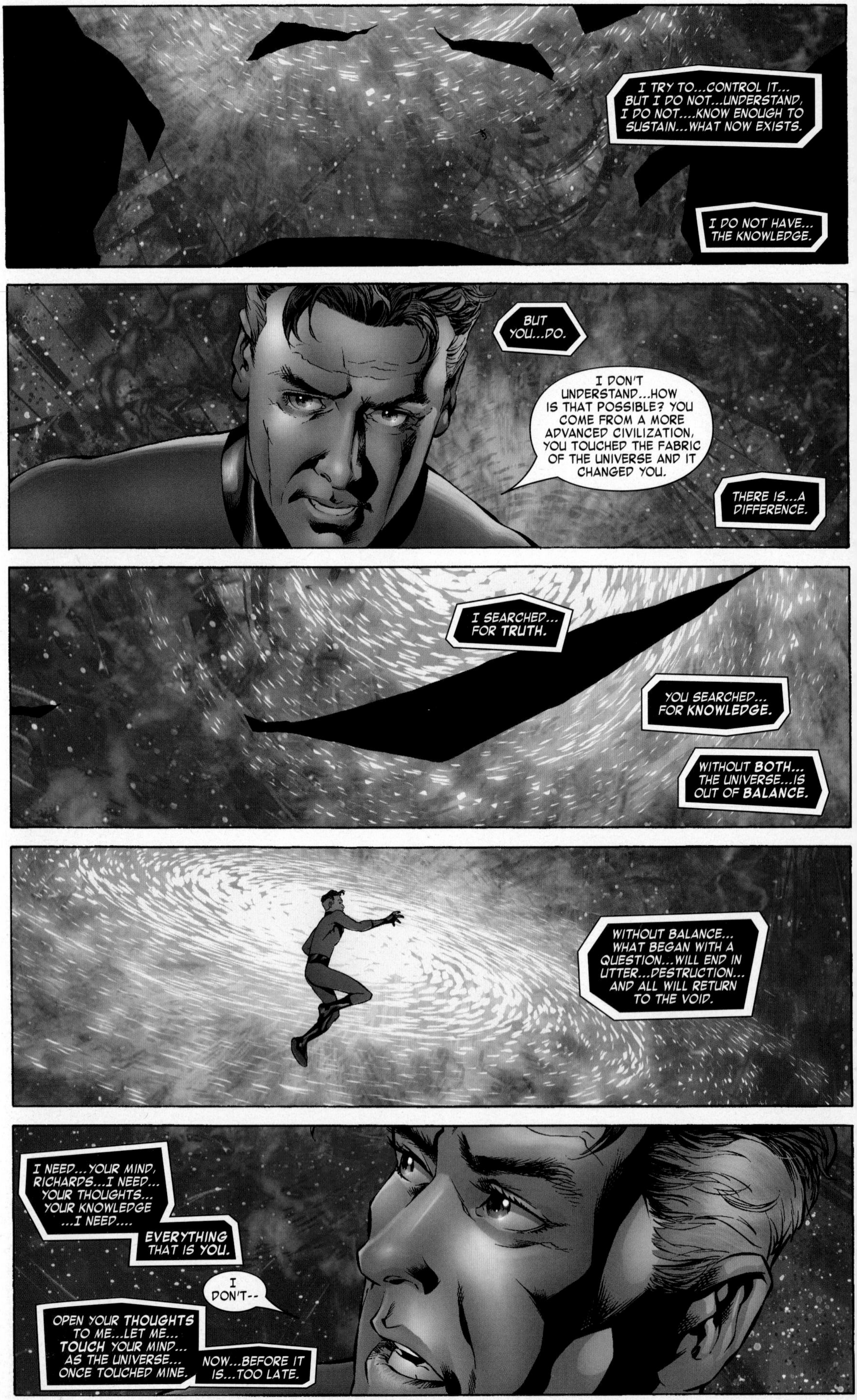

I TRY TO...CONTROL IT... BUT I DO NOT...UNDERSTAND, I DO NOT....KNOW ENOUGH TO SUSTAIN...WHAT NOW EXISTS.
I DO NOT HAVE... THE KNOWLEDGE.
BUT YOU...DO.
I DON'T UNDERSTAND...HOW IS THAT POSSIBLE? YOU COME FROM A MORE ADVANCED CIVILIZATION, YOU TOUCHED THE FABRIC OF THE UNIVERSE AND IT CHANGED YOU.
THERE IS...A DIFFERENCE.
I SEARCHED... FOR TRUTH.
YOU SEARCHED... FOR KNOWLEDGE.
WITHOUT BOTH... THE UNIVERSE...IS OUT OF BALANCE.
WITHOUT BALANCE... WHAT BEGAN WITH A QUESTION...WILL END IN UTTER...DESTRUCTION... AND ALL WILL RETURN TO THE VOID.
I NEED...YOUR MIND, RICHARDS...I NEED... YOUR THOUGHTS... YOUR KNOWLEDGE ...I NEED.... EVERYTHING THAT IS YOU.
I DON'T--
OPEN YOUR THOUGHTS TO ME...LET ME... TOUCH YOUR MIND... AS THE UNIVERSE... ONCE TOUCHED MINE.
NOW...BEFORE IT IS...TOO LATE.

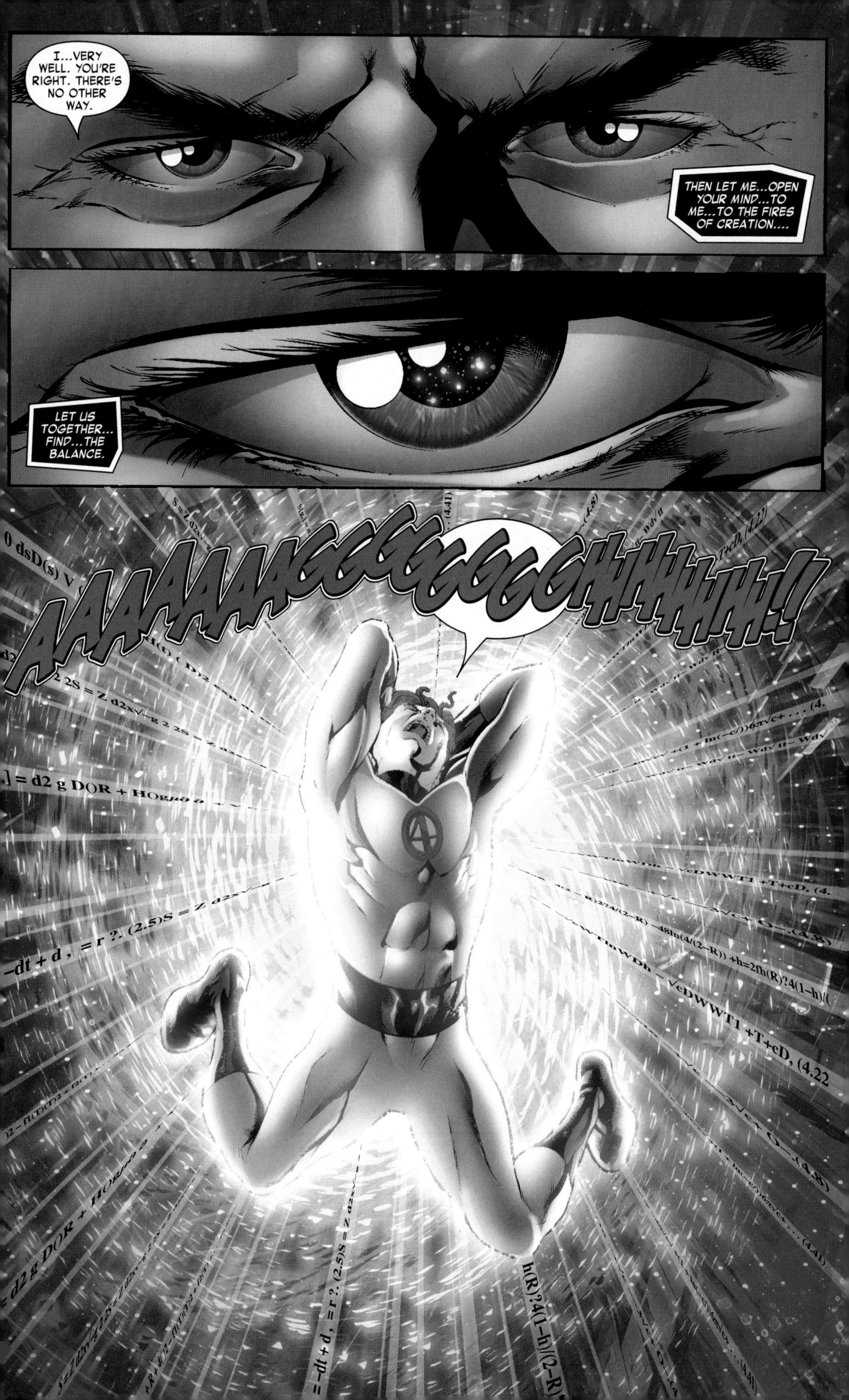
I...VERY WELL. YOU'RE RIGHT. THERE'S NO OTHER WAY.
THEN LET ME...OPEN YOUR MIND...TO ME...TO THE FIRES OF CREATION....
LET US TOGETHER... FIND...THE BALANCE.
AAAAAAAGGGGGGGGGHHHHHHHH!!

A MILLION YEARS... FLASH PAST...IN A SECOND...THE LAWS OF THERMODYNAMICS SET IN FIERY MOTION... THE MECHANISM OF THE COSMOS... ACCELERATING FROM CHAOS...INTO ORDER....

PLANETS STABILIZE AROUND A BILLION, BILLION STARS... CLINGING TO THE FRAGILE TRACERY OF GRAVITATIONAL ORBITS LIKE...MOLTEN PEARLS ON TRILLION-MILE STRINGS....

I TRY DESPERATELY... TO CLING TO MY SANITY... BECAUSE IF I FALTER... IF I FAIL TO HOLD ONTO THE BALANCE...ALL OF IT...WILL SPIRAL BACK INTO CHAOS.

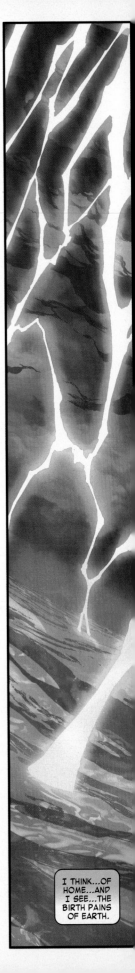

I THINK...OF HOME...AND I SEE...THE BIRTH PAINS OF EARTH.

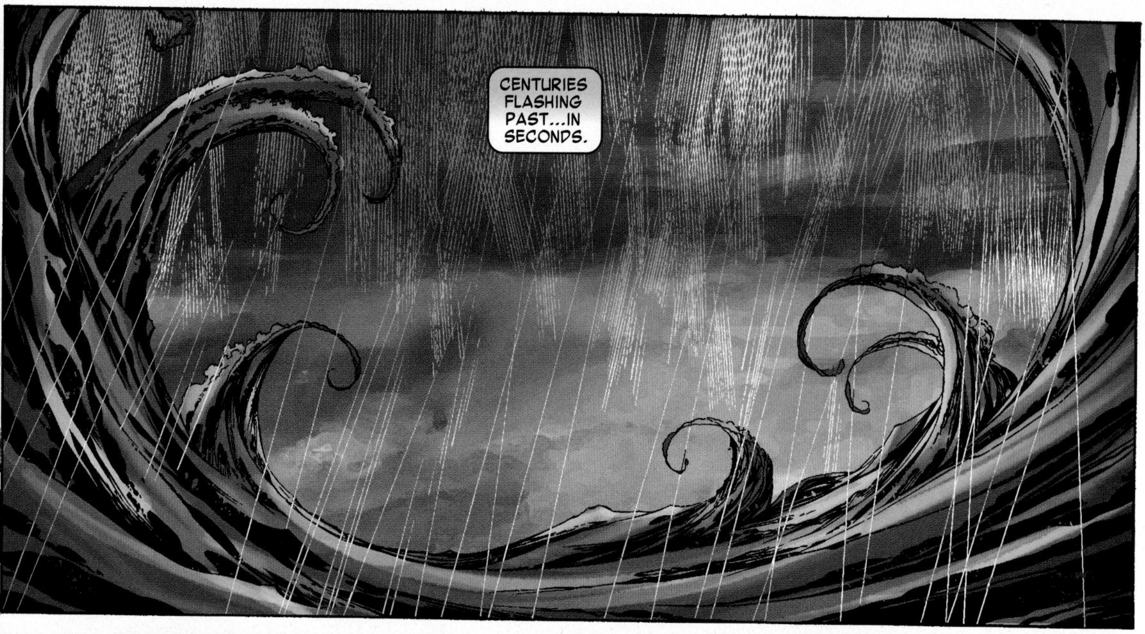
CENTURIES FLASHING PAST...IN SECONDS.

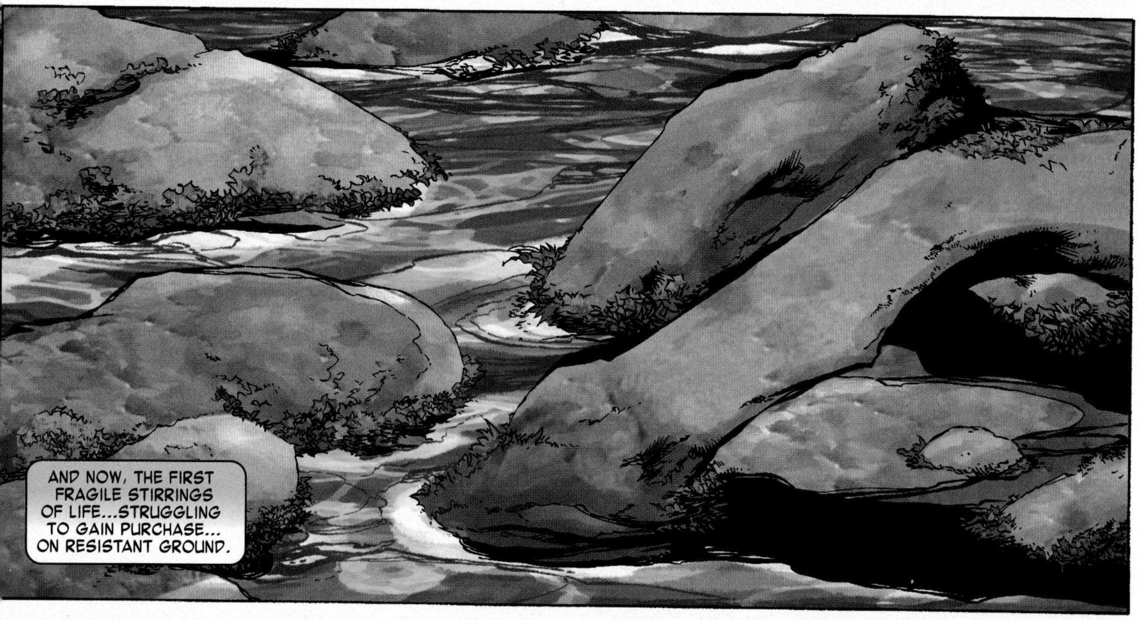
AND NOW, THE FIRST FRAGILE STIRRINGS OF LIFE...STRUGGLING TO GAIN PURCHASE... ON RESISTANT GROUND.

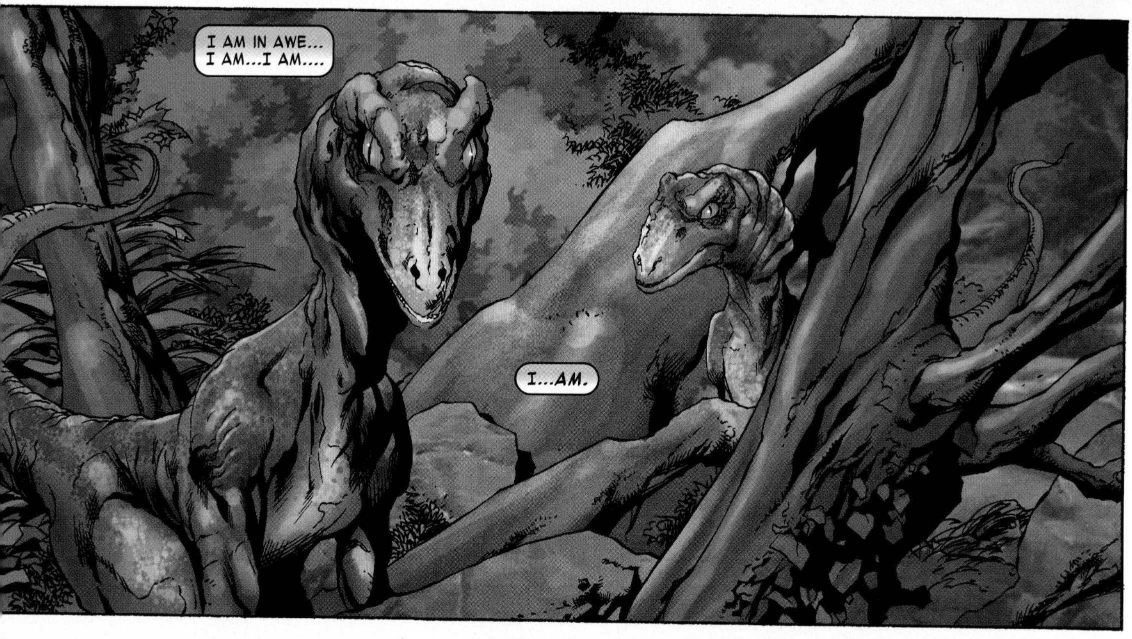
I AM IN AWE... I AM...I AM....
I...AM.

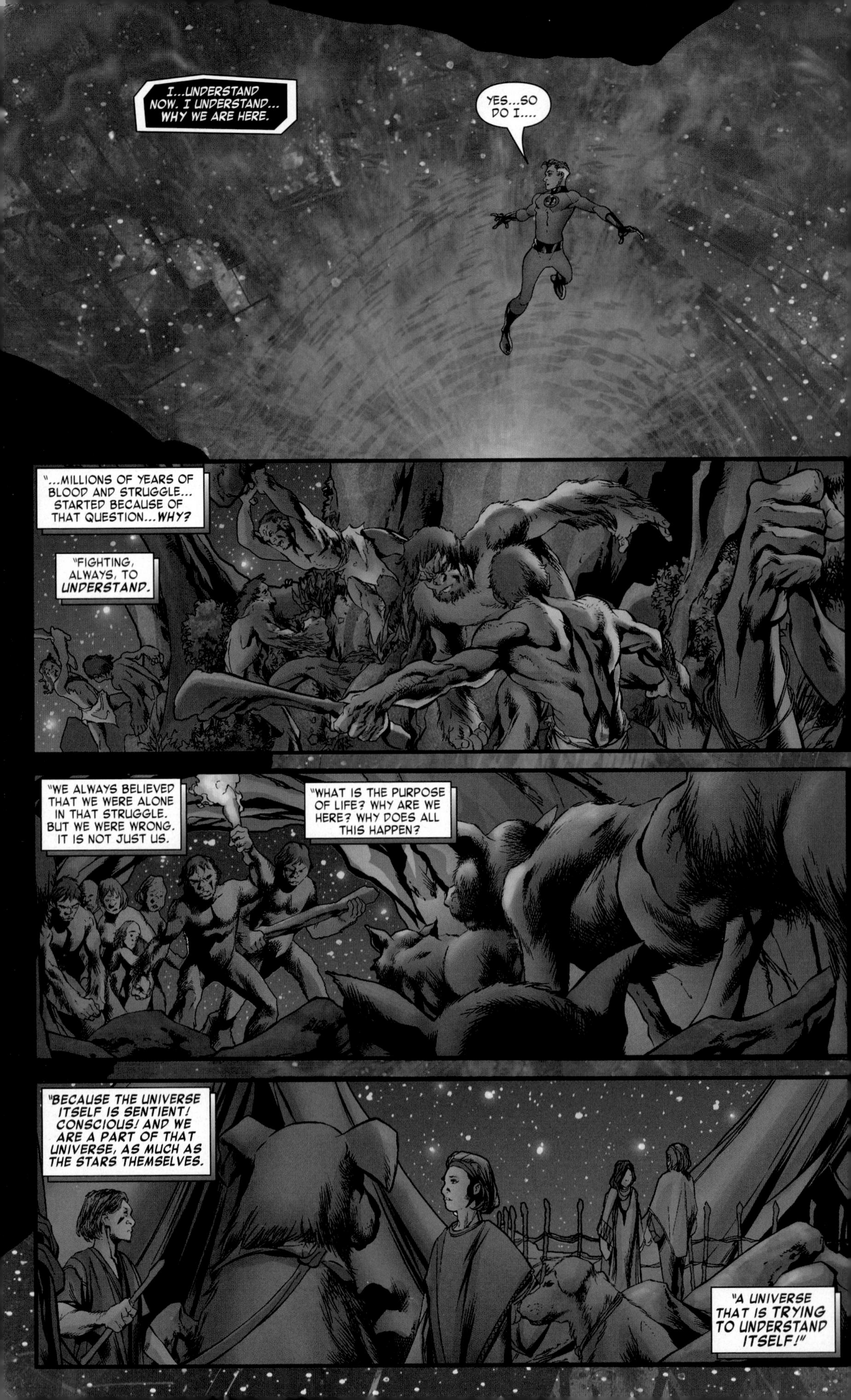
I...UNDERSTAND NOW. I UNDERSTAND... WHY WE ARE HERE.
YES...SO DO I....
"...MILLIONS OF YEARS OF BLOOD AND STRUGGLE... STARTED BECAUSE OF THAT QUESTION...WHY?
"FIGHTING, ALWAYS, TO UNDERSTAND.
"WE ALWAYS BELIEVED THAT WE WERE ALONE IN THAT STRUGGLE. BUT WE WERE WRONG. IT IS NOT JUST US.
"WHAT IS THE PURPOSE OF LIFE? WHY ARE WE HERE? WHY DOES ALL THIS HAPPEN?
"BECAUSE THE UNIVERSE ITSELF IS SENTIENT! CONSCIOUS! AND WE ARE A PART OF THAT UNIVERSE, AS MUCH AS THE STARS THEMSELVES.
"A UNIVERSE THAT IS TRYING TO UNDERSTAND ITSELF!"

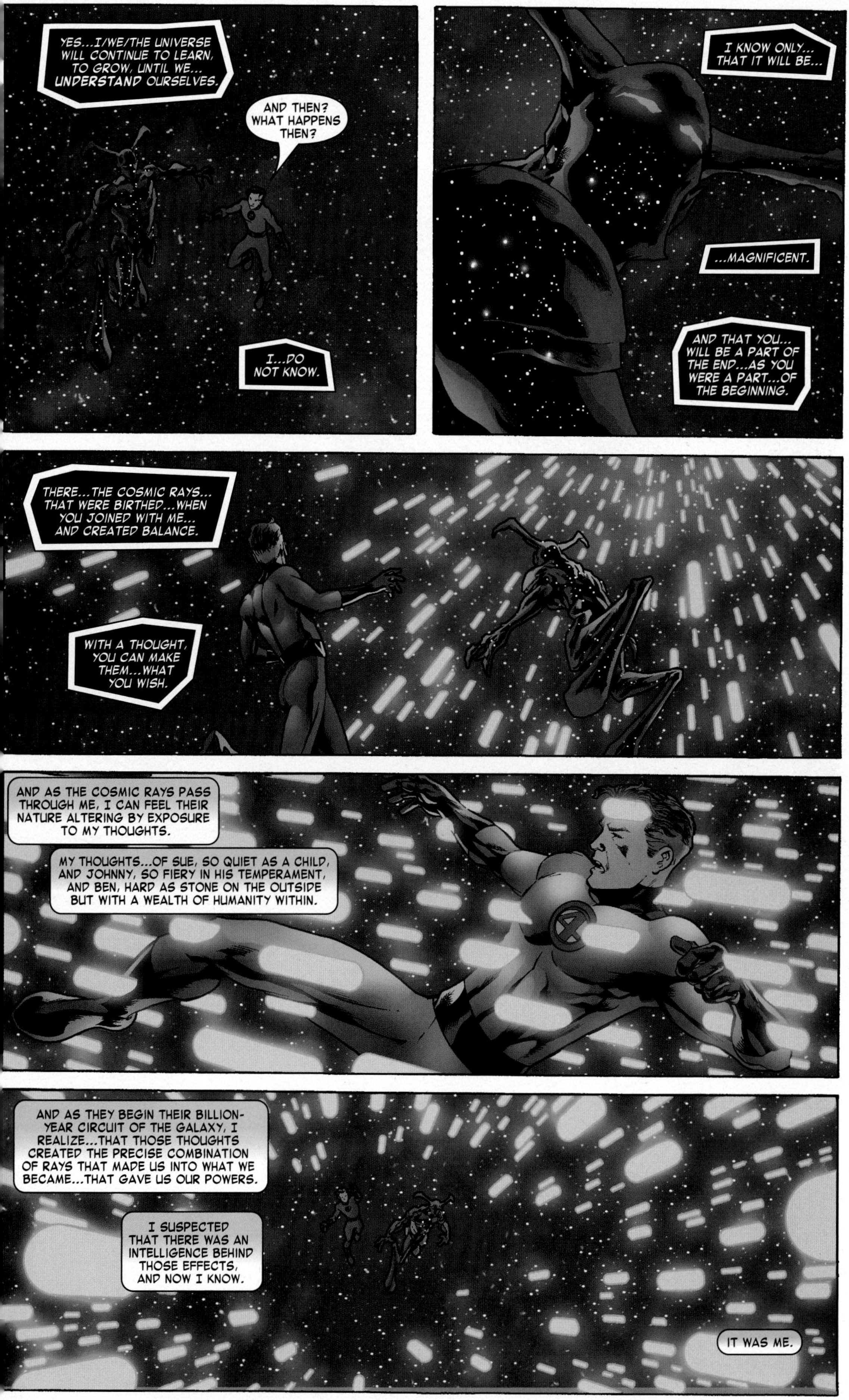
YES...I/WE/THE UNIVERSE WILL CONTINUE TO LEARN, TO GROW, UNTIL WE... UNDERSTAND OURSELVES.
AND THEN? WHAT HAPPENS THEN?
I...DO NOT KNOW.
I KNOW ONLY... THAT IT WILL BE...
...MAGNIFICENT.
AND THAT YOU... WILL BE A PART OF THE END...AS YOU WERE A PART...OF THE BEGINNING.
THERE...THE COSMIC RAYS... THAT WERE BIRTHED...WHEN YOU JOINED WITH ME... AND CREATED BALANCE.
WITH A THOUGHT, YOU CAN MAKE THEM...WHAT YOU WISH.
AND AS THE COSMIC RAYS PASS THROUGH ME, I CAN FEEL THEIR NATURE ALTERING BY EXPOSURE TO MY THOUGHTS.
MY THOUGHTS...OF SUE, SO QUIET AS A CHILD, AND JOHNNY, SO FIERY IN HIS TEMPERAMENT, AND BEN, HARD AS STONE ON THE OUTSIDE BUT WITH A WEALTH OF HUMANITY WITHIN.
AND AS THEY BEGIN THEIR BILLION-YEAR CIRCUIT OF THE GALAXY, I REALIZE...THAT THOSE THOUGHTS CREATED THE PRECISE COMBINATION OF RAYS THAT MADE US INTO WHAT WE BECAME...THAT GAVE US OUR POWERS.
I SUSPECTED THAT THERE WAS AN INTELLIGENCE BEHIND THOSE EFFECTS, AND NOW I KNOW.
IT WAS ME.

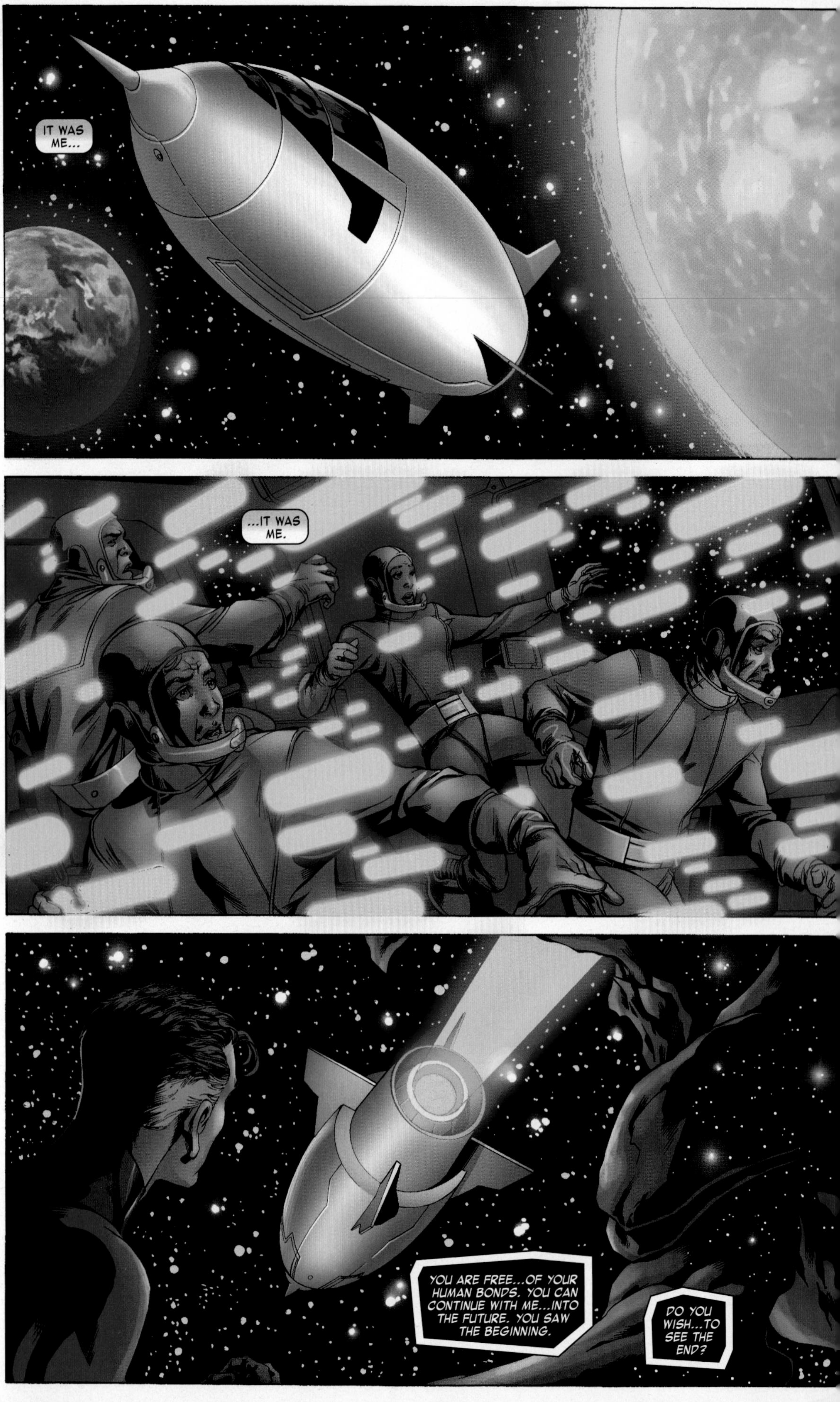
IT WAS ME...
...IT WAS ME.
YOU ARE FREE...OF YOUR HUMAN BONDS. YOU CAN CONTINUE WITH ME...INTO THE FUTURE. YOU SAW THE BEGINNING.
DO YOU WISH...TO SEE THE END?

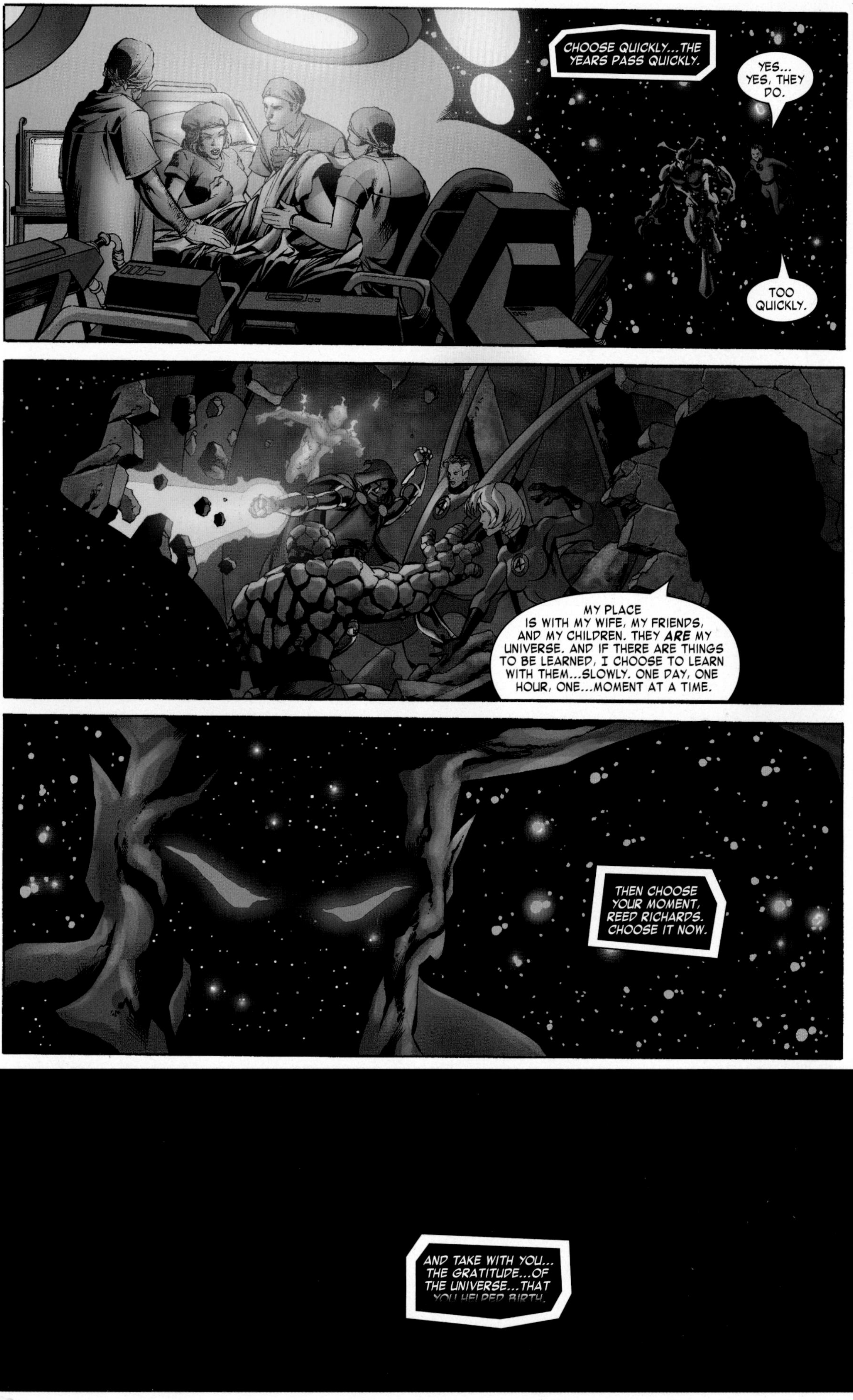
CHOOSE QUICKLY...THE YEARS PASS QUICKLY.
YES... YES, THEY DO.
TOO QUICKLY.
MY PLACE IS WITH MY WIFE, MY FRIENDS, AND MY CHILDREN. THEY ARE MY UNIVERSE. AND IF THERE ARE THINGS TO BE LEARNED, I CHOOSE TO LEARN WITH THEM...SLOWLY. ONE DAY, ONE HOUR, ONE...MOMENT AT A TIME.
THEN CHOOSE YOUR MOMENT, REED RICHARDS. CHOOSE IT NOW.
AND TAKE WITH YOU... THE GRATITUDE...OF THE UNIVERSE...THAT YOU HELPED BIRTH.

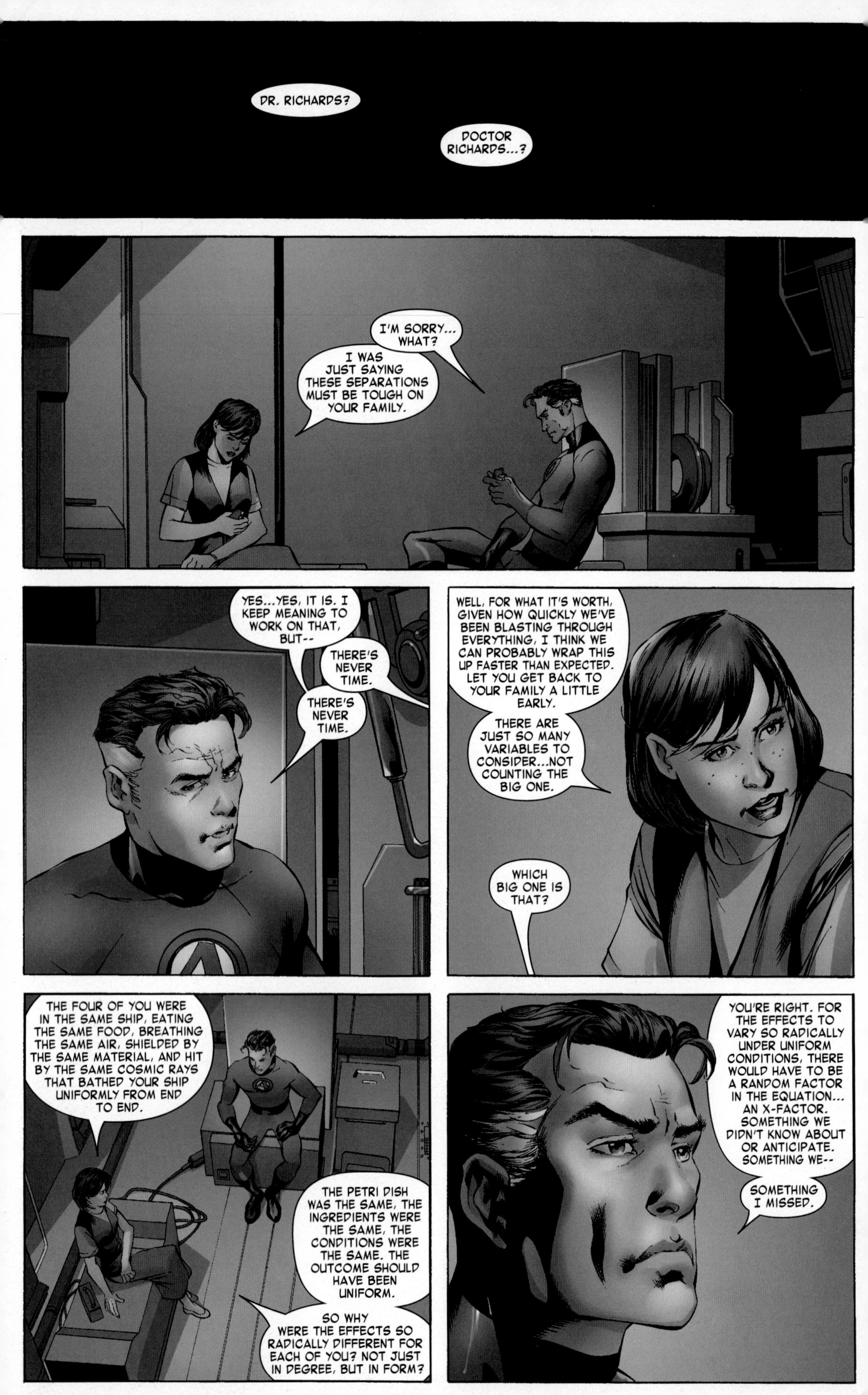
DR. RICHARDS?
DOCTOR RICHARDS...?
I'M SORRY... WHAT?
I WAS JUST SAYING THESE SEPARATIONS MUST BE TOUGH ON YOUR FAMILY.
YES...YES, IT IS. I KEEP MEANING TO WORK ON THAT, BUT--
THERE'S NEVER TIME.
THERE'S NEVER TIME.
WELL, FOR WHAT IT'S WORTH, GIVEN HOW QUICKLY WE'VE BEEN BLASTING THROUGH EVERYTHING, I THINK WE CAN PROBABLY WRAP THIS UP FASTER THAN EXPECTED. LET YOU GET BACK TO YOUR FAMILY A LITTLE EARLY.
THERE ARE JUST SO MANY VARIABLES TO CONSIDER...NOT COUNTING THE BIG ONE.
WHICH BIG ONE IS THAT?
THE FOUR OF YOU WERE IN THE SAME SHIP, EATING THE SAME FOOD, BREATHING THE SAME AIR, SHIELDED BY THE SAME MATERIAL, AND HIT BY THE SAME COSMIC RAYS THAT BATHED YOUR SHIP UNIFORMLY FROM END TO END.
THE PETRI DISH WAS THE SAME, THE INGREDIENTS WERE THE SAME, THE CONDITIONS WERE THE SAME. THE OUTCOME SHOULD HAVE BEEN UNIFORM.
SO WHY WERE THE EFFECTS SO RADICALLY DIFFERENT FOR EACH OF YOU? NOT JUST IN DEGREE, BUT IN FORM?
YOU'RE RIGHT. FOR THE EFFECTS TO VARY SO RADICALLY UNDER UNIFORM CONDITIONS, THERE WOULD HAVE TO BE A RANDOM FACTOR IN THE EQUATION... AN X-FACTOR. SOMETHING WE DIDN'T KNOW ABOUT OR ANTICIPATE. SOMETHING WE--
SOMETHING I MISSED.

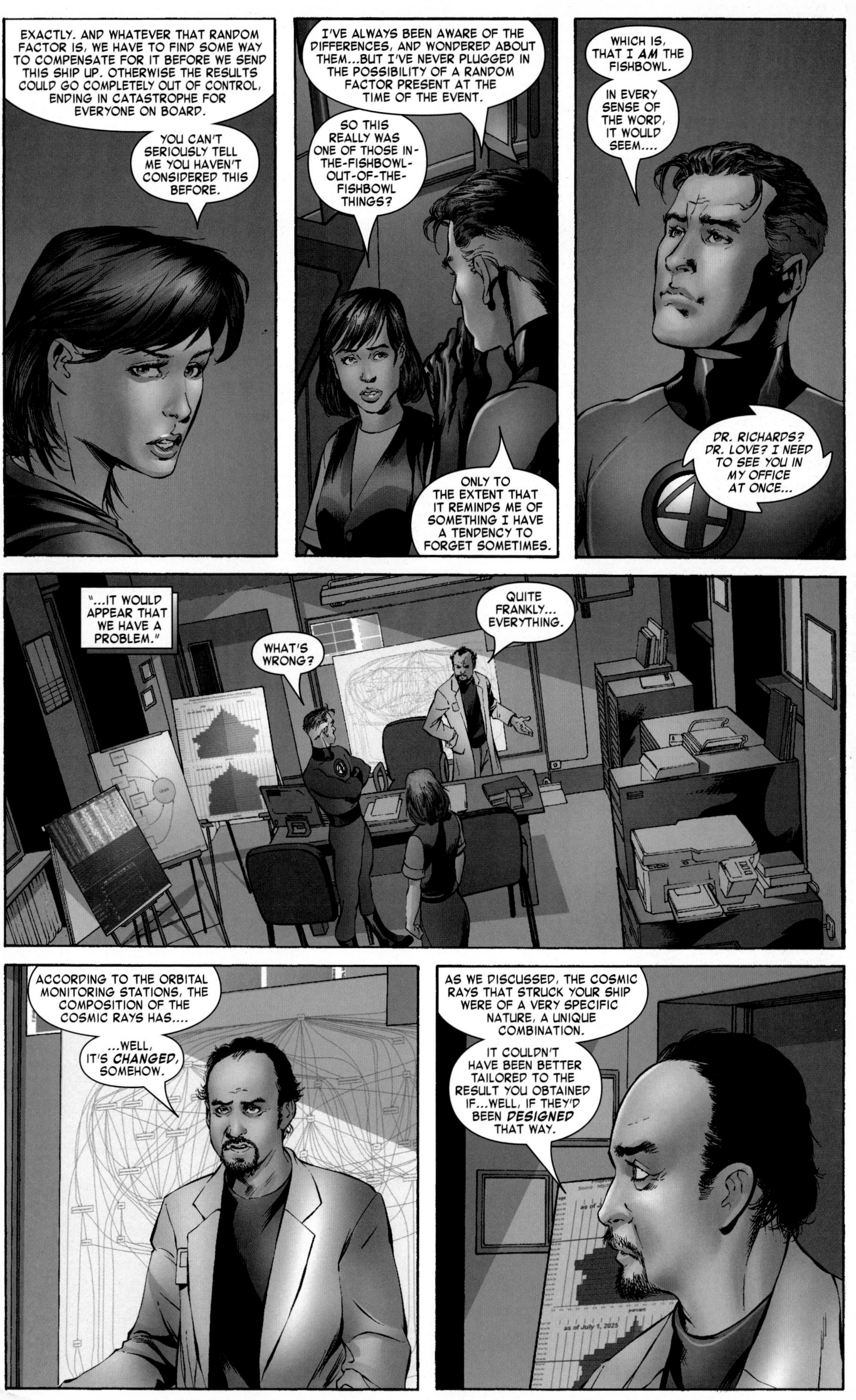
EXACTLY. AND WHATEVER THAT RANDOM FACTOR IS, WE HAVE TO FIND SOME WAY TO COMPENSATE FOR IT BEFORE WE SEND THIS SHIP UP. OTHERWISE THE RESULTS COULD GO COMPLETELY OUT OF CONTROL, ENDING IN CATASTROPHE FOR EVERYONE ON BOARD.
YOU CAN'T SERIOUSLY TELL ME YOU HAVEN'T CONSIDERED THIS BEFORE.
I'VE ALWAYS BEEN AWARE OF THE DIFFERENCES, AND WONDERED ABOUT THEM...BUT I'VE NEVER PLUGGED IN THE POSSIBILITY OF A RANDOM FACTOR PRESENT AT THE TIME OF THE EVENT.
SO THIS REALLY WAS ONE OF THOSE IN-THE-FISHBOWL-OUT-OF-THE-FISHBOWL THINGS?
ONLY TO THE EXTENT THAT IT REMINDS ME OF SOMETHING I HAVE A TENDENCY TO FORGET SOMETIMES.
WHICH IS, THAT I *AM* THE FISHBOWL.
IN EVERY SENSE OF THE WORD, IT WOULD SEEM....
DR. RICHARDS? DR. LOVE? I NEED TO SEE YOU IN MY OFFICE AT ONCE...
"...IT WOULD APPEAR THAT WE HAVE A PROBLEM."
WHAT'S WRONG?
QUITE FRANKLY... EVERYTHING.
ACCORDING TO THE ORBITAL MONITORING STATIONS, THE COMPOSITION OF THE COSMIC RAYS HAS....
...WELL, IT'S *CHANGED*, SOMEHOW.
AS WE DISCUSSED, THE COSMIC RAYS THAT STRUCK YOUR SHIP WERE OF A VERY SPECIFIC NATURE, A UNIQUE COMBINATION.
IT COULDN'T HAVE BEEN BETTER TAILORED TO THE RESULT YOU OBTAINED IF...WELL, IF THEY'D BEEN *DESIGNED* THAT WAY.

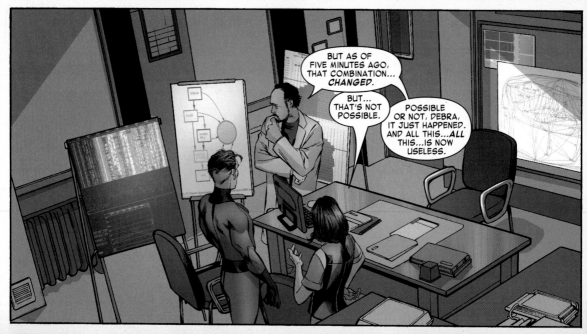

BUT AS OF FIVE MINUTES AGO, THAT COMBINATION... CHANGED.

BUT... THAT'S NOT POSSIBLE.

POSSIBLE OR NOT, DEBRA, IT JUST HAPPENED. AND ALL THIS...ALL THIS...IS NOW USELESS.

BUT DR. CRANE, WE'RE SO CLOSE, THE SHIP IS ALMOST READY TO FLY--

THE SHIP WAS DESIGNED TO COINCIDE WITH THE PRECISE REPLICATION OF COSMIC RAYS...BUT THAT CONDITION NO LONGER EXISTS. IF WE LAUNCH NOW, WE DON'T KNOW WHAT KIND OF SITUATION WE'D BE RUNNING INTO UP THERE.

SO WHAT'RE YOU SAYING?

I'M SAYING...

...THAT THE ENTIRE OPERATION IS SUSPENDED WHILE WE TRY AND FIGURE OUT WHAT THE HELL HAPPENED.

AND IF WE CAN'T?

THEN WE'LL PROBABLY HAVE TO SHUT DOWN THE WHOLE THING.

NOT MY PREFERENCE, BUT I'M BETTING THE PROGRAMMER WHO DIDN'T CONVERT METRIC TO STANDARD MATH ON THE PROBE THAT CRASHED INTO MARS FELT THE SAME WAY.

WELL, DR. RICHARDS? YOU HAVEN'T SAID A WORD DURING ALL THIS. ANY THOUGHTS?

JUST ONE. I THINK...

...I'D LIKE TO GO HOME NOW.

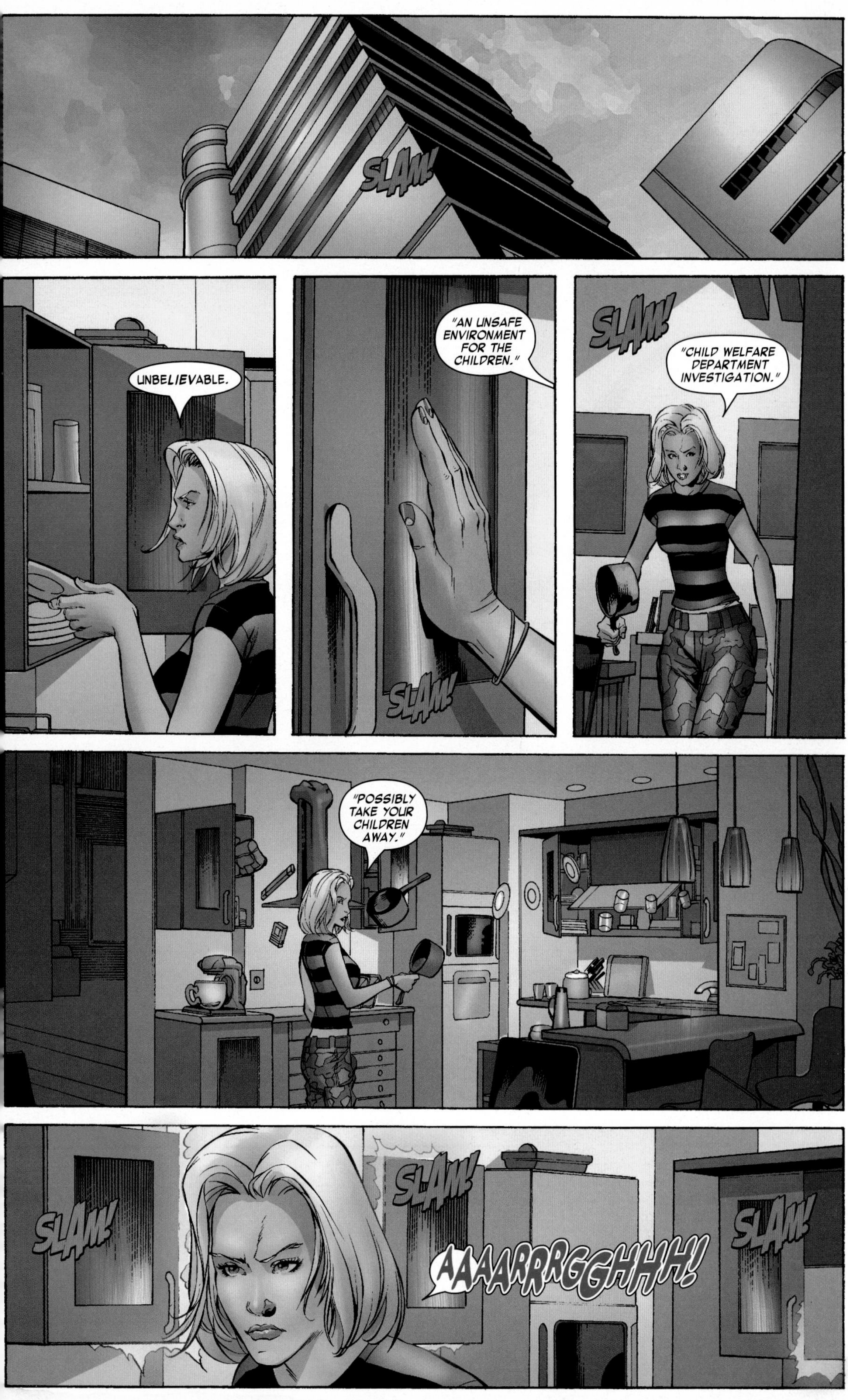
SLAM!
UNBELIEVABLE.
"AN UNSAFE ENVIRONMENT FOR THE CHILDREN."
SLAM!
SLAM!
"CHILD WELFARE DEPARTMENT INVESTIGATION."
"POSSIBLY TAKE YOUR CHILDREN AWAY."
SLAM!
SLAM!
AAAARRRGGHHH!
SLAM!

OKAY SUE, YOU'VE HAD YOUR TANTRUM, SLAMMED EVERY CABINET DOOR WITHIN RANGE, NOW YOU HAVE TO *THINK.*

WHAT WOULD REED DO IN A SITUATION LIKE THIS?

WELL, FOR STARTERS....

...HE'D KISS YOU HARD ENOUGH TO MAKE YOU SEE STARS.

REED? WHAT'RE YOU--

--MRMPH... MMMMMMMMRPH...

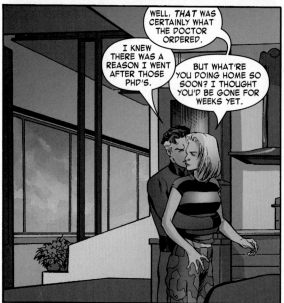

WELL, *THAT* WAS CERTAINLY WHAT THE DOCTOR ORDERED.

I KNEW THERE WAS A REASON I WENT AFTER THOSE PHD'S.

BUT WHAT'RE YOU DOING HOME SO SOON? I THOUGHT YOU'D BE GONE FOR WEEKS YET.

THERE WAS... A CHANGE OF PLAN.

GOOD, BECAUSE WE'VE GOT A PROBLEM HERE THAT --

I KNOW. MRS. DEBOUVIER FROM THE CHILD WELFARE DEPARTMENT THINKS WE ARE BRINGING UP OUR CHILDREN IN AN UNSAFE ENVIRONMENT AND IS INVESTIGATING WHETHER OR NOT TO TAKE THEM AWAY.

YES, BUT... HOW DID YOU KNOW?

I HEARD YOU TALKING TO YOURSELF.

BUT...I COULD SWEAR I DIDN'T MENTION HER NAME, I...

REED, ARE WE GOING TO THE BEDROOM?

DOCTOR'S ORDERS.

BUT IT'S THE MIDDLE OF THE DAY.

HOW ELSE ARE YOU GOING TO READ THE PRESCRIPTION?

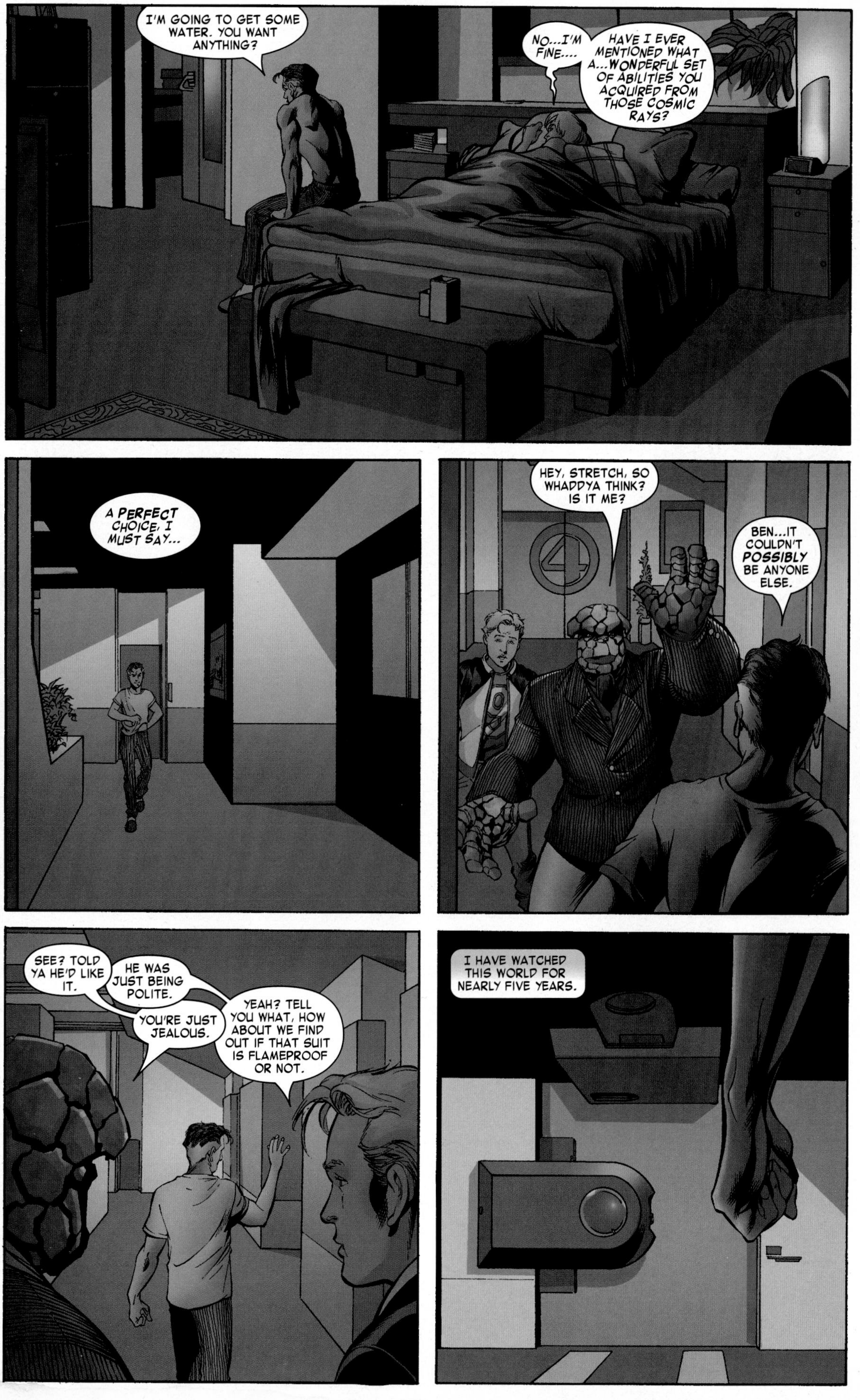

I'M GOING TO GET SOME WATER. YOU WANT ANYTHING?
NO...I'M FINE....
HAVE I EVER MENTIONED WHAT A...WONDERFUL SET OF ABILITIES YOU ACQUIRED FROM THOSE COSMIC RAYS?
A PERFECT CHOICE, I MUST SAY...
HEY, STRETCH, SO WHADDYA THINK? IS IT ME?
BEN...IT COULDN'T POSSIBLY BE ANYONE ELSE.
SEE? TOLD YA HE'D LIKE IT.
HE WAS JUST BEING POLITE.
YOU'RE JUST JEALOUS.
YEAH? TELL YOU WHAT, HOW ABOUT WE FIND OUT IF THAT SUIT IS FLAMEPROOF OR NOT.
I HAVE WATCHED THIS WORLD FOR NEARLY FIVE YEARS.

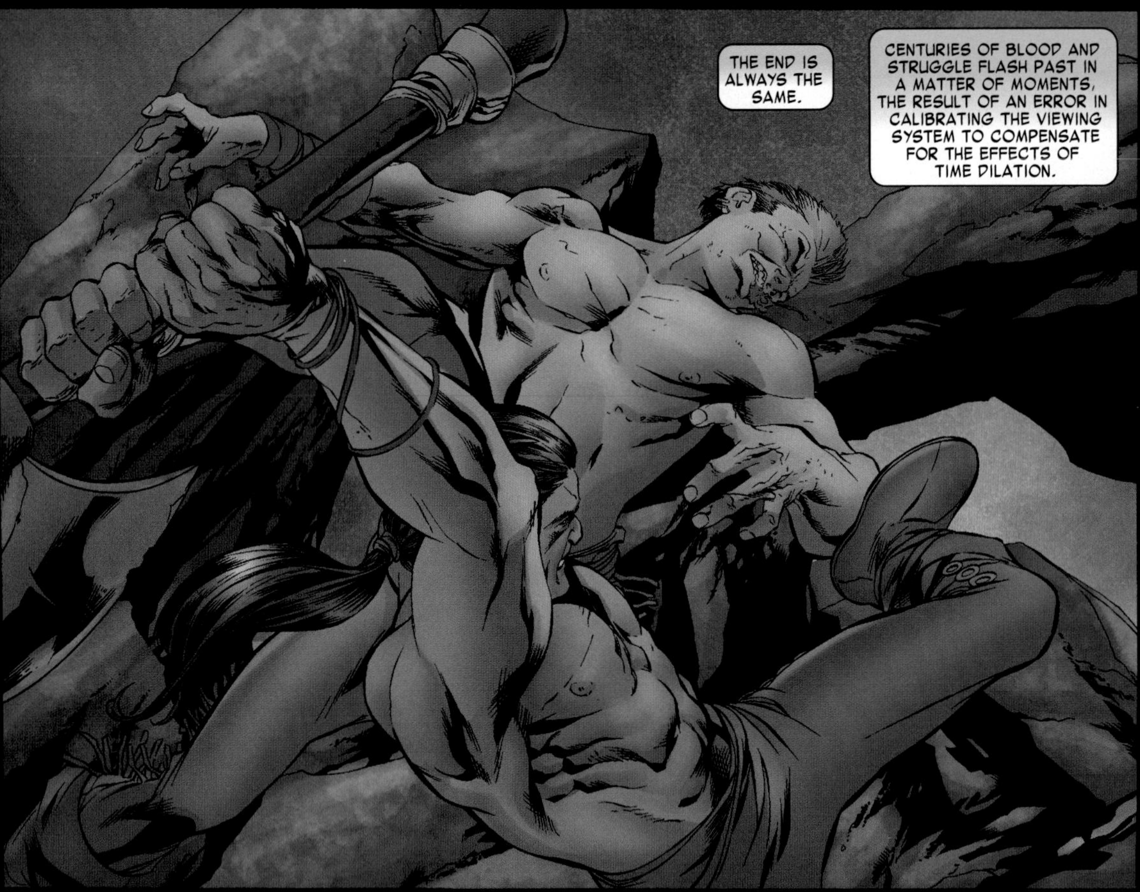
THE END IS ALWAYS THE SAME.
CENTURIES OF BLOOD AND STRUGGLE FLASH PAST IN A MATTER OF MOMENTS, THE RESULT OF AN ERROR IN CALIBRATING THE VIEWING SYSTEM TO COMPENSATE FOR THE EFFECTS OF TIME DILATION.

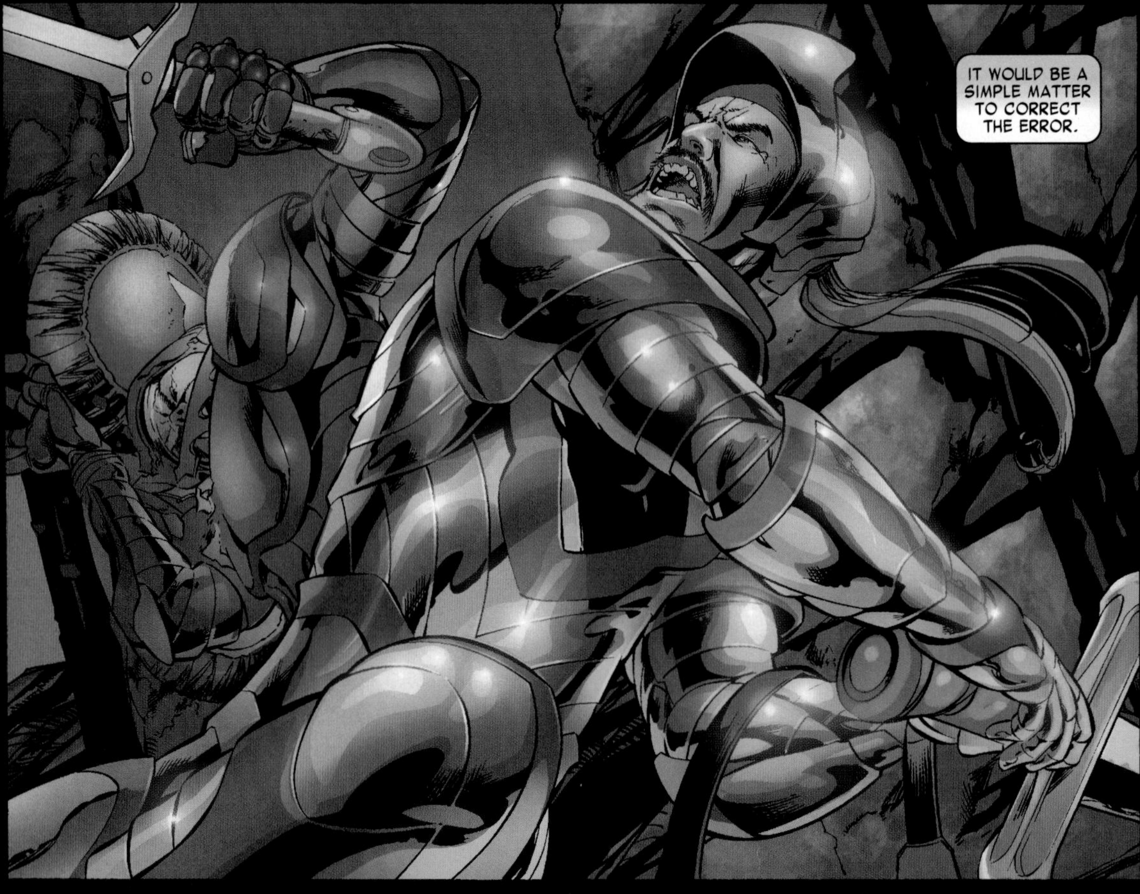
IT WOULD BE A SIMPLE MATTER TO CORRECT THE ERROR.

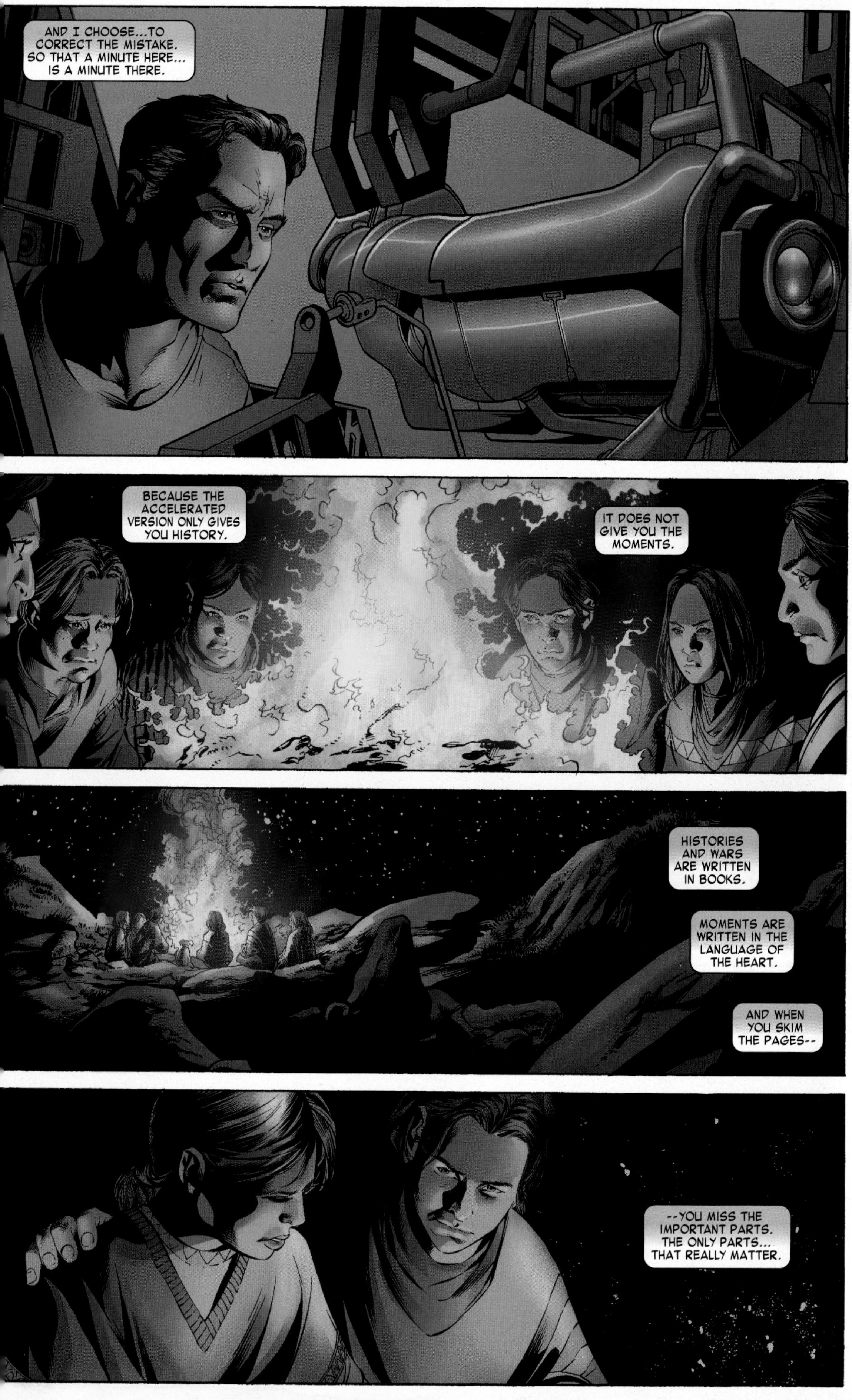
AND I CHOOSE...TO CORRECT THE MISTAKE. SO THAT A MINUTE HERE... IS A MINUTE THERE.
BECAUSE THE ACCELERATED VERSION ONLY GIVES YOU HISTORY.
IT DOES NOT GIVE YOU THE MOMENTS.
HISTORIES AND WARS ARE WRITTEN IN BOOKS.
MOMENTS ARE WRITTEN IN THE LANGUAGE OF THE HEART.
AND WHEN YOU SKIM THE PAGES--
--YOU MISS THE IMPORTANT PARTS. THE ONLY PARTS... THAT REALLY MATTER.

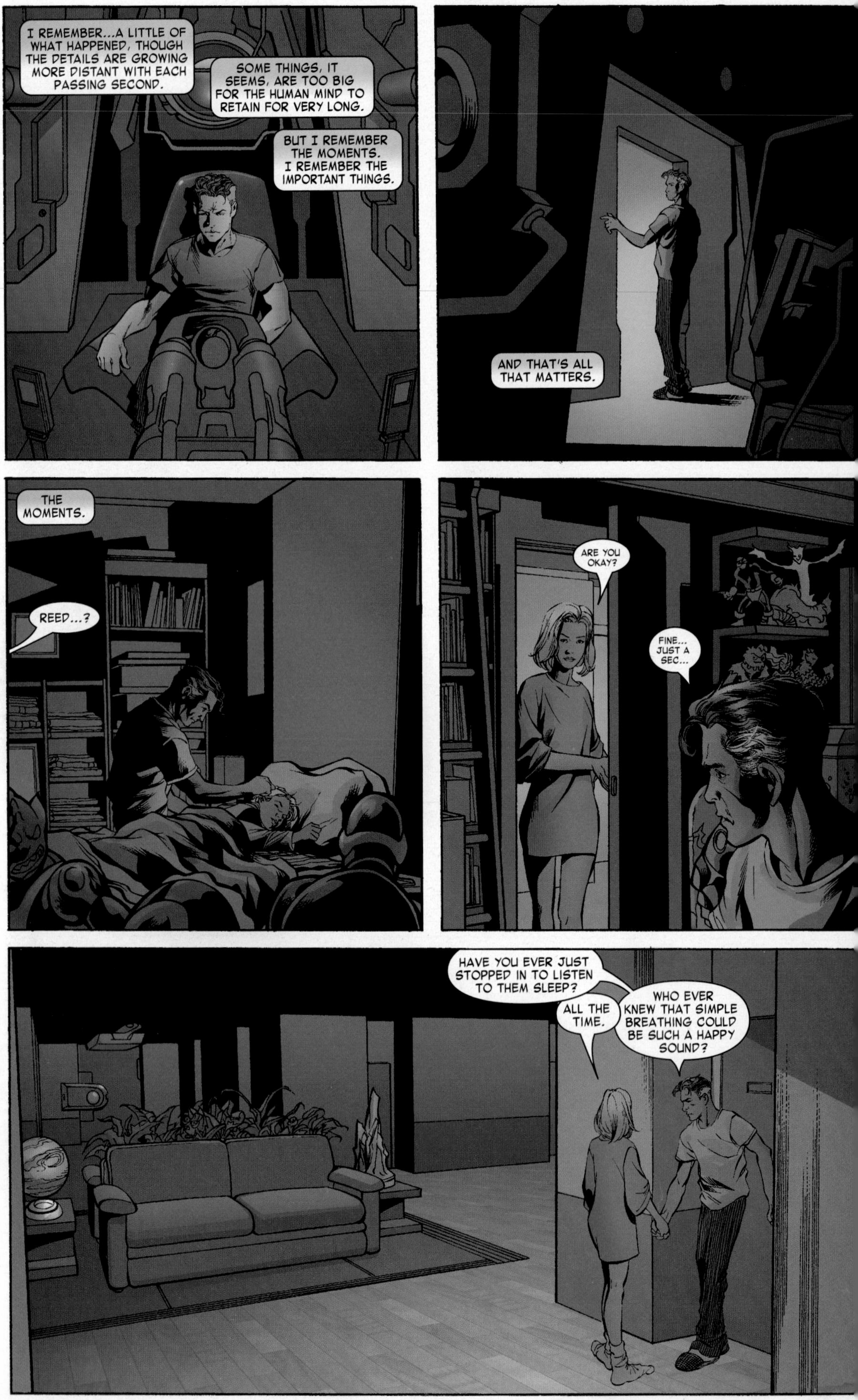
I REMEMBER...A LITTLE OF WHAT HAPPENED, THOUGH THE DETAILS ARE GROWING MORE DISTANT WITH EACH PASSING SECOND.
SOME THINGS, IT SEEMS, ARE TOO BIG FOR THE HUMAN MIND TO RETAIN FOR VERY LONG.
BUT I REMEMBER THE MOMENTS. I REMEMBER THE IMPORTANT THINGS.
AND THAT'S ALL THAT MATTERS.
THE MOMENTS.
REED...?
ARE YOU OKAY?
FINE... JUST A SEC...
HAVE YOU EVER JUST STOPPED IN TO LISTEN TO THEM SLEEP?
ALL THE TIME.
WHO EVER KNEW THAT SIMPLE BREATHING COULD BE SUCH A HAPPY SOUND?

SO WHAT'S GOTTEN INTO YOU?

NOTHING... EVERYTHING... IT'S A LONG STORY.

REED, WITH YOU, *EVERYTHING* IS A LONG STORY.

OKAY, THEN LONG...ER.

DID YOU SEE BEN'S NEW OUTFIT?

I DID. HE LOOKED... AMAZING.

JOHNNY SAID HE LOOKED LIKE A PIMP, BUT I THINK HE LOOKED DASHING.

I'M JUST GLAD TO SEE HIM HAPPY FOR A CHANGE. HE *DESERVES* TO BE HAPPY, DON'T YOU THINK, REED?

I DO, SUE...

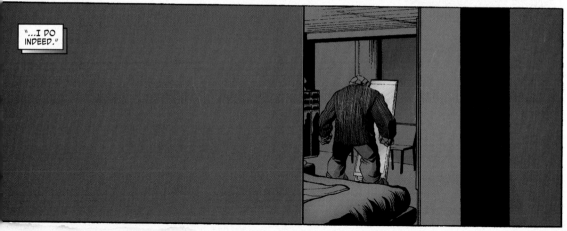

"...I DO INDEED."

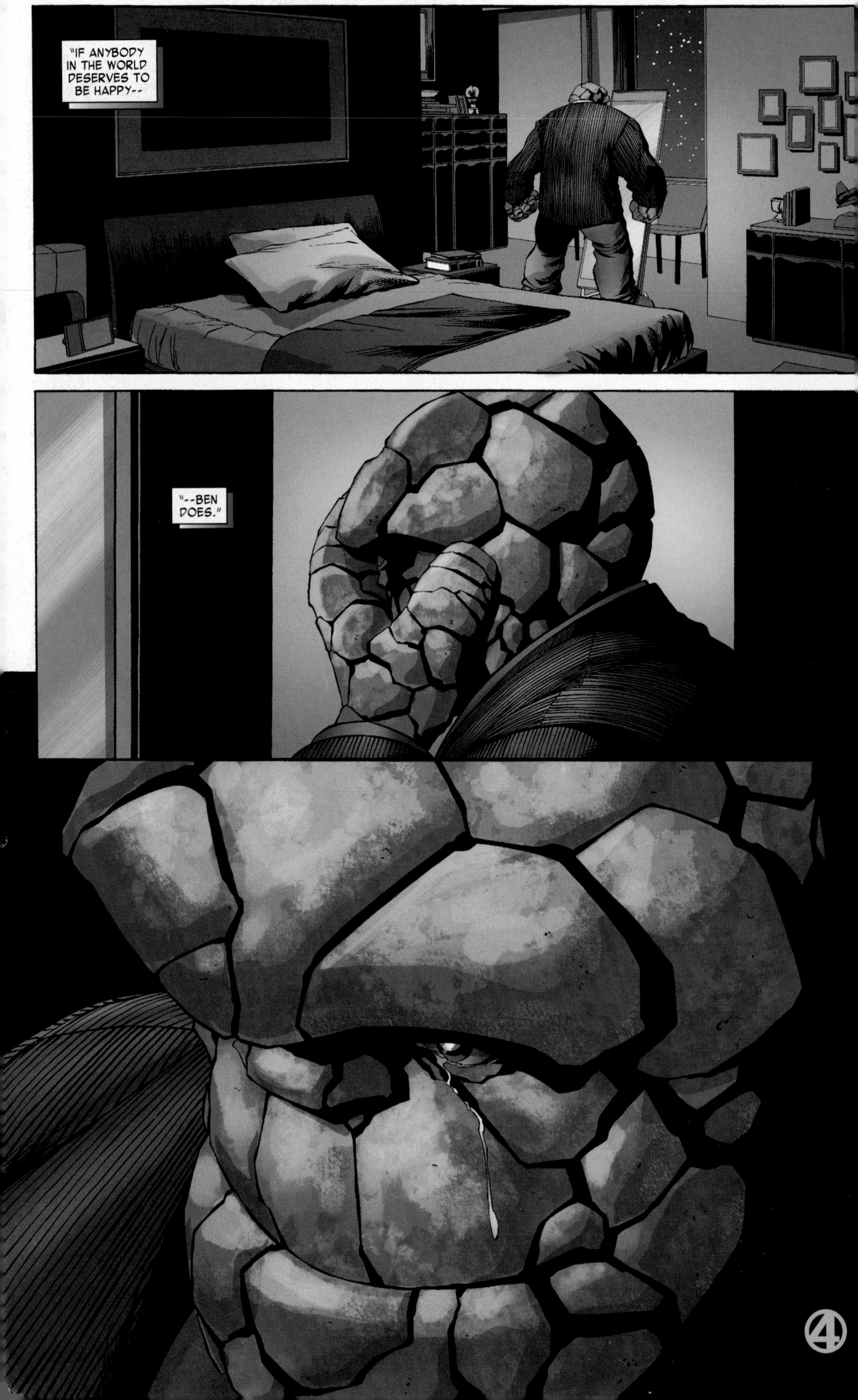
"IF ANYBODY IN THE WORLD DESERVES TO BE HAPPY--
"--BEN DOES."

#527 VARIANT COVER

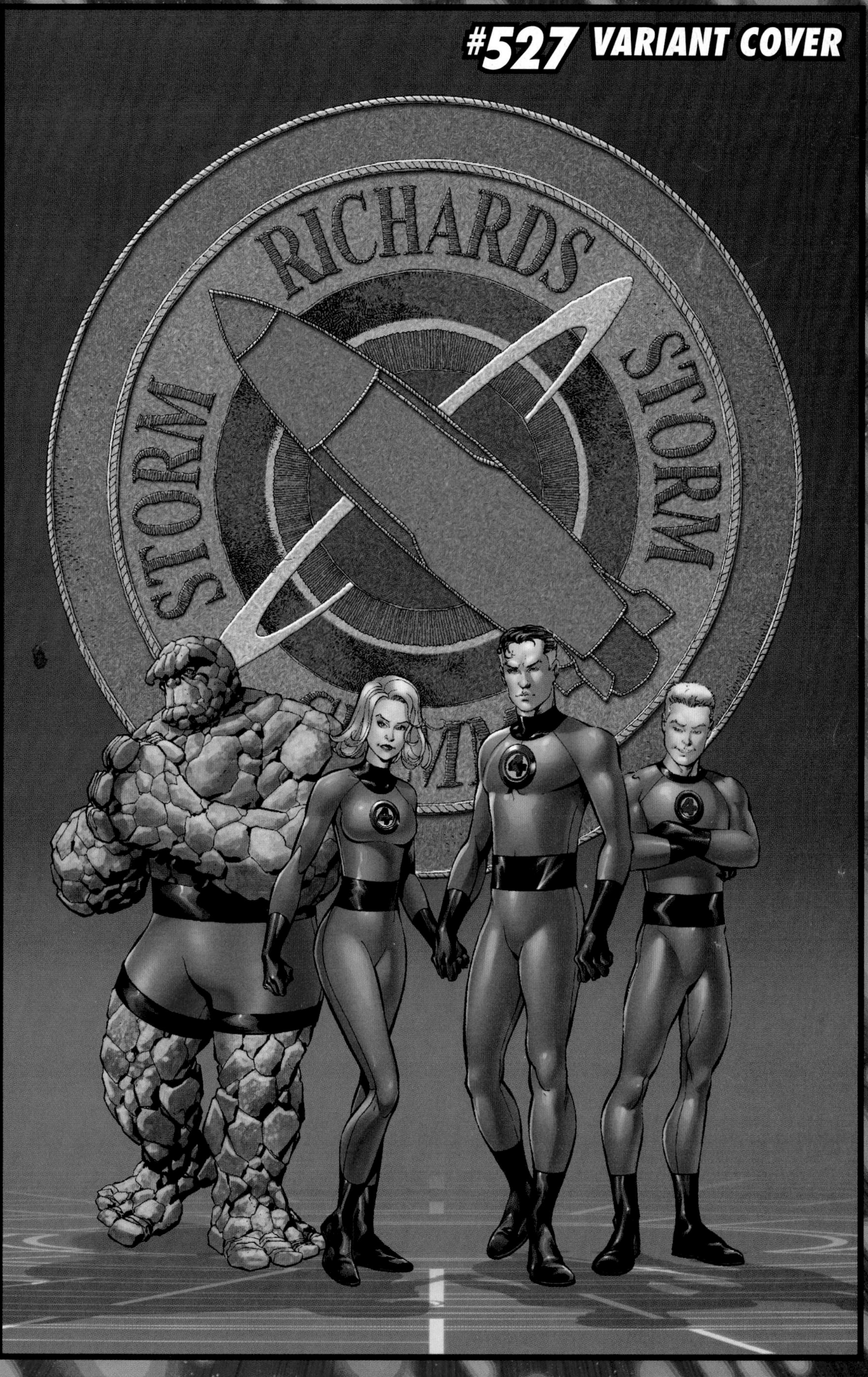
RICHARDS
STORM
STORM

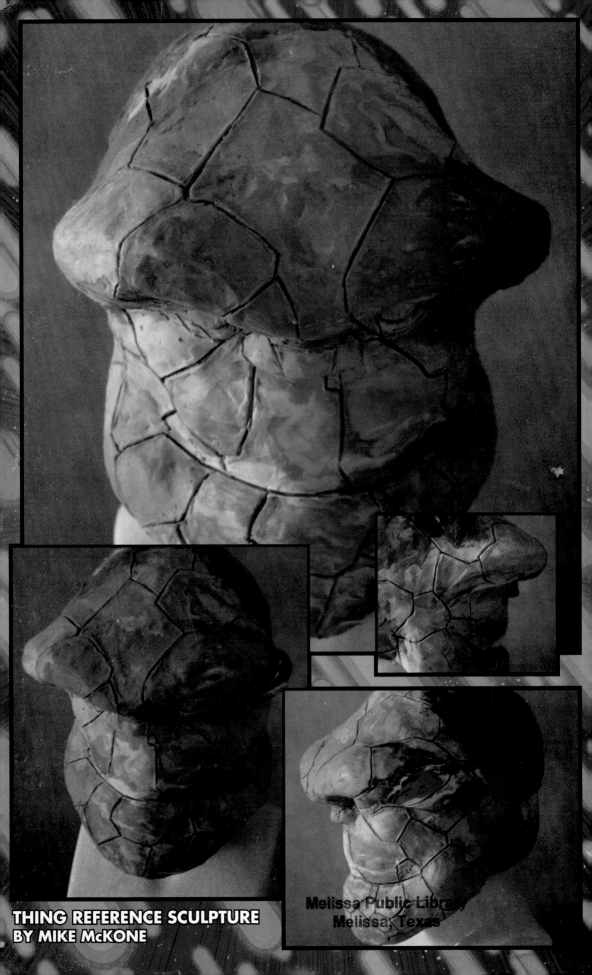

THING REFERENCE SCULPTURE
BY MIKE McKONE

Melissa Public Library
Melissa, Texas